PSALMS 73—150

A COMMENTARY ON BOOKS III-V OF THE PSALMS

by

THE REV. DEREK KIDNER, M.A., A.R.C.M.
formerly Warden of Tyndale House, Cambridge

INTER-VARSITY PRESS
LEICESTER, ENGLAND
DOWNERS GROVE, ILLINOIS, U.S.A.

Psalms 73-150
Inter-Varsity Press
38 De Montfort Street, Leicester LE1 7GP, England
Box 1400, Downers Grove, Illinois 60515 U.S.A.

© *Inter-Varsity Press, London 1975*

*Inter-Varsity Press, England, is the publishing division of the Universities and
Colleges Christian Fellowship (formerly the Inter-Varsity Fellowship), a student
movement linking Christian Unions in universities and colleges throughout the United
Kingdom and the Republic of Ireland, and a member movement of the International
Fellowship of Evangelical Students. For information about local and national
activities write to UCCF, 38 De Montfort Street, Leicester, LE1 7GP.*

*InterVarsity Press, U.S.A., is the book-publishing division of Inter-Varsity
Christian Fellowship, a student movement active on campus at hundreds of
universities, colleges and schools of nursing. For information about local and regional
activities, write IVCF, 233 Langdon St., Madison, WI 53703.*

*Distributed in Canada through InterVarsity Press, 860 Denison St., Unit 3,
Markham, Ontario L3R 4H1, Canada.*

Text set in Great Britain
Printed in the United States of America

UK ISBN 0-85111-629-9 (hardback)
UK ISBN 0-85111-830-5 (paperback)
Library of Congress Catalog Card Number: 75-7247
USA ISBN 0-87784-959-5 (hardback)
USA ISBN 0-87784-265-5 (paperback)
USA ISBN 0-87784-880-7 (set of Tyndale Old Testament Commentaries, hardback)
USA ISBN 0-87784-280-9 (set of Tyndale Old Testament Commentaries, paperback)

21	20	19	18	17	16	15	14	13	12	11
96	95	94	93	92	91	90	89	88	87	86

CONTENTS

Note on the numbering of the pages in this volume

Since this volume completes the commentary on the Psalms, its pages are numbered from the point at which the volume on Psalms 1–72 ended. The fairly frequent references to the Introduction, and other allusions to the earlier part of the commentary, are therefore identified simply by page numbers between 1 and 257. This avoids, incidentally, the possible confusion between the two volumes of the commentary and the five books into which the Psalter is traditionally divided.

CHIEF ABBREVIATIONS

Anderson	*The Book of Psalms* by A. A. Anderson (*New Century Bible*, Oliphants), 1972.
ANET	*Ancient Near Eastern Texts* by J. B. Pritchard, ²1955.
AV	English Authorized Version (King James), 1611.
BDB	*Hebrew-English Lexicon of the Old Testament* by F. Brown, S. R. Driver and C. A. Briggs, 1907.
BH	*Biblia Hebraica* edited by R. Kittel and P. Kahle, ⁷1951.
Briggs	*Psalms* by C. A. and E. G. Briggs (*International Critical Commentary*, T. & T. Clark), 1906–07.
Dahood	*Psalms* by M. J. Dahood (*Anchor Bible*, Doubleday), 1966–70.
Delitzsch	*Psalms* by F. Delitzsch, ⁴1883.
Eaton	*Psalms* by J. H. Eaton (*Torch Bible Commentaries*, SCM Press), 1967.
EV	English versions.
Gelineau	*The Psalms: A New Translation* arranged for singing to the psalmody of Joseph Gelineau (Fontana), 1963.
G-K	*Hebrew Grammar* by W. Gesenius, edited by E. Kautzsch and A. E. Cowley, ²1910.
Gk.	Greek.
Heb.	Hebrew.
HTR	*Harvard Theological Review.*
JB	Jerusalem Bible, 1966.
JTS	*Journal of Theological Studies.*
K-B	*Lexicon in Veteris Testamenti Libros* by L. Koehler and W. Baumgartner, 1953.
Keet	*A Study of the Psalms of Ascents* by C. C. Keet (Mitre), 1969.
Kirkpatrick	*Psalms* by A. F. Kirkpatrick (*Cambridge Bible for Schools and Colleges*, CUP), 1891–1901.
Kissane	*Psalms* by E. J. Kissane (Browne and Nolan), 1953–54.
LXX	The Septuagint (pre-Christian Greek version of the Old Testament).
mg.	margin.

CHIEF ABBREVIATIONS

Moffatt	*A New Translation of the Bible* bv James Moffatt (Hodder and Stoughton), 1934.
Mowinckel	*The Psalms in Israel's Worship* by S. Mowinckel (Blackwell), 1962.
MS(s)	manuscript(s).
MT	Massoretic Text.
NBD	*The New Bible Dictionary* edited by J. D. Douglas *et al.* (IVP), 1962.
NEB	The New English Bible, 1970.
PBV	Prayer Book Version, 1662.
Perowne	*The Psalms* by J. S. Perowne (G. Bell), 1864.
RP	The Revised Psalter (SPCK), 1964.
RSV	American Revised Standard Version, 1952.
RV	English Revised Version, 1881.
Syr.	The Peshitta (Syriac version of the Old Testament).
Targ.	The Targum (Aramaic version of the Old Testament).
TEV	Today's English Version, the Psalms: *Sing a New Song* (Fontana), 1972.
TRP	*The Text of the Revised Psalter.* Notes by D. W. Thomas (SPCK), 1963.
VT	*Vetus Testamentum.*
Vulg.	The Vulgate (Jerome's Latin version of the Bible).
Weiser	*Psalms* by A. Weiser (*Old Testament Library*, SCM Press), 1962.

Book III: Psalms 73-89

The eleven psalms 73-83, which make up the bulk of this third 'book', bear the name of Asaph, founder of one of the temple choirs (1 Ch. 25:1). Psalm 50 is their isolated forerunner in Book II. Four of the remaining psalms belong to the Sons of Korah (84f., 87f., supplementing the group in Book II, 42-49); the rest are divided between David (86), Heman (who shares with the Korahites the heading to Ps. 88) and Ethan (89). For some further details see the Introduction, II, pp. 5f.; VI.*b*, p. 35.

Psalm 73

'Beyond Compare'

This great psalm is the story of a bitter and despairing search, which has now been rewarded beyond all expectation. It recalls the kind of questions that distracted Job and Jeremiah; but at the end they no longer seem unanswerable, and the psalmist has a confession and a supreme discovery to share.

Title
On *Asaph*, see Introduction, p. 35.

73:1-14. The blight of envy
Verse 1 stands somewhat by itself, and is the key to the whole psalm, telling not merely of what God can do for a man but of what He can be to him. The phrase, *pure in heart*, is more significant than it may seem, for the psalm will show the relative unimportance of circumstances in comparison with attitudes, which may be either soured by self-interest (3, 13) or set free by love (25). *Pure* means more than clean-minded, though it certainly includes it (see the ruinous effect of impurity in Tit. 1:15; 2 Pet. 2:14); basically it is being totally committed to God. As for *heart*, its occurrence six times in the psalm emphasizes, as Martin Buber has pointed out, that 'the state of the heart determines whether a man lives in the truth, in which God's goodness is experienced, or in the semblance of

truth, where the fact that it "goes ill" with him is confused with the illusion that God is not good to him'.[1]

The upright (1) is an emendation (see mg.), made by dividing the consonants of 'Israel' (*yśr'l*) into two words, *yśr 'l* (but RSV, NEB then omit the second of them, a synonym for 'God'). This is unsupported and hardly necessary, since 'Israel' makes good sense and is an appropriate reminder, at the outset, of God's grace and covenant, which precede the individual's response.

2, 3. Unsettling doubt. The NEB conveys the precarious situation better than RSV, with 'My feet had almost slipped, my foothold had all but given way'. On the reasons for this crisis of faith the psalmist is refreshingly frank. Where he might have affected a disinterested passion for justice he confesses to envy and to having judged only by what he *saw* (contrast Is. 11:3).

4-9. Daunting display. It is curious that to be physically *sound and sleek* is still viewed in some circles as the believer's birthright, in spite of passages such as this and, *e.g.*, Romans 8:23; Hebrews 12:8. In the very description the psalmist reveals the temptation to arrogance which goes with too much well-being; which indeed would have become his own temptation had his original wish been granted.

4. This verse as read by RSV, *etc.*, makes excellent sense, though it involves dividing one Hebrew word into two. While this was hardly justified in verse 1 (see comment there on *the upright*), here the awkwardness of the alternative makes a case for it.[2]

7. NEB is preferable in the second line: 'while vain fancies pass through their minds.'

The whole passage is a masterly picture of these darlings of fortune: overblown, overweening; laughable if they were not so ruthless; their vanity egging them on to hector the very universe. There are companion portraits in, *e.g.*, Psalms 12 and 14; and in the present psalm a telling contrast of attitude to *the heavens* and *the earth* (9) in verse 25.

---

[1] *Right and Wrong* (SCM Press, 1952), p. 37. The six occurrences are in verses 1, 7, 13, 21, 26, 26.

[2] *Cf.* RV: 'For there are no bands (or 'pangs') in their death.' Death seems to be introduced too early in the passage. 'In their death' is a single Heb. word, *lᵉmôṭām*; divided it is read as *lāmô; tām, i.e.* as the italicized words in the sentence: '. . . no pangs *for them*; *sound* and sleek is their body.'

10–14. Lonely dissent. The idea that 'we needs must love the highest when we see it'[1] finds no support here, unless by 'highest' we mean whatever appears to have the upper hand. The *Most High* (11) receives the least respect of all, and the psalmist has the mortification of seeing sin not only well paid but well thought of (10; see comment). It is not a purely modern phenomenon.

10. The text of this verse seems to have suffered in transmission. Literally the first line reads either '. . . he will bring back his people here' or '. . . his people will return here'; and the second line (*cf.* RV) 'and water of a full (vessel) will be drained by them'. But the lack of any clear connection with the context has prompted attempts by RSV and others to restore the original text. The Hebrew emendations are fairly small,[2] and most modern versions find here the popular worship of success.

13. The phrase, *and washed my hands in innocence*, is a bitter echo of the devoted resolve of 26:6. To decide that such earnestness has been a waste of time is pathetically self-centred—what did I get out of it?—but the very formulating of the thought has shocked the writer into a better frame of mind, which he now describes.

73:15–28. The radiance of faith
The transformation of his outlook had its decisive moment, pinpointed by the *until* of verse 17, but there was heart-searching before it, and much to explore beyond it.

15–20. The dawn of truth. The first step to enlightenment was not mental but moral: a turning from the self-interest and self-pity revealed in verses 3 and 13 to remembering basic responsibilities and loyalties (15). The writer had still no inkling of an answer (16), but this shift of attention was itself a release after his fixation on one part of the scene, the worldlings. The high title he uses for his fellow-believers, 'the family of God' (NEB), or lit. 'thy sons' (15), introduces a forgotten factor, a relationship which is wealth of quite another kind.

17. The light breaks in as he turns to God Himself, and to

---

[1] Tennyson, *Guinevere*, l. 647 (*Idylls of the King*).

[2] *E.g.*, *ᵃlēhem* ('to them') for MT *hᵃlōm* ('hither'); and *mûm lōʾ yimṣᵉʾû* ('find no fault') for MT *mê mālê yimmāṣû* ('water of a full [vessel] will be drained'). In defence of the Massoretic Text (MT) *cf.* perhaps our own metaphors of 'imbibing', 'drinking in', 'lapping up' what people say (*cf.* Eaton here).

Him as an object not of speculation[1] but of worship. Against His eternity, sovereignty and underived being, these men of the moment are seen as they are. *Their end* is literally 'their afterward', their future which will unmake everything they have lived for. By contrast, a related word for 'afterward' in verse 24 will introduce a quite different and glorious prospect.

18-20. Judgment is not simply the logical end or 'afterward' of evil, though it has this quality (see on verse 17); it is ultimately God's personal rejection, His dismissal of someone as of no further account or interest (20) which is the 'shame and everlasting contempt' of Daniel 12:2, and the 'I never knew you' of Matthew 7:23. 'We can be left utterly and absolutely *outside*—repelled, exiled, estranged, finally and unspeakably ignored.'[2]

21-26. The full blaze of glory. 'On the other hand' (to continue the quotation above) 'we can be called in, welcomed, received, acknowledged.' It was this that the writer had forgotten—for nothing is so blinding (and his terms are still stronger, 22) as envy or grievance. This was the nerve the serpent had touched in Eden, to make even Paradise appear an insult. Now the true values come to light, in a passage which must be unsurpassed, brief as it is, in the record of man's response to God.

21, 22. There is a new depth in the singer's repentance of his former mood. In verse 2 he had noticed his own peril from it; in verse 15 he saw it as a betrayal of his fellows; now he confesses the affront he has been offering to God. This has come of finding himself in God's presence (*cf.* 'into the sanctuary', 17), for *toward thee* is literally 'with thee'; but that presence, at first accusing, will now become his delight. The same expression, 'with thee', is taken up at once in 23a, and again in 25b (see note), transformed by its new context.

23, 24. The tenses, while they are not always as sharply temporal in Hebrew as in English, seem designed here to bring out the long span of the phrase, *continually with thee*. The sequence can be read (somewhat as in JB):

> 'You took hold of my right hand,
> You guide me with your counsel,
> And in the end you will receive me with glory.'

---

[1] JB (*cf.* Gelineau) has 'until . . . I pierced the mystery', but this is an unwarranted spiritualizing of the straightforward statement 'until I went into the sanctuary'.

[2] C. S. Lewis, 'The Weight of Glory', *Transposition* (Bles, 1949), p. 30.

The word *afterward*,[1] or 'in the end', makes it clear that the ast line looks beyond the steady progress of the middle sentence, to the climax of the whole. Whether that climax (which can be translated either *to glory* or 'with glory') is the comparatively modest one of promotion to earthly honour, as some would judge, or the crowning joy of passing into God's presence, is something of an open question. To the present writeɪ, the second is altogether the more likely. Verbally, the word *receive* suggests it, and doubly so by its use in the story of Enoch (Gn. 5:24, 'for God took him'; the verb is the same) and in Psalm 49:15. In the latter, the line 'for he will receive me' completes a couplet which begins 'But God will ransom my soul from the power of Sheol'. Further, the thrust of the present paragraph is towards God alone, from its opening theme, 'continually with thee', to its supreme confession in 25f., 'Whom have I in heaven but thee?' This mounting experience of salvation, 'grasped, guided, glorified', is a humble counterpart to the great theological sequence of Romans 8:29f., which spans the work of God from its hidden beginning, 'whom he foreknew', to the same consummation as here, 'he also glorified'. We may well conclude that if eternal life was visible to a discerning eye even in the saying 'I am the God of Abraham, . . . Isaac, and . . . Jacob', as our Lord pointed out, here it lies open for all to see. For some other passages where this hope comes into view, see the final comment on Psalm 11.

25. Having reached assurance on what God is doing for his salvation ('hold . . . guide . . . receive', 23f.), the psalmist comes to rest in what God is to him, however unpromising his situation.

Heaven and *earth* are, at one level of language, simply a way of saying 'anywhere at all'. But addressed to God, the two words keep their full meaning. Certainly the Bible's presentation of heaven is wholly God-centred—

> 'Thou its light, its joy, its crown,
> Thou its sun which goes not down'[2]

---

[1] This word, *'aḥar*, can be used either as an adverb, *i.e.* 'afterward(s)', 'after that', *etc.* (*e.g.* Gn. 10:18; 18:5; Lv. 14:8, 19; *etc.*), or as a preposition 'after'. The latter ('*after* glory') would make little sense here; but LXX understood it so, and RP emended it to *'ōraḥ* ('*along the path of* honour'). The sense 'afterwards' involves no such difficulty.

[2] W. C. Dix, 'As with gladness men of old'. *Cf.* Rev. 4:2ff.; 21:22 – 22:5.

—and in its view of earth it shows that the motto, 'To me to live is Christ', is not an excluding but an enriching of other relationships.[1]

Note in passing tha. *besides thee* is the same Hebrew expression here as 'toward thee' (22) and 'with thee' (23); a link which is not translatable but real enough, emphasizing the poet's sense of standing in God's presence, which has transformed his outlook. NEB may well be right in rendering this line not '. . . besides thee', but *'And having thee*, I desire nothing else on earth'.

26. Here death itself is faced, for the word *fail* looks in this direction, meaning 'come to an end' rather than 'be inadequate'.[2] But with true realism the psalmist refuses to modify either this or the contrasted eternity of God (note the uncompromising words 'rock', RSV mg., and *for ever*); and he invokes the indissoluble bond between the two parties, which, as our Lord pointed out, must override death (Mt. 22:32). As a Levite, furthermore, he had an explicit assurance that God was his *portion* (Nu. 18:20), an assurance which David could claim only by analogy: see on 16:5, 6.

27, 28. The real comparison. From this vantage-point the singer can look back at his fretting and jealousy, and see them truly. 'Envious of the arrogant' (3)? But they are doomed. 'All in vain' my godliness (13)? But I possess the chief and only *good* (28), which is *to be near God.*

So, whereas at one point the best thing he could do was to keep his thoughts to himself (15), now his lips are open. In the light of his discovery we turn back to his first exclamation with new understanding: 'Truly God is good . . . to those who are pure in heart.'

Psalm 74

Havoc

This tormented psalm has the marks of the national disaster that produced Psalms 79 and 137 and the book of Lamenta-

---

[1] Phil. 1:21. *Cf.* the warm and enduring friendships of Paul, whose motto this was.

[2] JB's 'pining with love' assumes too much. The verb can have this sense when it is linked to its object by the preposition 'for', as in 84:2; 119:81; but here it stands by itself.

tions: *i.e.*, the Babylonian destruction of Jerusalem and the Temple in 587 BC. Perhaps the closest parallel is in Lamentations 2:5–9, where the silencing of prophecy is, as here (verse 9), one of the most disorientating blows of all. In AV, RV, a mention of 'synagogues' (8) gives an impression of a later age, such as the great persecution by Antiochus Epiphanes in 168–165 BC (when we are again told of the absence of any prophet: 1 Macc. 4:46). But 'synagogues' is a debatable translation here, and most interpreters agree in placing the psalm within a lifetime, at most, after the events of 587.

The complete change of tone in verses 12–17, not unlike the triumphant interlude in Psalm 60, suggests a new voice breaking in (note the singular, 'my', after the 'us' and 'our'), or else a breath of fresh air from another psalm otherwise unknown to us. The tragic note will return, but at least the discipline of offering praise and of facing other facts will have made the plea more confident, if no less urgent.

Title
On *Maskil* and *Asaph* see Introduction, pp. 38, 35.

74:1–3. The cast-off heritage
It is faith, more than doubt, that precipitates the shower of questions which begins and ends this half of the psalm (verses 1, 10, 11), since the real perplexity is not over the bare fact of punishment but over its apparent finality. 'Is it for ever?' (1a, NEB; *cf.* 10)—yet how can it be, when this is '*thy* pasture ... *thy* congregation ... *thy* heritage'? We might add, it is thine by choice and long standing; for such is the implication of the series in verse 2: *thou hast gotten of old ... redeemed ... dwelt*. On this theme see Romans 11:1f., 29.

2. On the practical implications of *Remember*, see on 13:1. In the Psalms, the theme of *Zion* as God's earthly dwelling evokes a great variety of moods, from the present bewilderment to the eager longings of Psalm 84, the jubilance of 68, the world-vision of 87, the defiant faith of 46, and more besides. Of the present verse Perowne has well said that 'the two great facts, the redemption from Egypt, and God's dwelling in the midst of them, ... seem here, as in the 68th Psalm, to sum up all their history'.

Tribe can also mean 'rod' or 'sceptre', and was so translated by the ancient versions; but the emphasis here is on belonging to God as His own folk, not on being wielded as His instrument (*cf.* likewise Je. 10:16 and the plural in Is. 63:17).

3. *Direct* is literally 'lift up'; hence JB has the vivid but doubtful touch, 'Pick your steps over these endless ruins'. It is more likely to mean 'hasten to';[1] and the ruins are seemingly irreparable, rather than endlessly extensive.

74:4–8. The pillaged temple

After the questions and entreaties, the facts are now spread before God. The sharp detail of the picture, evidently an indelible memory, adds greatly to its force.

4. For *roared* . . . , NEB has, more realistically, 'The shouts of thy enemies filled the holy place'. But 'roared' was probably meant to convey a comparison with wild beasts. 'Bellowed' might be a better combination of realism and metaphor. The word used here for *thy holy place* is 'thy meeting place' (*cf.* 8), which recalls the term 'tent of meeting', *i.e.*, the place where God promised to be available to His people (Ex. 29:42). Already the scene is a brutal enough contrast to the setting in which Isaiah heard the seraphim's *Sanctus* and the voice of God.

The *signs* would be the military ensigns (*cf.* the same word in Nu. 2:2). The explanatory note, *for signs*, which may look superfluous, directs our attention to some very different 'signs' appointed for the sanctuary: the beaten-out censers from Korah's rebellion, and Aaron's miraculous rod (Nu. 16:38; 17:10 [17:3, 25, Heb.]). To these reminders of inviolable holiness the heathen emblems were a humiliating retort. There were worse abominations to come, but both the Old Testament and the New contemplate them as signs of the enemy's last onslaught and imminent defeat (Dn. 11:31; Mt. 24:15).

5. The RV is the most faithful to this difficult verse, with 'They[2] seemed (or, 'made themselves known',[3] mg.) as men that lifted up axes upon a thicket of trees'. It is a picture of furious destructive energy.

---

[1] NEB ('Now at last restore') uses a common meaning of the verb, but modifies 'thy steps' to make the word (without 'thy') an adverb as in, *e.g.*, Gn. 2:23. It is ingenious but unwarranted.

[2] The verb is singular, but this can have the force of 'each one of them'. LXX attaches this verb to the previous verse, but reads it as 'and they knew not'; *cf.* JB, Gelineau, who further modify it by assuming an original reading '(which) we knew not'.

[3] It is this verb which AV translates as 'a man was famous'.

6, 7. 1 Kings 6:21f., 29 reveals that the *carved* work was overlaid with gold (RSV adds the word *wood*). If any of this plating remained (*cf.* 2 Ki. 18:16), verse 6 may describe its stripping off before the burning of the woodwork: *cf.* the careful collecting of metals for removal to Babylon, 2 Kings 25:13-17.

8. *Meeting places* is the plural of the word translated 'holy place' in verse 4, where see comment. If this is the sense here, their multiplicity is a problem, since only one sanctuary was recognized by God (Dt. 12:13f.). Possibly, however, this verse sees the Jerusalem temple as the last of God's successive meeting places (Ex. 20:24), all of which had now been destroyed. *Cf.* Shiloh (Ps. 78:60-64). If, instead, it means 'assembly places' (*cf.* 'synagogues', AV, RV), there is no clear supporting evidence for such buildings at this early date, apparently within living memory of the events of 587 BC. The LXX offers a third possibility by understanding it as 'appointed feasts', a sense which it often has; but it would require a different verb, *e.g.* 'made to cease'. There is, so far, no clear solution, but on balance the first seems the most likely.

74:9-11. The impenetrable silence

The lack of any 'sign of thy favour' (*cf.* the plea of Ps. 86:17), let alone any word through a prophet, are deeper wounds than the enemy's, for 'by these things men live' (Is. 38:16; *cf.* Dt. 8:3). The only *signs* within memory had been the enemy's (*cf.* 4b). Incidentally, the role of a *prophet* emerges clearly here as one who was entrusted with inside knowledge (Am. 3:7) and could see ahead. *Cf.* the expression, 'your eyes, the prophets' (Is. 29:10).

Historically, this cry could well be that of the derelict community left in the homeland after the deportations to Babylon and the emigration to Egypt (Je. 43:5-7) which had removed first Ezekiel and then Jeremiah.[1] We can see, at this distance, how fruitful the fallow period of God's apparent neglect was to be, in dissolving Judah's political structures in readiness for its next phase, as a church rather than a kingdom The *How long* (10), as always, had a limit, and the *Why* . *why* (11) an answer.

---

[1] See, however, the other possibilities discussed in the opening paragraph and in the comment on verse 8.

74:12-17. The ancient exploits

On the sudden burst of praise, see above, in the second introductory paragraph.

12. The psalm is swung into a new direction on the pivotal opening, *Yet God . . .* , as are many other passages of Scripture: *e.g.* Psalm 22:19 (see comment); Ephesians 2:4. While the pronoun *my* may imply that a single voice now takes the lead, it speaks for the nation, as in the similar utterance of 44:4ff. (where 'I' and 'we' alternate). With the words *God my King* there is a tacit turning from the earthly monarchy to the heavenly; the former a brief episode in history, late on the scene and soon overpowered; but the latter immemorial and irresistible. (The contrast would disappear with the Messiah, who is also *from of old*: Mi. 5:2 [1, Heb.].) The human enemies and their havoc (4-8) now look small against the powers which God has quelled and the universe He formed. What the heathen had done 'in the midst' of the sanctuary (4) was as nothing to what God at the exodus had done *in the midst of the earth* (12)—their earth, as they had thought.

13-15. The parting of the Red Sea and the crushing blow to Egypt, that dragon of the deep (*cf.* Ezk. 32:2ff.), invite comparison with the Canaanite boast of Baal's victories over the personified Sea and River, over the Dragon (*tnn*; *cf.* the plural *tannînîm*, *dragons*, here) and over the seven-headed serpent Lotan (the equivalent word to *Leviathan*[1]). The point here is that what Baal had claimed in the realm of myth, God had done in the realm of history—and done for His people, *working salvation*. Scripture will also use this language for the battle with 'the spiritual hosts of wickedness in the heavenly places' (*cf.* Is. 27:1; Rev. 12:7ff.; 13:1ff.); but here verses 12-15 survey the earthly scene, clothing the exodus events in its lively imagery, from the Red Sea (13a) to the Jordan (15b), and from the realm of judgment on the enemy (13b, 14a) to that of God's turning the wilderness into a scene of plenty (14b, 15a). It was highly relevant to the current crisis of verses 1-11, as indeed it is to the vicissitudes of the Christian church.

On *Leviathan* (14) see above. The slaying of a monster has its

---

[1] The allusion to the Canaanite material is unmistakable in Is. 27:1, where the unusual adjectives as well as the nouns are those of the Baal poem. See *Documents from Old Testament Times*, ed. D. Winton Thomas (Nelson, 1958), pp. 129-133. For comparable passages see Ps. 89:10; Is. 51:9f.

natural sequel in the devouring of its carcase, a picture elaborated with relish in Ezekiel 32:4ff., where Egypt is again the dragon (*tannîn*). To RSV, the feast is enjoyed by *the creatures of the wilderness* (*cf.* JB, Gelineau), while NEB conjectures 'the sharks'; but these are emendations of the Hebrew text,[1] which reads 'to a people, to desert-dwellers' (or desert-creatures, interpreting 'people' as in Pr. 30:25; but see 72:9 mg., and comment *ad loc.*). At the risk of over-pressing a poetic image, we may perhaps see a reference to the wealth which the Israelites brought away with them from Egypt; 'thus they despoiled the Egyptians' (Ex. 12:35f.). The mention of *food* corresponds to the metaphor of Egypt as a carcase, not necessarily to the literal provision it yielded.

16, 17. Now the thought takes wings, to God as Creator, not only as Redeemer. It is tempting to read a parable in the phrase, *thine also the night*; likewise in the final word, *and winter*; but the psalmist gives no sign of speaking figuratively. Nevertheless he is claiming the whole created order, with all its contrasts, powers and changes, for God. In the psalm's context of suffering, it forestalls our hasty conclusions in the same way as the closing chapters of Job, by looking beyond the immediate problem to the total scene which God co-ordinates in wisdom.

74:18–23. The continuing ordeal

The suffering remains, and the psalm ends with a stream of urgent prayers. But, perhaps significantly, the questions of verses 1–11 ('Why?' 'How long?' 'Why?') have ceased.

Some inconspicuous, probably unconscious, features of the prayer are instructive. Its first request, as in the Lord's prayer, is for God's good *name* (18); and this concern shows through again in 21. Another fingerprint is the frequent use of '*thy*', which relates friend and foe to God, not only to one another (see further on 72:1–4). And the appeal to God's *covenant* gives a steadying foothold where all else is in movement.

A few further details call for comment:

18. *Impious*, here and in verse 22, is *nābāl*, the word for the

---

[1] MT reads *leʿām leṣiyyîm*; RSV simply omits the former word (*cf.* mg.); Wellhausen suggested *lā ʿas*, a conjectured synonym for food: NEB ('sharks') retains the consonants but reads as *leʿamleṣê yām*, from a conjectured derivative of the root *mlṣ*, 'be smooth'. See K–B, s.v. *ʿamlāṣ.

blasphemous and overbearing fool who meets us in 14:1, where see comment.

19. *The soul of thy dove* was read by the ancient versions as 'the soul that confesses thee' (NEB), a difference of one letter (*d* for *r*, easily confused in Hebrew). But 'dove', a term of tender affection (*e.g.* Ct. 6:9), makes equally good sense.

20. This verse is particularly haunting in its AV form, where *the land* is translated 'the earth', and *violence* 'cruelty'. The RSV is more accurate, since the setting of the psalm is local,[1] and the meaning of the final word is not as specialized as our word 'cruelty'. But when the details are filled in, as in Lamentations 5:11ff. ('Women are ravished . . . Princes are hung up by their hands . . . '), or as in man's continuing record, 'cruelty' is not too strong a word, nor 'the earth' too wide a scene.

Psalm 75

Disposer Supreme

Joy in God's great reversals, His 'putting down one and lifting up another' (7), is a note which this psalm shares especially with the *Magnificat* and the Song of Hannah. It is happily placed to follow the plea of 74:22f. that God will bring His case to court. Here He is no reluctant plaintiff but the Judge: the case will open when He chooses (2), and be settled without compromise.

Title
On *the choirmaster* and *Do Not Destroy*, see Introduction, pp. 40, 43. On *Asaph*, see p. 35.

75:1. The wondrous story
Here are the *thanks* that are prompted by memory, and memory by 'recital'; that is, by a re-telling of the great things God has done (*cf.* 78:4; Dt. 31:10ff.). This is still an indispensable part of worship: *cf.* 1 Corinthians 11:23–26.

On the expression, *wondrous deeds*, see on 9:1. In this line the

---

[1] NEB widens it in this verse by revocalizing *bᵉrît*, 'covenant', as *bᵉriyyōt*, 'creatures', a word found only in Nu. 16:30 (singular); a gratuitous and unconvincing alteration.

RSV follows the ancient versions,[1] whereas NEB keeps closer to the existing Hebrew with 'thy name is brought very near to us in the story of thy wonderful deeds'.[2] God's *name* is part of His self-giving: a revelation of who He is (Ex. 34:5ff., 14) and an invitation to call upon Him (Acts 2:21). Brought 'near' in all His acts, it was brought right among us in Christ (Jn. 17:6, 26).

75:2-5. Word from the Judge

Now (perhaps initially through a prophet) the voice of God breaks in, with the same massive authority as in 60:6-8: first to reassure (2f.) and then to warn (4f.).

2. *The set time* is an important word in the Old Testament account of God's ordering of the world. It is used for the 'seasons' of the year, with their steady rhythm (Gn. 1:14), for the 'appointed feasts' (Lv. 23:2)[3] which gave the annual pattern of worship (and, unknown to Israel, set the times when Christ would suffer, rise and send the Holy Spirit), and for the 'time, times and a half' which, unknown to us, mark the approaching end (Dn. 12:7). No word could better express His control, and no word better befits a judge than *equity*, its companion here.

3. There is an almost panic-stricken glimpse of crumbling foundations in Psalm 11:3, with an answering reminder of the throne set in heaven. Here is the other aspect: God as the stabilizing strength within the structure. It can be spelt out in terms of 'common grace', His gift of wholesome influences and institutions which shore up even a godless society; but also more directly, by His holding all things in being (Acts 17:25), by His guiding hand on events and by His truth in certain men's lives. *Cf.* the 'he' of Isaiah 33:6 and the 'you' of Isaiah 58:12.

4, 5. After the reassurance, the warning; for those who think themselves 'pillars' of society (3) may be only the pushers in the herd. NEB brings 5a to life, with 'toss not your horns against high heaven'; but in 5b it unnecessarily follows LXX and Vulg. in finding a reference to God ('arrogantly against your

---

[1] *E.g.*, *qārō' b-*, 'call on', where MT has *qārôb*, 'near (is)'.
[2] Lit. 'thy name is near, thy wonders declare (it)'; *cf.* Ex. 9:16.
[3] The same word also served for the 'appointed place' where God would meet His people (see on 74:8), and, rarely, for the 'assembly' itself (Nu. 16:2). AV, PBV choose the latter meaning here, not very intelligibly. NEB is straightforward: 'I seize the appointed time'.

Creator').[1] The 'insolent neck' (RSV, as MT) is well suited to the figure of the tossing horns; it refuses the yoke, as the wicked refuse God.

75:6–8. Vision of justice

This is the responsive comment on God's oracle, driving home two of its points in particular.

6, 7. The root word for *lifting up*, in both these verses, is picked up from God's rebuke to the self-promoted (4, 5; this is the drawback of NEB's vivid '*toss not* your horns'). In verse 6 the Hebrew nouns are less stereotyped than ours, and emphasize not the points of the compass but the element of inaccessibility (the place of going forth (of the sun), the place of evening, and the wilderness; and the latter is not the Negeb in the south, but any wilderness). In other words, search where you will, there is no other arbiter but God;[2] therefore no worldly rank that is anything but provisional.

8. Now God's pledge of ultimate action (2) is translated into a powerful vision. The figure of a *cup* of judgment meets us often elsewhere, and its final occurrence in Scripture presents it as retribution: in our phrase, a dose of one's own medicine; 'a double draught for her in the cup she mixed' (Rev. 18:6). Other passages give further play to the metaphor, picturing the recipients reeling, vomiting, crazed, prostrate (*e.g.* Is. 51:17; Je. 25:15f., 27f.). *Well mixed* is a reference to the spices which might be added for pungency; so NEB, 'hot with spice'.

75:9, 10. Endless glory

Rejoice is what LXX read; a difference of one letter from 'declare'. But the latter is the text we have, and matches the concern of the second line to give God the glory.

With verse 10 the theme of tossing horns and of true exaltation returns. Strictly, the one who will act is not 'he' (RSV) but 'I'. This may mean that the worshipper pledges

[1] For *ṣawwā'r*, 'neck', LXX and Vulg. may have read *ṣûr*, 'Rock', a difference of one consonant. But if so, the fact that they paraphrased it to 'God' is an admission of its slight awkwardness here. There is no need to alter MT ('neck').

[2] In 6b, *hārîm*, 'lifting up' could alternatively be the noun 'mountains', which finds support in MT's pointing of the previous word, yielding the phrase 'wilderness of the mountains' (*cf.* LXX, Vulg.). This underlies JB, RP and Gelineau, but it involves some small adjustments to make sense. RSV, NEB are preferable.

himself to fight God's battles; but in view of the emphasis on the one Judge, more probably this echoes God's own proclamation of 4 and 5. So patience and suffering are not the end of the story: there will be a time for power without aggression, and glory without pride.

Psalm 76

Lion of Judah

There is a strong simplicity in the pattern of this psalm, which first looks back to a great deliverance (1–6), and then on to a greater judgment (7–12). The former is local and defensive, with Zion, God's earthly base and residence, under concerted attack; the latter half is cosmic, with heaven as God's seat, the world His kingdom, and all who suffer injustice His concern. So it is to some extent a miniature of the biblical story itself, from the circumscribed and fiercely fought beginnings to the end-time when, through all man's opposition, God's salvation and judgment will have reached their climax and full spread.

Title
On *the choirmaster* and *Asaph*, see Introduction, pp. 40, 35. On *A Song*, see p. 37.

76:1–3. God in His stronghold
Nothing could be narrower or more provincial than this beginning, taken as a statement of *God*'s glory; but as the glory of Israel nothing could be richer or more fruitful for the world. The fact that in Judah God was *known* has become the blessing of all men, 'for salvation is from the Jews' (note the connection of this with the claim that 'we worship what we know', in Jn. 4:22). Likewise for the church, these are still the priorities: that God be *known* (Phil. 3:10) in it, and His *name* held *great* (Jn. 12:27f.).

2. Not His '*abode*' but His 'covert' or 'lair'[1] is the bold expression here, with its tacit comparison of the Lord to a lion

---

[1] The longer form of this word is used for a man-made shelter or hut (*cf.* 'tent', NEB, JB, here); but the word used here denotes a natural thicket, the latter as impenetrable as the former is flimsy.

273

(*cf.* Je. 25:38, and see on Ps. 27:5, with the references there; also, for His defence of Jerusalem, Is. 31:4). *Salem* is a shorter form of Jerusalem (*cf.* Gn. 14:18; Heb. 7:2); its alternative name of *Zion* was that of the hilltop and fortress which David captured. On God's choice of this city, a major theme in the Psalms, see on 46:4; 68:15-18; 87.

3. The *flashing arrows* are literally 'thunderbolts (*cf.* 78:48) of the bow'. The great deliverance will be enlarged upon in the next section.

76:4-6. The helpless aggressor

The occasion that springs to mind here is the elimination of Sennacherib's army overnight by the angel of the Lord (Is. 37:36). The LXX brings in an allusion to it in its version of the title, and no event could be more strongly suggested than this by verses 5f. While Psalms 46-48 sing of Zion's salvation in figurative terms, as if to avoid confining it to any one occasion, this language seems designed to recall a particular night in history,[1] as if to remind us that miracles are actual and datable, not picturesque statements of general truths.

4. *The everlasting mountains* is a reading borrowed from the LXX, probably rightly, in place of the somewhat obscure 'mountains of prey' (AV, RV).[2] Various other suggestions have been made (*e.g.* JB, TEV), but have no textual evidence to support them.

5. The phrase, *were unable to use their hands* (lit. 'did not find their hands') is put better by NEB: 'cannot lift a hand'. So God fulfilled His promise: 'He shall not come into this city, or shoot an arrow there . . .' (Is. 37:33). There is a series of such miraculous restraints on the enemy, within Scripture and without, in the history of God's church; but not an unbroken series (as Pss. 74 and 44, to look no further, make clear enough). What one's expectation of miracles should be, has never been better put than by the three friends in Daniel 3:17f.

---

[1] On the theory that such references arise from a cultic drama, see Introduction, pp. 8ff.

[2] This may be a compressed expression for the mountains which are the haunts of predators. *Cf.* note on verse 2. D. W. Thomas, however (*TRP, ad loc.*), suggests that '*ad*, 'for ever', may have been the original reading, but through its proximity to the root for 'spoil' (5a) a copyist mistook it for the other '*ad*, a rare word meaning 'prey' (Gn. 49:27), and inserted the more usual word to clarify it. Such association of ideas is not unknown. Both words occur in Gn. 49:27.

76:7-9. God rises for judgment

The action is no longer localized, or past, or defensive. God is foreseen striking the final blow against evil everywhere, as Judge; and, in the concluding stanza, receiving the world's homage, as its King.

7. *Who can stand . . . ?* is echoed (perhaps quoted) as the climax of the judgment vision of Revelation 6:12–17, which is a most powerful exposition of this verse.

8. This is the end-time, and the vision of it is so certain as to be presented to us as past and complete. (This happens often enough in the Prophets to have given rise to the term 'the prophetic perfect', often translated by the future.[1]) The picture of the earth hushed into silence is akin to that of verses 5f., which like all God's judgments gives a foretaste of His final day. God is now seen, however, not entrenched in Zion but enthroned in heaven.

9. Note the purpose of *judgment*, which is *to save* those who commit their cause to God. This is the chief aspect of justice in the Psalms, where the plight of those who either cannot or will not hit back at the ruthless is a constant concern. Here the victims are the latter sort: the 'humble' (NEB, JB) or 'meek' (AV, RV) rather than simply the 'oppressed'. See the comments on the word '*ānāw* at 18:27 (the second word discussed there). Note, too, the breadth of God's care: His little kingdom of verses 1–3 was His bridgehead, never His boundary. This was as wide as *the earth*, and His objective the salvation of '*all*' (9b) poor men and humble'.

76:10-12. The rebels submit

Verse 10, one of the most striking sayings in the Psalter, creates some problems of detail by its very boldness. But most of our translations agree on the first line, well conveyed by Coverdale in 'The fierceness of man shall turn to thy praise'. This statement of God's providential control (to have its supreme demonstration at Calvary, *cf.* Acts 2:23) is the main thrust of the verse. The familiar sequel, 'the remainder of wrath shalt thou restrain' (AV, *cf.* PBV), distorts the meaning of the verb, which is always used in the Old Testament to mean 'gird' or 'gird on', not 'bind' in the sense of 'restrict'.

---

[1] An example from a well-known prophecy is Is. 9:6 (5, Heb.), where the whole verse has the form of narrative, but is usually translated by a mixture of perfects and futures.

The picture then is probably like that of Isaiah 59:17, where the Lord 'wrapped himself in fury as a mantle',[1] and it is a moot point whether *the residue of wrath* is thought of as man's or God's. If it is the latter, it implies that whatever is lacking in the judgment man brings on himself (thereby vindicating God's name), the wrath of God will supply when He arises to judge the world.

11. The expression *your God* suggests that the first half of the verse is addressed to the covenant people; but the second half summons the surrounding world, since their *gifts* are properly translated 'tribute' (NEB; *cf.* this word in 68:29 (30, Heb.); Is. 18:7). In speaking of *him who is to be feared* (a single word in Heb.) the last line uses a term for God which (in spite of NEB mg.) need not be forbidding; it is expounded in Isaiah 8:12f.

12. If verse 11 left the matter open, this closes it. The first line can mean either 'he snuffs out the lives' (JB) or 'he breaks the spirit' (NEB). The second line takes a related word to 'feared', discussed above (11); but now, as in verse 7, its context can only allow the meaning *terrible*.

If this is an Old Testament ending, the New Testament presents the same alternatives of willing or unwilling submission. But it adds to this the daunting dimension of eternity.

Psalm 77

Musings in Two Moods

All who have known the enveloping pressure of a dark mood can be grateful for the candour of this fellow-sufferer,[2] but also for his courage. The memories which at first brought only tormenting comparisons are resolutely re-examined, no longer coloured with the present despair but allowed to shine with

[1] LXX, however, has 'keep festival' (Heb. *ḥgg*) instead of 'gird' (*ḥgr*), which raises the further question whether 'the residue' should mean 'the survivors' (as it often does). Hence TEV, 'those who survive the wars will keep your festivals'. NEB adopts a similar starting-point, but also revocalizes 'man' in the first line and 'wrath' in the second, to read 'Edom' and 'Hamath' respectively (kingdoms to the south and north of Israel).

[2] There is a poignant setting of verses 8f., with parts of other psalms, in Vaughan Williams, *The Pilgrim's Progress*, Act III, Scene 2.

their own light and speak with their own logic. By the end of the psalm the pervasive 'I' has disappeared, and the objective facts of the faith have captured all his attention and all of ours.

Title

On *the choirmaster* and *Asaph*, see Introduction, pp. 40, 35. On *Jeduthun*, see on Psalm 39.

77:1-3. Cries of distress

1. If we think it naïve to cry to God *aloud . . . , that he may hear me*, God, reading the heart, may think otherwise. Jesus Himself prayed 'with loud cries and tears . . . , and he was heard for his godly fear' (Heb. 5:7).

2. In this verse the tenses should probably be translated as past, helping to show the long span of the ordeal, but also the persistence of the prayer.[1] In the last line there may be a further hint of this tenacity by an echo of Jacob's refusal to be comforted over Joseph (Gn. 37:35). Love will not easily accept a parting; and this is how God's silence seems to the sufferer.

3. *I think* is literally 'I remember'—a word which will play an important part in the poem as a whole: see verses 5 (6) and 11, and the opening comments on the psalm.

77:4-9. Searchings of heart

We are now given a closer insight into the distress, first as to its symptoms of sleeplessness and confusion (4), but chiefly as to its root condition, a state of doubt.

5, 6. Most modern translations follow the ancient versions here, transferring *I remember* from verse 6 to verse 5, and accepting other small variations, which hardly affect the general sense. But the existing Hebrew text has some striking features which may well be original. RV renders it:

> 'I have considered the days of old,
>   The years of ancient times.
> I call to remembrance my song in the night:
>   I commune with mine own heart;
>   And my spirit made diligent search.'

[1] NEB, however, renders the penultimate sentence 'I lay sweating and nothing would cool me'. The verbs give some support to this, since the primary sense of *stretched out* and *wearying* (RSV) is 'flowed' and 'growing numb'. But the latter verb is used elsewhere only figuratively, of helplessness; also NEB's rendering involves eliminating *my hand*.

277

The last line could indeed be translated 'And He searched my spirit',[1] which would bring out the other side of this self-communing; but the ensuing questions follow more naturally from the usual translation. 'My song'[2] is probably not a 'song in the night' like that of 42:8, but one remembered in the night from happier days—making the contrast all the sharper, but the homeward pull so much the stronger.

7-9. This is a clear example of the value of confessing one's doubts to God. As the broad misgivings of verse 7 are spelt out more precisely in verses 8f. their inner contradictions come to light, and with them the possibility of an answer. If *steadfast love* is pledged in His covenant (see on 17:7), it can hardly disappear, or *his promises* come to nothing. The words *for ever* and *for all time* underline the point. And to ask '*Has God forgotten?*' is to invite only one reply. The remaining question (9b) is admittedly more uncomfortable, since only sin arouses God's *anger*, and only impenitence perpetuates it. But that, if it arises, is a challenge rather than a problem.

77:10-15. Courage from the past

Verse 10 is the turning-point (as the *Selah* indicates), in spite of RSV's paragraphing. But since two of its key words are open to various interpretations,[3] the translation of the verse must ultimately be controlled by its compatibility with the passage it introduces. That passage (10-20) is an exultant act of worship, recalling the miracles of salvation.

This tells against RSV and most moderns, with their tone of pained surprise at God's lost prowess[4] (*cf.* especially TEV's 'What hurts me most is this—'). Our older translations did better justice to the sense by supplying the verb 'I will remember' (anticipating its two occurrences in the next verse).

---

[1] The verb is masculine, and 'spirit' is usually, though not invariably, feminine.

[2] For this word, *neĝînātî*, the ancient versions evidently read *hāĝîtî*, 'I mused'.

[3] *Grief* (RSV; *cf.* JB, Gelineau, TEV) could alternatively be read as 'infirmity' (AV, RV, PBV; *cf.* RP, NEB) or translated as 'entreaty' (Eaton); while *changed* (RSV; *cf.* Gelineau, JB, RP, NEB, TEV) could mean 'years' (AV, RV, PBV) or 'renewal' or 'recital' (Eaton).

[4] This tone, however, can be modified if, with some commentators, the emphasis is thought to lie on God's *right hand* (*i.e.*, on His current mode of operation) as distinct from His unchanging character, and if, further, *my grief* is taken to be an attitude now repudiated by the psalmist. It remains, if so, a somewhat muted act of praise.

Thus PBV: 'And I said, It is mine own infirmity: but I will remember the years of the right hand of the most Highest.' The verse then makes a strong pivot between the two sections, and its roughness of form may be partly due to its variation on verse 5b (another verbless line)[1] which it lifts to a higher plane—as if to say, 'The years of long ago?' 'The years of His right hand!' So memory, which was enervating before, is now invigorating. That right hand, so far from failing, links the past to the present, full of promise.[2]

11, 12. *I will call to mind* is, strictly speaking,[3] 'I will make mention of'; *i.e.*, it is a public recounting of these deeds (Ps. 78 is an extended example of this), just as 11b, 12 speaks of one's private pondering of them—the one enriching the other. On the meaning of *wonders*, here and at verse 14, see on 9:1, where 'wonderful deeds' is a word from this root.

13, 14. Although the translation, 'Thy way . . . is in the sanctuary' (AV, RV; *cf.* LXX, *etc.*), would find a telling counterpart in verse 19, 'thy way was in the sea', the phrase should almost certainly be taken as (lit.) 'thy way is in holiness', for this echoes the victory song at the Red Sea ('majestic in holiness', Ex. 15:11), while the companion phrases echo first its question 'Who is like thee . . . among the gods?', then its epithet 'doing wonders' (as in our verse 14a), and finally its allusion to the effect of these things on 'the peoples' (14b; Ex. 15:14). *Holy*, in such a context, is a formidable word, conveying the aspect of God as one who 'dwells in unapproachable light'; fearful as an enemy but glorious as a friend.

15. And it is closer than friendship. In contrast to *the peoples* (14), these are *thy people*, joined to God in covenant and counted as virtually His kinsmen. This is the common implication of the word *redeem*, since the redeemer (*gō'ēl*) was normally the relative who must buy one out of trouble when all else failed. The deliverance from Egypt implied no less than that.

The coupling of *Jacob* and *Joseph* as ancestors of the people

---

[1] See on verses 5, 6, above.
[2] Eaton, with no textual changes, offers two translations which speak of prayer rather than grief or infirmity, and of the renewal or the recital of God's acts, rather than 'years' or 'change'. His translations, though they may be too ingenious, have the important merits of fitting the context and of showing a smooth construction.
[3] Following the *ketîb*, *i.e.*, the consonants as written.

redeemed from the Egyptians may be due to the insistence of both of them that the Promised Land, not Egypt, must be their final rest (Gn. 47:29ff.; 50:24f.).

77:16-20. 'Thunder of thy power'

The tremendous events at the Red Sea and at Sinai fire the poet's mind as he gives himself to the thought of them and to conveying what he sees. Not only is his trouble dwarfed and forgotten, but our picture of the world is given a corrective against any impression of autonomous forces and an absentee creator. Poetic freedom, of course, as in 114:3ff., heightens and personalizes the drama, with the waters not merely in turmoil but in travail (the lit. sense of *afraid*, 16), and the lightning and thunder pictured as God's flaming *arrows* (17) and, perhaps, roaring chariot-wheels (a frequent sense of the word translated *whirlwind*, 18; *cf.* NEB mg. and, *e.g.*, Is. 5:28; Je. 47:3; Ezk. 10:2). But it is a true picture of God's sway over nature. Even when He was incarnate, the winds and waves would obey Him and the sea provide a path for Him.

20. The closing verse, if it is an anticlimax, is a calculated one. Displays of power (as Elijah was to find) are means, not ends; God's overriding concern is for His *flock*. With that unflattering but reassuring word, and with the mixed human leadership of *Moses and Aaron*, the psalm comes to a close which is within hailing distance of the psalmist and his day of small things, yet one which marked a stage in Israel's pilgrimage destined to be no less formative than its spectacular beginning.

Psalm 78

Lest We Forget

This could be sub-titled, in view of verses 12 and 68, *From Zoan to Zion*, for it reviews the turbulent adolescence of Israel from its time of slavery in Egypt to the reign of David. Like the parting song of Moses (Dt. 32) it is meant to search the conscience: it is history that must not repeat itself. At the same time, it is meant to warm the heart, for it tells of great miracles, of a grace that persists through all the judgments, and of the promise that displays its tokens in the chosen city and chosen king.

The Christian user of the psalm knows that history did repeat itself, and that finally the chosen tribe refused its King, and did so in the chosen city (68); but he also knows that God has more than kept the promise to David, and has established a Mount Zion that is 'the mother of us all' (Gal. 4:26, AV). He can also reflect, however, that just as Israel's story in the psalm breaks off abruptly, for subsequent generations to complete and to learn from, so the New Testament breaks off its history of our own beginnings (Acts 28:30f.), for us to continue with the fidelity which is expounded in verse 7.

Title
On *Maskil* and *Asaph*, see Introduction, pp. 38, 35.

78:1–8. A sermon from history
Verses 1 and 2 are in the style of the Wisdom writings; for example, the word for *parable* (*māšāl*) gives the book of Proverbs its title. Basically this means a comparison, *i.e.*, a saying which uses one realm of life to illuminate another. Matthew 13:35 quotes verse 2 as a prophecy of the way Jesus would teach; but His method would be more imaginative and less explicit than this example. The psalm makes its point (as Stephen did in Acts 7) by its selection of material from the past, and drives the lesson home relentlessly. Our Lord, when He based a parable on history (Mt. 21:33ff.), re-shaped the events by a vivid miniaturization (as Nathan did in 2 Sa. 12) which invited the hearers to draw conclusions. Both methods make the past hold up a mirror to the present, and bring its *dark sayings*, or riddles (NEB), to light—for the true pattern of history is not self-evident.

4. On the use of the word *wonders* (translated 'miracles' in verse 11), see on 9:1.

5, 6. The certainty and the clarity of what God has delivered to us are emphasized in the twin expressions, *testimony* and *law*; see the comment on 19:7–10 and on 119:1f. For the classic passage on teaching this faith to one's *children* see Deuteronomy 6:6–9, for Scripture has no room for parental neutrality.

7, 8. Here is the main burden of the psalm, in positive and negative terms. The three phrases of verse 7 show a threefold cord of faith, as personal trust,[1] informed and humble thinking,

[1] *Hope* here means reliance.

and an obedient will. If these qualities strike us as un-adventurous, verse 8 depicts the rebel against the covenant in his true colours, not a hero but a renegade: perverse, infirm of purpose and unfit for trust. The next verses develop the thought.

78:9-16. Miracles forgotten

9. *The Ephraimites* will reappear in verse 67 as those who were passed over for the leadership. As the largest of the breakaway tribes, their subsequent history was to make them almost a symbol of backsliding and apostasy (*cf.* Ho. 4–13, *passim*), and this is how their name is used here. As there is no record of any special cowardice on their part (they tended in fact to be hot-tempered: Jdg. 8:1ff.; 12:1ff.), their desertion in battle is probably a metaphor, a powerful way of expressing the facts of the next verse and bringing out the shame of it, a shame which belongs to the whole nation.[1]

12. *Zoan* is better known as Tanis, in the north-east of the Nile Delta, a city which was either identical with Rameses II's capital (Raamses, which the Israelites helped to build: Ex. 1:11) or not many miles from it. The *fields* would be better translated 'the country round' or 'the region of'.

78:17-31. Murmurs of unrest

17, 18. Evidently the more God gives, the less we appreciate it. This grudging response to a string of miracles is not unlike the sequel to the feeding of the five thousand: a demand for a further and better sign (Jn. 6:26, 30f.). The whole history of unbelief in the wilderness supports our Lord's refusal; it is also an answer to the perennial demands for better proofs. In appealing to this very psalm (24; *cf.* Jn. 6:31), the arguers were handling too sharp a weapon.

19, 20. The expression, *spread a table*, uses the same words as Psalm 23:5, whose serenity is a shining contrast to this. If the question, *Can God . . . ? Can he . . . ?* always deserves some degree of rebuke (*e.g.* Gn. 18:14; Mk. 9:23), God knows the

---

[1] The Heb. of this verse is difficult, with an extra word, 'shooters of', before the word 'bow' (*cf.* mg.). As the root (*rmh*) of this extra word is similar to that of 'deceitful' in verse 57, there may be some word-play between the two verses, which are also linked by the expressions 'turned back'/'twisted' (both from the root *hpk*). See also Ho. 7:16, where Ephraim is again called a deceitful bow.

difference between struggling faith and contemptuous unbelief (*no faith*, 22).

21, 22. Verses 21-31 are based on Numbers 11, from which
we learn that the *fire* of verse 21 was more than a mere
metaphor (*cf.* Nu. 11:1-3). God's reply to the challenge of 19f.
was in fact a fiery 'No' to the spirit of the demand, and a
prodigious 'Yes' to the substance of it. Through both of these,
in different ways, Israel was brought into judgment. The
second of them is memorably summed up in Psalm 106:15
(where see comment).

23-25. While the quails (26ff.) were the climax of the *food
in abundance* (25), the *manna* was likewise a quite searching gift
of grace. The stipulations surrounding it made it a gentle test
of obedience (Ex. 16:4) and its unfamiliarity made it (together
with the hunger that had preceded it) a simple training in
priorities and in humility (Dt. 8:3).

Jesus pointed out the limited sense in which it could be
called *the grain of heaven* ('bread from heaven', Jn. 6:31f.), and
yet a foretaste, for all that, of the greater reality. If this bread
came from the skies, He, the bread of life, was from the Father;
and if this nourished the body for a while, He would satisfy a
deeper hunger and be made the food of immortality (Jn.
6:30-40, 47-51). We may note perhaps a further parallel, in
that neither of these gifts from above, for all their miraculous
and kindly qualities, evoked much gratitude.

26-31. If the manna, with its unexciting provision, was one
kind of test, the sudden glut of quails was quite another. It was
met with an abandoned greed (commemorated in the name
of the spot, 'the graves of craving', Nu. 11:34 mg.; *cf.* our
verses 29b, 30a) which spoke its own language of utter
impatience with the pilgrim call and the filial spirit. The swift
judgment of 30f. shows not that God acted prematurely but
that this behaviour was symptomatic, this attitude contagious
and this moment crucial.

78:32-39. Meaningless repentance
A passage that may usefully be read with this is Hosea 5:15 –
6:6, where Israel is seen responding to God's chastening, as
here, with apparent earnestness (*cf.* 34), and with a touching
eloquence which may deceive the reader (Ho. 6:1-3), until he
hears God's answer: 'Your love is like a morning cloud, like
the dew that goes early away.' The flattery and lies of our

verse 36 were possibly of this kind: a deception which was the self-deception of empty verbalizing: in which case the guilt of Israel was not unlike the guilt which James attacks in Christians (*e.g.* Jas. 1:22ff.; 2:14ff.). But the sin which was so shallowly repented of, here and in Hosea, was the crucial sin of disloyalty to God (*towards him*) and *to his covenant* (37; *cf.* verse 8b, above). In the light of this apostasy, the equivalent of marital unfaithfulness, God's compassion and restraint (38f.) are overwhelming. In this respect, too, the passage is reminiscent of Hosea: 'What shall I do with you, O Ephraim?' (Ho. 6:4), 'How can I give you up!' (11:8).

78:40–53. Ingratitude for the Exodus

40, 41. The expressions, *How often . . . !* and *again and again*, give the other side of the sudden judgment of verses 30f. and the pious prayers of 34f. The verbs add their contribution to the picture of both Israel and God: on Israel's side a combination of stubbornness (*rebelled*; *cf.* Dt. 21:18) and insolent scepticism (*tested*; *cf.* Ex. 17:7; Ps. 95:8f.), and on God's side grief and pain. The rare verb in 41b probably means hurt or *provoked* (LXX and most moderns), rather than AV's 'limited', appropriate though the latter might seem.[1] On the name, *Holy One of Israel*, see on 71:22.

42. Here is the crux of the matter (*cf.* verse 7), for if redemption itself is forgotten (in Israel's case, the exodus; in ours, the cross and resurrection), faith and love will not last long.

43–53. So the psalm makes sure that our memory is refreshed. In a free survey of the 'miracles in the fields of Zoan' (43; see on verse 12) six or seven of the ten plagues are mentioned,[2] in language designed to show not only the power of God but the privilege of Israel. Have they forgotten that the wrath which was restrained for them (38) was let loose on their oppressors (49f.), or that they were shepherded while others perished (52f.)?

---

[1] 'Limited' is a rather precarious derivation from a noun meaning a mark, supposing it to mean, by extension, a boundary.

[2] In verse 48 two Heb. mss have *deḇer*, 'plague', 'murrain' (as in Ex. 9:3), where *bārāḏ*, 'hail', would repeat verse 47. If this is original it adds the cattle-plague of Ex. 9:3ff. to the other six, leaving only the lice, boils and darkness unmentioned. *Thunderbolts* (48) can also mean 'fevers'; *cf.* JB, NEB, and see Dt. 32:24.

78:54-64. Ingratitude for the promised land

Privilege again sharpens the reproach, with the mention of the evicted *nations* (55); for the old attitudes of Israel persisted, summed up in the words *tested and rebelled* (56; *cf.* 40f.) and in the metaphor of the useless *bow*, failing on the day of battle (57; *cf.* verse 9).

58. But the characteristic sin is no longer discontent (the paradox of the wilderness years with their daily miracles) but idolatry—the paradox of the years in Canaan, whose idolaters God had used Israel to judge.

59-64. The history behind these verses is told in 1 Samuel 4, the chapter which gave us the word Ichabod and the phrase 'The glory has departed'. This *glory* (61) was the ark of God, captured by the Philistines, its departure a symbol of His own withdrawal (60f.). It would happen again. Jeremiah would use *Shiloh* (60) as his text against the temple (Je. 7:11ff.), and Ezekiel would see the glory of the Lord departing from Jerusalem (Ezk. 11:23). Jesus would speak in similar terms, and not only to the Jewish church (*cf.* Rev. 2:5; 3:16).

64. The allusion is to the death of Eli and his two sons, and to the stunned silence of Phinehas's widow (1 Sa. 4:20), broken only by her cry of 'Ichabod' and her comment on its meaning. *Cf.* Ezekiel 24:15–24.

78:65-72. A new beginning

The blackest moment in Israel's early history had in fact been swiftly followed by stirrings of power. The boisterous verses 65f. scarcely exaggerate the tragi-comedy played out at Ashdod (1 Sa. 5), and the next half-century was to see Israel brought to its zenith. By this point in the psalm such a development is utterly unexpected, and shows the steadfast love of God in the most robust and unsentimental colours.

67ff. Now it is God's sovereignty of choice which comes to the fore. Despite the fame of *Joseph*, and the central position and power of his son *Ephraim*, God's choice was *Judah*, a tribe which had won no glory in the days of the judges. Within Judah He chose *Mount Zion*, a stronghold still in enemy hands (2 Sa. 5:6f.); and to capture it and reign there He took a *shepherd* from the flock. In all this the only motivation which is mentioned is in the phrase 'Mount Zion, *which he loves*'. Certainly the rejected Ephraim (67) was stigmatized in verse 9 as a renegade, but all Israel has since been shown in the same light. The emphasis is not on man's deserts but on God's 'own purpose and . . . grace' (2 Tim. 1:9). To this, Zion owes its stability (69); to this God's people owe the gift and gifts of David as their skilful shepherd. If Israel's record is her shame, God's persistent goodness emerges as her hope (and ours) for the unfinished story.

Psalm 79

Outrage

With Psalm 74, this cry comes down to us, it seems, from eyewitnesses of the fall of Jerusalem to Nebuchadnezzar. Probably these were the survivors left in its neighbourhood, rather than deportees like the singers of Psalm 137.

The gloom is almost unrelieved, but never reaches despair: it is in fact largely the product of bewilderment that God's 'great power' (11) should be withheld so long from His undoubted people. In other words it is a cry of faith in perplexity, not of fundamental doubt.

Title
On *Asaph*, see Introduction, p. 35.

79:1–4. Desecration
While there is pathos in the psalm, its prevailing tone is one of indignation, and its appeal is to God's honour. It is *thy* inheritance and temple, not simply ours, that have suffered; *thy servants* and *thy saints*, viewed not merely as our friends and compatriots, who have been treated as carrion. The word *holy* (1) adds to this emphasis. What has happened is more than tragedy: it is sacrilege. (But the word for *saints*, in verse 2, means 'loyal', not 'holy'; see on 18:25.) So was fulfilled the prophecy of Jeremiah 16:4.

3. To lie unburied was the final humiliation, as though one had departed unloved and of no account, as disposable as an animal. David had honoured Rizpah for fighting off this last indignity for her sons (2 Sa. 21:10–14); the tyrant Jehoiakim was promised just such a fate: 'the burial of an ass . . . , dragged and cast forth' (Je. 22:18f.). Whether in popular imagination the departed suffered in Sheol for lack of burial rites, as is often assumed, one can hardly tell; it is certainly not a doctrine of the Old Testament,[1] which discourages super-stitious attitudes to death (*cf.* Lv. 19:28). What *is* taught in the Old Testament is the human solidarity and individual worth which decent burial and mourning customs instinctively affirm.

79:5-7. Strange friendship!

There is no pretence here of innocence; the word for *jealous wrath* is too reminiscent of the second commandment for that (Ex. 20:5). But there is a twofold perplexity, that the fire should burn so long, and the covenant count for so little. For us, this is doubly valuable, first as insight into the feelings of the hard-pressed in our own age; but secondly through hind-sight, for history shows us God's answer to Israel. The ordeal was not for ever; the jealous wrath had another side to it (see Zc. 8:2); and the answer to verse 6 had already been given through Amos (Am. 3:2; *cf.* Lk. 12:48), if they could bear to hear it.[2]

79:8-10. Strange severity!

8. Two prophets in this period quote a bitter saying that was going the rounds: 'The fathers have eaten sour grapes, and the children's teeth are set on edge' (Je. 31:29; Ezk. 18:2). There was truth in it (see again the second commandment), which one could either humbly accept, as here, recognizing one's continuity with the past, or indignantly reject as a gross injustice. The present humility shows itself in the plea for *compassion* (whose vivid phrase, *come speedily to meet us*, may put us in mind of another encounter: Lk. 15:20), and in the people's confession of their own sins (9).

9. The appeal rests on God's character (as *God of our salvation*) and His good *name*, much as in Ezekiel 36, where the highest of blessings are promised in terms not even of com-

---

[1] Ezk. 32:27 (where see comment) may seem to penalize Meshech and Tubal for burial without full military honours; but the text is insecure (LXX omits the crucial 'not', and is followed by most commentators) and the details of the vision are poetic rather than didactic.

[2] Nevertheless the New Testament upholds the plea for judgment, on the ground that man's ignorance of God is, at bottom, wilful: Rom. 1:18-23; 2 Thes. 1:6ff.

passion but of God's self-consistency and honour. It is strong ground.

10. This fiercer demand is equally well founded, since every tongue must confess the Lord (Is. 45:23), and every drop of innocent blood be requited (*cf.* Mt. 23:35; Lk. 18:7). What the psalmists could not know of was the blood of Christ which 'speaks more graciously than the blood of Abel' (Heb. 12:24). See further, Introduction, pp. 25–32.

79:11–13. Sighs, taunts or praise

Such are the three tones of voice which, in the main, ascend to God. The prayer of the psalm is that the first two will be answered so decisively that only the third remains. It is a prayer to echo; but not lightly. The Old Testament searches the reader in relation to verse 11 (see Pr. 24:11f.) and the New Testament in relation to verse 12, at least as regards the taunts that spread to us (*cf.* 1 Pet. 3:9, 16f.; 4:14).

13. To look back to verse 1 is to wonder at the faith which enabled such a psalm, from such distress, to end, even if only in anticipation, with such a word as *praise.*

Psalm 80

Turn, Lord, and Turn Us!

Not the fall of Jerusalem, it seems, but the last days of its northern counterpart, Samaria, about a century-and-a-half earlier, gave rise to this strong cry for help. The refrain, 'Restore us . . . ' (3, 7, 19), reiterates the theme of the psalm, and the extended simile of the vine gives it a memorable form. The prayer reveals how deep was the shock felt in Jerusalem (the psalm belongs to the Asaphite temple-singers) at the sweeping away of almost the whole of Israel—ten tribes out of the twelve—between 734 and 722 BC, leaving the little realm of Judah exposed now on the north to a new Assyrian province instead of to its sister-kingdom of Israel. There is no thought here of the old rivalries of north and south, only distress at the wreck of so much promise and the break-up of the old family. There was another glimpse of this solidarity in the invitation to the passover at Jerusalem, which was sent by Hezekiah to the survivors of the northern tribes, soon after the disaster. But the rebuff which he received (2 Ch. 30:1, 10f.) revealed something of the Israelite obduracy which had helped to make inevitable the judgment which this psalm laments.

Title
See Introduction, pp. 42, 35, 37. LXX adds 'A psalm concerning the Assyrian', which seems a valid inference from the psalm, whether or not it belonged originally to the title.

80:1-3. Distant shepherd, hidden sun
Just as prayer itself adds nothing to God's knowledge, and yet plays a large part in His economy, so the impassioned pleas for His attention, that He will rouse Himself and act, have a proper place within prayer although they add nothing to His will to help. This psalm abounds in them: see the spate of imperatives in the first and last sections. God, it seems, prefers an excess of boldness in prayer to an excess of caution, as long as the boldness is something more than loquacity (Ec. 5:2; Mt. 6:7). We come to Him as sons, not as applicants.

1. It was mostly the king who was called his people's *Shepherd; cf.* 78:71. This prayer acknowledges that ultimately there is only One who lives up to such a title (*cf.* 2 Sa. 24:17; Ezk. 34:1ff.). He is also named as Shepherd in the Blessing of *Joseph* (Gn. 49:24). Pictured in Psalm 22:3 as 'enthroned on the praises of Israel' (since a people's love is a king's glory), God is seen elsewhere in the Old Testament *enthroned upon the cherubim*, guardians of holiness and agents of judgment (see on 18:10). These, together with His dazzling brightness, were features of a theophany, *i.e.*, of God's majesty made visible; and the psalm prays for no less.

2. These tribes, the Rachel tribes (Gn. 46:19f.), give us the clue to the situation, for they had ceased to exist as independent units long before the fall of Jerusalem. The prayer therefore concerns their own crisis and downfall, near the end of the eighth century BC; see the opening remarks on the psalm. Only Benjamin survived, since it had stayed with Judah at the split of the kingdom after Solomon. Samaria, the capital of Israel, was in the territory of Ephraim, and this powerful tribe, with its brother Manasseh, dominated the centre of the promised land. The kingdom of Israel, as distinct from Judah, was often referred to as 'Ephraim', especially by Hosea; so it was doubly difficult for this proud tribe to accept help from Jerusalem (*cf.*, again, 2 Ch. 30:5-12). But this prayer shows how genuine was Jerusalem's concern: note the fellow-feeling in the use of 'us' and 'our'.[1]

3. This refrain returns at verses 7 and 19, each time with the divine title a little fuller than before. The plea, *restore us*, can be taken in more than one way, and it is debatable whether it is simply a cry for rescue or whether it goes deeper, as in AV, RV, 'Turn us again'. The confession of disloyalty in verse 18 suggests that it has indeed a spiritual dimension as well as the material one; if so, this will apply, too, to the word *saved* (*cf.* Ezk. 37:23), although in the Old Testament the latter seldom has this richer meaning. The prayer, *let thy face shine*, takes up the words of the Aaronic Blessing (Nu. 6:25), invoking not the blinding glory of verse 1b but the glow of kindness and friendship. The paraphrases of JB and TEV, 'let your face smile on us', and 'Show us your love' (to match the latter's paraphrase of 2b, 'Show us your strength'), are vivid and expressive, but are comments rather than translations.

80:4-7. The bread of tears

Instead of the shining face of God (see above) there is the darkness of smoke, like that of Sinai, in the word used here for *be angry*; *cf.* JB, 'smoulder'.[2] Instead of green pastures and a cup running over, the Shepherd of Israel (1) offers monotonously *tears . . . tears* (*cf.* 42:3). The word for *in full measure* is characteristically specific; a rough equivalent would be 'by the quart'[3]—a vivid touch.

6. For *scorn* (*mānôd*) the MT has 'strife' (*mādôn*). The latter makes some sense, as in our expression 'a bone of contention', but the former is supported by the Syriac version and makes a closer parallel with the second line; it assumes that two consonants have changed places in the copying.

7. On this refrain, see on verse 3.

[1] Another possibility is that this is the prayer of devout refugees from these tribes. Even so, its presence in the Asaphite collection reveals this sense of Israel's unity.

[2] NEB's 'resist' is conjectured from a Syriac root, 'be strong', *i.e.*, unyielding. *Cf.* G. R. Driver, *HTR* 29 (1936), pp. 186f. But it is hardly necessary to look for an alternative to 'smoke', even though the subject of the verb is usually God's wrath rather than God Himself. See on 18:8.

[3] To be exact, 'by the third'; evidently a standard size of container, though we have no further details of it as yet. It occurs also in Is. 40:12.

80:8–13. The ravaged vine
This may well have been the chief background to our Lord's
saying, 'I am the true vine'. What Israel had only begun to be,
He wholly was and is. Other relevant passages are Isaiah 5:1–7,
written perhaps at about this time, and Ezekiel 15. Possibly
the 'fruitful bough' of Joseph (*cf.* verse 1) in Genesis 49:22
suggested the metaphor here.

8–11. The story of Israel's exodus, conquest and settlement
is carried through to the great days of its expansion[1] under
David and Solomon, in a figure of simple beauty and clarity.
What is also brought out is the wonder of so small a tree
overshadowing *mountains* and *mighty cedars*. But is there a hint
of incongruity, as in the fable of the vine tempted to leave its
fruit-bearing to lord it over the trees (Jdg. 9:12f.)?

12. The answer to this *Why?* is given clearly enough to the
men of Judah, in a like situation sung of in Isaiah 5:1–7. The
unanswerable question is not this, but the 'why?' of Isaiah 5:4.

13.[2] The expression *all that move* represents a single Hebrew
word, *zîz*, which may mean 'swarms of insects' (*cf.* NEB) or
perhaps the small creatures of the countryside. In 50:11 it is
parallel to 'birds of the air'. Unprotected, Israel lies open to
casual (12b) and piecemeal (13b) plundering, as well as to
more formidable foes (13a), the one kind completing what the
other has begun. *Cf.* Song of Solomon 2:15; Isaiah 56:9f.

80:14–19. The final plea
14. *Turn again* matches the recurrent prayer, 'Turn us again'
(or 'Restore us', RSV; see note on verse 3), and makes this verse
a variant of the refrain in 3, 7 and 19. It reaches back behind
God's power to save, seen in those verses, to the compassion
which motivates it. On the expression, *have regard*, see on 8:4
('care').

15. Now the appeal is to God's faithfulness as well as to His
compassion, since the planting of the vine was no casual
operation; *cf.* the allusion to God's *right hand, i.e.,* His power

---

[1] On *sea* and *River* (11) see on 72:8.
[2] The middle consonant of *ya'ar, forest,* is suspended above the line in the
MT, to identify it as the middle letter of the Psalter—an example of the
Massoretes' care for accurate copying. Likewise the *waw* in the Heb. for
'belly' in Lv. 11:42 is reckoned the middle letter of the Pentateuch. See
further C. D. Ginsburg, *Introduction to the Hebrew Bible* (Trinitarian Bible
Society, 1897), p. 69.

fully exerted; see again verses 8f. He is not the one to begin a
great work and lose interest in it.

But the verse has a second line, arbitrarily relegated to the
margin by RSV and others (but not TEV). RV renders it: 'And
the branch (Heb. 'son') that thou madest strong for thyself.'
The word 'son',[1] used here for the vine-shoot, will be up-
graded in 17b, a line which carries the whole thought a stage
further. Here it simply continues the metaphor and emphasizes
the growth of what was planted, as in 9b–11.

17. Two expressions are picked up here from verse 15 and
strengthened. *Thy right hand* is now used to mean the place of
honour (*cf.* 110:1), and the 'son' is now *the son of man*. This
sounds Messianic, but the context points to Israel in the first
place, as God's 'firstborn'[2] and right-hand man among
humanity. It is in other passages that Israel's calling becomes
focused in a single figure who alone fulfils it: the true Vine and
Son of man.

18. *Turn back* is not the same expression as the 'turn again'
of verse 14, but is from the verb used in 53:3 (4, Heb.) for
apostasy: 'they have all fallen away'. By the linking word
Then (or 'And') it faces the fact that only God's hand (17) can
avert this,[3] as only His breath of life (18b) can awaken faith.

19. So the psalm ends with the refrain (see on verse 3), now
at its fullest with the addition of the name Yahweh (*Lord*),
and with its thought enriched by the history just reviewed and
by the call and grace of God re-emphasized.

Psalm 81

Trumpet Call

This powerful psalm leaves no doubt of its festal character, and
little doubt of the particular feast it was designed to serve: in
all probability the Feast of Tabernacles (see on verse 3). This

---

[1] It is the word used for 'bough' in Gn. 49:22; see on verses 8–13, above.
The Targum took it as a Messianic title, and paraphrased it as 'King
Messiah'. On this interpretation, see on verse 17.

[2] Ex. 4:22, RV. See also Introduction (IV: 'The Messianic Hope'),
pp. 18–25.

[3] NEB turns the thought upside-down, by omitting the opening conjunction and putting the verb in the past: 'We have not turned back . . . ,
so grant us new life. . . .'

commemorated the wilderness journey, and included a public reading of the law, every seventh year (Dt. 31:10ff.), of which verses 8–10 seem to preserve some echoes.

The psalm nearest to the spirit of this is the *Venite*, Psalm 95, where a similarly joyous opening leads to the reminder that God looks for listeners as well as singers, on whom the sober lessons of the wilderness will not be lost.

Title

On *the choirmaster* and *according to The Gittith*, see Introduction, pp. 40, 41. On *Asaph*, see p. 35.

81:1–5. Rejoice

This rousing call, *Sing aloud*, was first heard in the Song of Moses (Dt. 32:43), whose praises and warnings, with other themes from Deuteronomy, have left a considerable mark on the psalm. The joyous *shout* was such as might greet a king (1 Sa. 10:24) or hail a victory (Zp. 3:14), for the scene in the temple court would have had all the excitement of a national occasion.

2. *Song* should probably be 'music' (possibly 'pipe', NEB), instrumental rather than vocal. The *timbrel* is the tambourine, its tapping sound suggested by the Hebrew, *tōp̄*. Miriam danced to it; so did the women who greeted Saul and David. On *lyre* (*kinnôr*) and *harp* (*nēḇel*; in the older versions 'psaltery') see the article 'Music and Musical Instruments' in *NBD*.

3. This word for *trumpet* is shophar (*šôp̄ār*), the ram's horn such as sounded the attack at Jericho and in Gideon's battle, and which announced certain festal days. Here the reference to *the new moon*, or 'the new month' (NEB), points to the seventh month, which was the climax of the festal year and was ushered in with the sound of this horn (Lv. 23:23) on the first day. On the tenth there followed the Day of Atonement, and on the fifteenth, *i.e.*, *at the full moon*, began the Feast of Booths, or Tabernacles (Lv. 23:34).

4, 5a. The mention of *statute*, *ordinance* and *decree* may raise the question of how one can rejoice to order. Neither the Old Testament nor the New finds this a difficulty, since there are 'always' solid grounds for joy, and valid means of awakening and sharing it (Eph. 5:19f.). The New Testament agrees with the Old in prescribing music as well as words for this; but makes no *statute* about feasts or fasts, speaking of them as 'only a shadow' of the reality which Christ brought, leaving their use or non-use to individual judgment (Col. 2:16f.; Rom. 14:5f.). But it warns against individual*ism* ('neglecting to meet together', Heb. 10:25), and here the common sense of Matthew Henry makes the useful comment: 'No time is amiss for praising God. . . . But some are times appointed, not for God to meet us (He is always ready) but for us to meet one another, that we may join together in praising God.'

5b. The 'he' in the phrase, *when he went out* (or 'forth'), is evidently God, who spoke of His judgment on the firstborn in these terms (Ex. 11:4). The word *over* can also mean 'against'. So TEV: 'when he marched out against the land of Egypt'.[1]

5c. This 'aside' (omitted in NEB[2]) has been taken in two main ways: as a reminiscence of life in a foreign land (the ancient versions, and PBV, AV, RV), and as a lead-in to God's oracle (6ff.) by the one who is inspired to speak it, who testifies to his inspiration (*cf.* RSV, TEV, Gelineau). The latter fits the context better.

81:6–10. Remember

The reminders are vivid. Instead of abstractions such as oppression and redemption, we read of *shoulder* and *hands*, *burden* and *basket* (the last of these an independent memory, not mentioned in the record, but confirmed by many pictures). To judge by this model, it is good to recall God's answers with some sharpness of detail.

7. But God's response was more than Israel had bargained for. The sequence, *I delivered . . . answered . . . tested*, goes beyond the bare rescue to the searching discipline that followed it, by exposure to God's person on the one hand, and to the impersonal, empty desert on the other. *The secret place*[3] *of thunder* was Sinai, shrouded in smoke and terrible with the voice of God (Ex. 19:16ff.; 20:18ff.). It was education by

---

[1] But the ancient versions refer it to Israel's departure; *cf.* NEB, 'when he came out of Egypt'. This, however, involves a change of preposition or an appeal to a cognate language (*cf. TRP*, Dahood).

[2] NEB evidently regards it as a marginal note which has crept into the text. *Cf.* A. Guilding, *JTS* (NS) 3 (1952), pp. 45f., who argues that it consists of three catchwords referring to three Torah Lessons in a triennial cycle. But the years, if so, are out of sequence, and 'I heard' has to be emended to 'guilt-offering'—a precarious procedure.

[3] This expression, a single word, could be rendered 'in concealment'; so NEB, 'unseen, I answered you in thunder'. *Cf.* Dt. 4:12.

encounter. *Meribah* was education by silence and apparent neglect; it left its name (strife, dispute) on two places in the desert where Israel failed the test of faith, both early and late in their pilgrimage (Ex. 17:7; Nu. 20:13). It is remembered again in Psalm 95:8, whose lessons for the Christian are drawn out in Hebrews 3 and 4.

8-10.[1] By snatches of God's wilderness words and deeds these verses give the pith and point of His schooling of Israel (and, by implication, of all generations of His followers): that they were to listen to, bow to and look to Him only. There are echoes of the 'Shema' (the great commandment, 'Hear, O Israel . . . ', Dt. 6:4); of the wistful 'if only' exclamations of Deuteronomy 5:29; 32:29; of the Song of Moses with its warnings against any 'strange god' (Dt. 32:12, 16, *etc.*); and of the Ten Commandments with their opening reminder of the exodus from Egypt (Dt. 5:6). The climax, at a point where one awaits, perhaps defensively, the rest of the Decalogue, changes suddenly from demand to the sheer bounty of 10c. Yet this was the message (if they could hear it) of even the physical hunger of the march (Dt. 8:3-10), and of the law's austerest demands ('for our good always, that he might preserve us alive', Dt. 6:24):

> 'All that Thou sendest me
> In mercy given.'[2]

81:11-16. Repent

The distaste of *my people* for *my voice* and for *me* is almost too common to seem inconsistent. Yet it is as if the lock rejected its key, or the fledgling its parent; such was the demented human material God handled, and handles.

12. The clause, *So I gave them over* (still more exactly, 'sent them off', NEB), shows an important aspect of judgment, as God's 'So be it!' to what we choose, which is best known from Romans 1:24, 26, 28. In the wilderness it was done almost literally.

13f. The affectionate tone of these verses is also worth noting in the context of judgment: it is something of an Old Testament counterpart to the lament for Jerusalem (Mt.

---

[1] NEB arbitrarily interposes 10c and 16, suitably emended, between verses 7 and 8.

[2] S. F. Adams, 'Nearer, my God, to Thee'.

23:37). But here the options are still open: there is time to repent.[1] Once again there are echoes, as in 8b, of Deuteronomy (Dt. 5:29; 32:28ff.).

15. On *cringe*, see on 18:37–45 (footnote on verse 44). *Fate* is literally 'time', which the older translations took to refer to Israel and its time of triumph, but which most modern versions more plausibly understand as the end of heathen ascendancy. Anderson points out this sense of the word in, *e.g.*, Jeremiah 27:7.

16. This verse again draws on the Song of Moses, and the Hebrew calls attention to it by falling into the Song's narrative form for the first line (lit. 'And he fed him with the fat[2] of the wheat': *cf.* Dt. 32:14), before reverting to the I-you form of address in the last line, to hold out the possibility of similar delights. *Honey from the rock* alludes to the companion verse in the Song (Dt. 32:13).

So the psalm ends with a strong reminder of God's grace and resource. The One whom Israel distrusts is neither niggardly nor impotent: He gives the best, and brings sweetness out of what is harsh, forbidding and wholly unpromising.

Psalm 82

The Gods on Trial

With its bold, dramatic form this judgment scene brings some clarity to a confused human situation. It takes us in a few words behind and beyond our present wrongs, to portray God's unbounded jurisdiction, His delegation of power, His diagnosis of our condition and His drastic intentions. The closing prayer responds fervently to the breadth of the vision.

The crux for the interpreter is the repeated reference to 'gods', who are reprimanded for injustice. Our Lord's reference to verse 6 in John 10:34f. leaves their identity an open question. On one view (*e.g.*, Delitzsch, Perowne, Briggs) they are human judges, given this title as God's deputies. This rests chiefly on Exodus 21:6; 22:8f., where for certain legal pro-

---

[1] AV and PBV are inaccurate in relegating the alternatives to the past.

[2] *I.e.* 'the finest', as RSV; but the word 'fat' and the similar-sounding word for 'milk' are prominent in the Heb. of Dt. 32:14.

cedures the parties were required to come before 'God' (or 'the god'[1]); also on Exodus 22:28 ('You shall not revile God,[2] nor curse a ruler of your people'), taking 'God' and 'ruler' to be synonymous. But these passages are far from conclusive. While the last reference does not exclude a synonym, it does not require it; and the former group need claim no more for the magistrates than what Moses claimed for himself: 'the people come to me to inquire of God; . . . and I make them know the statutes of God and his decisions' (Ex. 18:15f.).

A second view is that these 'gods' are 'principalities and powers', 'the world rulers of this present darkness' (*cf.* Eph. 6:12). There are a few Old Testament references to such potentates, good and bad (Is. 24:21; Dn. 10:13, 20f.; 12:1), for whom the New Testament uses the term 'angels' (Rev. 12:7). Admittedly they are shown as princes rather than judges, but the distinction is not a sharp one in Scripture (*cf.* Ps. 72). On the whole this view seems truer than the former to the language of the psalm (*e.g.* verse 7) and to the occasional Old Testament use of the term 'gods' or 'sons of God' for angels (see on Ps. 8:5; *cf.* Jb. 1:6; 38:7).

A third interpretation sees here a relic of polytheism, that these are the gods of the heathen, not yet denied but domesticated and brought to account. It is true that 1 Corinthians 10:20 speaks of pagan worship as the worship of demons, but this is to make the point that idolatry is never neutral but a surrender to Belial[3] and his hosts; it is not an acceptance by Paul of heathen mythologies. Likewise the Old Testament never wavers in its abhorrence of heathen gods. For Yahweh to authenticate their claim with the words, 'I say, "You are gods" ' (6), would be totally out of character.

Title
On *Asaph*, see Introduction, p. 35.

82:1. The court of heaven
The word *council* is misleading here. The Old Testament does use the term (see on 25:14) to speak vividly of God's sharing

---

[1] The definite article is used in these three verses, but is far from uncommon, especially after a preposition. *Cf.*, *e.g.*, Gn. 5:24, where 'God' occurs with and without the article in the same sentence.

[2] 'God' is used here without the article.

[3] *Cf.* 2 Cor. 6:15f.

His thoughts with His servants; but here the word is simply 'assembly'. This company is present to be judged, not consulted. On *the gods*, see the discussion above.

As to the occasion, this is 'continuous assessment', dramatized as a single scene in court, though it looks ahead to the end. There is rebuke and warning, but the sentence is yet to be carried out (*cf.* 7f.).

82:2–7. Indictment and sentence

God's '*How long?*', addressed to the loftiest of 'the powers that be', chimes in with the observation of Ecclesiastes 5:8 that local injustices are but the tip of the iceberg (to invert the metaphor), 'for the high official is watched by a higher, and there are yet higher ones over them'. Here the spiral reaches 'the spiritual hosts of wickedness in the heavenly places'. But what verses 2–4 make clear is that the Highest of all has no patience with this chain of misrule; we cannot yet read off His will from the way things are on earth. Scripture, from the flood story onwards, shows the patience of God orientated to perfecting salvation, not towards condoning the corruption which meanwhile abuses it (*cf.* 2 Pet. 3:9, 13, 15).

5. Against the majority of commentators, who see this verse as an 'aside', a comment on the corrupt rulers,[1] I take it to describe the plight of the misgoverned and misled, who are 'destroyed for lack of knowledge' (Ho. 4:6), and groping for lack of light or of any moral certainties (*cf.* Is. 59:9ff.). 'If the foundations are destroyed, what can the righteous do?'[2]

6, 7. The opening is emphatic: 'It was I who said, "You are gods." ' Our Lord took up the point in His phrase '. . . to whom the word of God came' (Jn. 10:35). But with verse 7 it underlines the principle that not even the highest credentials can be brandished against God their giver: *cf.* His word to the presumptuous Eli: ' "I promised . . ." ; but now the Lord declares: "Far be it from me . . ." ' (1 Sa. 2:30). If this can be said to the most exalted, it is also a warning to the least. On the meaning of *gods* here, see the opening comments on

---

[1] *Cf.* RSV, JB, which close their quotation marks before this verse; also NEB, TEV, which substitute 'you' for the 'they' of the Heb. text (without warrant).

[2] Ps. 11:3 (using a different word for 'foundations'). *Cf.* 75:3 (4, Heb.), with yet another word.

the psalm. Verse 7, with its simile, *like men*,[1] seems fatal to the view that these are human judges; and there is no reason whatever to make them Canaanite gods by taking *the Most High* in its Canaanite rather than its biblical sense, as in NEB. See on 7:17. As for their death sentence, the New Testament confirms that the devil and his angels will share the fate of human rebels (Mt. 25:41; Rev. 20:10, 14f.), which is 'the second death'.

82:8. The cry from earth

The psalm, having traversed some of the ground which Revelation will explore, ends very much as that book ends with its 'Come, Lord Jesus!'. True to the Bible's emphasis, it shows no further interest in the 'gods' and their mysterious role: only in God Himself and His salvation.

In the final line, NEB follows G. R. Driver's dictum that 'the only possible translation' is one which gives the last verb the meaning 'to sift';[2] hence its rendering, 'for thou dost pass all nations through thy sieve'. This gives good sense, but so does the more usual meaning of the verb, which makes the whole world God's possession. So much for the devil's claim (Lk. 4:6), still urged on us by various means: 'I give it to whom I will.'

Psalm 83

Encircled

Here is an Israel ringed by an unholy alliance dedicated to her destruction. If we look for an episode to match the psalm and its long list of enemies, the nearest is probably that of 2 Chronicles 20, where Jehoshaphat of Judah was threatened by a group which included Edom and was headed by Moab and Ammon (*cf.* our verses 6f., and the prominence of 'the children of Lot', 8). A further link, at first sight, with this

---

[1] This could be translated 'like Adam', but the parallel expression, 'like any prince', is too general to make this likely. 'Like man' (*Twenty-five Psalms*, Church Information Office, 1973) is nearer the mark.

[2] *HTR* 29 (1936), p. 187. This is based on an Assyrian root, with Syriac and Arabic cognates.

psalm of Asaph is the fact that it was an Asaphite who prophesied Jehoshaphat's victory, and the levitical singers who paved the way for it (2 Ch. 20:14, 19, 22).

But the latter were not Asaphites, and the psalm they are quoted as singing was not the present one; moreover the list of enemies here is much longer than Jehoshaphat's. It may well be, then, that this is a prayer concerned with something bigger than a single threat and a particular alliance: rather with the perennial aggression of the world against God and His people. The psalm may have been the product of a habitual consciousness of this; equally it could have arisen in the context of a ritual which dramatized the conflict, if such a ritual existed.[1]

Whatever the occasion that gave rise to it, the psalm has more than victory in view. True, it would have the enemy routed and destroyed, but still more it wants him convinced: made to acknowledge, and even seek, the Lord. So the beleaguered minority has not lost its vision. However narrow the enemy's objective, Israel's remains no less than to see 'all the earth' (18) bow to the Most High.

Title

On *A Song* and *Asaph*, see Introduction, pp. 37, 35.

83:1-8. 'See how Thy foes . . .'

'. . . *Thy* foes their banners are unfurling'[2]—for the strength of the psalm is its emphasis on 'thy' and 'thee'. There is no mention of 'us' or 'Israel' (except on the enemy's lips, 4); the attack is seen to be basically against God (2, 5; *cf*. Ps. 2:1-3), and while the immediate target is Israel, the prayer takes its stand not on the people's plight but on their relationship, *thy people . . . thy protected ones* (3). The second of these terms is well paraphrased in NEB, 'those thou hast made thy treasure'. It uses the verb found in 27:5a; 31:19a, 20b (20a, 21b, Heb.).

4. The bitter enmity against Israel goes deeper than the politics and rivalries of the time. In view of the promise to Abraham it should probably be seen as a phase of the long conflict announced in Genesis 3:15, one attempt among many others by the kingdom of darkness to wipe out the bearers of

---

[1] This is discussed in the Introduction, pp. 8ff.
[2] P. Pusey, 'Lord of our life'.

salvation (*e.g.* through Pharaoh, Sennacherib, Ahasuerus, Herod).

6, 7a. Some of these peoples were close relatives of Israel, and thereby all the more intense in their hostility. *Edom* was the people of Esau, Jacob's brother; the *Ishmaelites* looked back to the half-brother of Isaac; *Moab* and *Ammon* were *the children of Lot* (8). With these eastern and south-eastern neighbours of Israel were now allied the smaller tribes of the same general area. The *Hagrites* are seen in 1 Chronicles 5:10 east of the Jordan; *Gebal* is probably not the northern city of that name (better known as Byblos, and associated with Tyre: Jos. 13:5; 1 Ki. 5:18) but a locality south of the Dead Sea. *Amalek*, Israel's oldest enemy after Egypt (Ex. 17:8ff.), was a roving tribe of Edomite ancestry (Gn. 36: 12, 16), centred mostly in the south.

7b, 8. To this coalition from the south and east were added the formidable coastal peoples of the south-west and north-west, *Philistia* and *Tyre*, almost completing the circle; and behind the scenes was the Great Power, *Assyria*, using the leaders, Moab and Ammon (*the children of Lot*), as its pawns. It intended, and eventually managed, to incorporate this entire group of peoples, friend and foe alike, in its empire. In view of Psalm 82's proximity, we may perhaps legitimately see Assyria itself as a pawn rather than a player.

83:9–12. 'Lord, Thou canst save . . .'

The past comes to life here in prayer and faith. All these are names of the defeated, from two campaigns in the book of Judges which emphasize the weakness of God's chosen victors. The destruction of *Midian* (9) and its four chieftains (11) was begun with Gideon's three hundred, armed with trumpets, jars and torches (Jdg. 7:19ff.). *Sisera*, Jabin's commander, was sold 'into the hand of a woman' (Jdg. 4:9).

12. If God's choice of the weak was one part of the pattern, another was His promise of the land. So the enemy's thoughts are re-phrased in the prayer, to bring out the truth about the territories they had coveted: these were *the pastures of God*, not simply the holdings of Israel (*cf.* the comments on verses 1ff.). In the New Testament there is a similar stress on God's protective care for what is His own: *e.g.* 'my church' (Mt. 16:18), 'my sheep' (Jn. 10:27–29), 'God's temple' (1 Cor. 3:17), *etc.*

83:13–18. '. . . till backward they are driven'
Unlike the hymn, the psalm prays for a rout (13–15), not a mere retreat; but the hymn, from the vantage-ground of the New Testament, can outdo the psalm's remaining verses, by praying for the full fruits of the enemy's seeking (16) and knowing (18): 'Grant them Thy truth, that they may be forgiven'; not simply 'dismayed for ever' (17).

13. *Whirling dust* is literally 'the wheel', a noun from the verb 'to roll'. So it may be a whirl of dust or chaff, or something like thistledown (NEB); such, in the long run, are the massive powers and the men of weight. *Cf.*, *e.g.*, 1:4; 62:9; 68:2.

16–18. Verse 16 comes to the brink of praying for the enemy's conversion, but its ruling thought is of God's vindication rather than man's conversion. The emphasis of the last verses falls where Ezekiel, under God, would place it in his refrain, 'Then you/they will know that I am the Lord'.[1] Other scriptures are concerned to distinguish between fruitful and fruitless seeking (16; *cf.*, *e.g.*, Je. 29:13; Ho. 5:4–6); this is content to pray for the time when 'every eye shall see him, . . . and all tribes of the earth will wail on account of him' (Rev. 1:7). The prospect of enforced submissions is small joy compared with the conversions of, *e.g.*, Psalm 87; but it is part of the final victory, and a vast advance on the spectacle of evil unabashed and encroaching. There is a richer knowledge of God than the reluctant assent which is envisaged in verse 18, but this is the minimum. The psalm will not settle for less, nor for a smaller realm than *all the earth*.

So end the Psalms of Asaph (50; 73–83).

Psalm 84

The Pull of Home

Longing is written all over this psalm. This eager and homesick man is one of the Korahite temple singers, and the mood of the psalm is not unlike that of Psalms 42 and 43, which are a product of the same group. Perowne suggests that here we

---

[1] *E.g.* Ezk. 6:7 and the seventeen references listed there in RV. The list is far from exhaustive.

may be listening to the self-same voice; if so, the singer has now come out of the gloom from which he was already beginning to break free in the earlier song.

Three times he uses the word 'Blessed', or 'Happy': once wistfully (4), once resolutely (5), once in deep contentment (12). These can guide us in exploring the movement of the psalm.

Title

This psalm is one of four Korahite psalms (84f.; 87f.) which supplement the eight found in Book II (Pss. 42–49). On *The Gittith*, see Introduction, p. 41.

84:1-4. Distant home

1. *How lovely* is more exactly 'How dear' or 'How beloved'; it is the language of love poetry. Psalms 42:4; 43:4 give a glimpse of the delight which a dedicated servant of the temple found in his role—a joy quite foreign to the un-committed (*cf*. Am. 8:5!). The Christian equivalent is 'love of the brethren', who are individually and collectively God's temple (1 Cor. 3:16; 6:19).

> 'Oh, my spirit longs and faints
> For the converse of Thy saints.'[1]

2. 'I pine, I faint with longing' (NEB) is a good translation of the first line, which makes the subsequent expression, *sing for joy* (or an equivalent, as found in almost every modern version) distinctly inappropriate. The word in question indicates a loud cry, not necessarily a joyful one (*cf*. 17:1; La. 2:19), and AV, RV were wise to translate it 'cry out'.

The living God, just as in 42:2, is the true object of this longing, which is not simply an attachment to a place, however hallowed. That can become an escape (1 Ki. 19:9) or a fetish (Acts 7:48, 54), whereas the rest of this psalm will show how constructive is a preoccupation with God Himself.

3. *Even the sparrow*—this sounds again like the language of love, where one may envy anyone or anything that has access to the distant beloved. The temple, incidentally, is not being pictured as derelict: see verse 4. The courtyards were open to the sky, and the temple eaves would give good nesting.

---

[1] H. F. Lyte, 'Pleasant are Thy courts above'.

Note here the two mentions of the word *house* (or *home*), close together: one for the sparrow (3), the other for God (4), a touch that brings out His tender hospitality; and if for the birds, then surely for the servant!

Another way of taking this (*cf.* Delitzsch) is to see the sparrow and swallow as figures of the psalmist himself, who has had to flit too long from place to place, but now pictures himself at home. So JB: 'The sparrow has found its home at last. . . .' But this makes him arrive, so to speak, too soon. The psalm has still a pilgrimage to make.

4. *Blessed.* . . . Here is the first of the three beatitudes (see the second of the opening paragraphs on the psalm). It sums up the musings of the verses so far, on the happy lot of those who are not exiles. But we may reflect that often it is the exile who appreciates home, while the stay-at-homes find fault with it.

84:5–8. Eager journey

5a. *Blessed.* . . . The singer takes up this word from the previous verse and gives it a new direction, refusing to settle down into vain regrets. The beatitude lends its bracing tone to the stanza. If he cannot be at Zion, he can be with God; if he cannot enjoy sweetness (*cf.* verse 1) he can find strength (7). He remembers the blessings of those who have to push through to Zion rather than reside there like the choirs of verse 4.

This may refer to those who plan a literal pilgrimage, or to those who must be content to make the journey in their hearts (5b), treating the present hardships as counterparts of the arduous road to Zion. In either case, he now visualizes that Pilgrim's Way, and appears to make some play with the names of its landmarks.

5b. *Highways* (or 'the pilgrim ways', NEB) is a word with two possible meanings (see on 68:4): either a raised road, and in particular a 'sacred way' for processions,[1] or, just possibly, the music that is raised to God in worship (*cf.* NEB mg., 'high praises'). But the latter is only an inference from one interpretation of 68:4 and from the probable meaning of *Selah* (see Introduction, p. 36). In its main sense the word carries

[1] See Is. 35:8ff., using a related word; also Is. 40:3; 62:10, *etc. Cf.* Mowinckel, I, pp. 170f. The additional words 'to Zion' (AV, RV, RSV) are an interpretative addition, not in the text.

the reminder that the way to God's presence is not as lonely or trackless as it may seem, but well prepared and well frequented. For us, the Psalms themselves are such a highway.

6. *Baca*,[1] evidently the singular of the word translated 'balsam trees' or (NEB) 'aspens' (2 Sa. 5:23), is thought to indicate a tree or shrub which grows in arid places; hence NEB, 'the thirsty valley'. The NEB emends the next line to make matters too easy for the pilgrims: 'they find water from a spring'. Rather, as RSV, *they make it a place of springs*, which is a classic statement of the faith which dares to dig blessings out of hardships.[2] But God may choose to send *rain*, which comes through nobody's enterprise and can bring a whole area to life, for He has more than one way of dealing with our dryness (*cf.* 81:7 with 107:35). *Pools* is a word with the same consonants as 'blessings' (RV), and the latter is in fact the word in the Hebrew text and in the ancient versions,[3] perhaps as a term for the green growth that springs up after a shower in such an area.

7a. The nearer the goal, the stronger its pull; so that the pilgrims, so far from flagging, press on more eagerly than at the start. In terms of a life's pilgrimage the analogy is perhaps not so much between the godliness of a man's youth and age (where extraneous factors disturb the comparison) as between following God at a distance and at closer quarters, since faith and love grow with exercise. With the expression *from strength to strength*,[4] *cf.* the New Testament phrase, 'from glory to glory'

---

[1] The verb 'to weep' is very similar in sound to this; hence 'the valley of Weeping' in RV, following LXX, *etc.* The name of the tree may be connected with this verb, perhaps as a tree which exudes or 'weeps' some substance (*cf.* K-B), in which case there may be a play on words here, which the 'Valley of Weeping' picks up.

[2] Appropriately enough, Rephaim, the only vale of such trees named in the Old Testament (2 Sa. 5:22f.), was once made a place of refreshing beyond all expectation for a thirsty and dispirited David, through the devoted daring of his friends (2 Sa. 23:13–17).

[3] These also take *môreh* (*early rain*) in its other sense of 'teacher' or 'lawgiver': so LXX, Vulg., 'the lawgiver will give blessings'. The psalm may be comparing this pilgrimage with that of the exodus.

[4] NEB 'from outer wall to inner' assumes that *ḥayil*, 'strength', is a mistake for *ḥêl* (consonants *ḥ-y-l*), 'rampart' ('from rampart to rampart', as the pilgrims enter Jerusalem). This is plausible, but has no textual support. Conceivably, by a word-play, the psalmist has substituted 'strength' for 'stronghold' ('rampart') in making the pilgrimage a figurative rather than a literal journey.

(2 Cor. 3:18, AV, RV), which is closely linked, as here, with a concentration on seeing and knowing God Himself.

7b. *The God of gods* is another expression which involves a vowel change (*'ēl* for *'el*), but this time it is supported by the ancient versions and it avoids the rather harsh construction which the AV italics acknowledge. It is probably right.

8. But the psalmist is alone; he cannot join the pilgrims whom he has just been visualizing. He returns from 'they' to *my*; yet he is alone with God, not with his 'sole self', however far he may be from the Zion of verse 7. His prayer will be heard.

84:9–12. Radiant presence

Verse 9 has the look of a parenthesis, interrupting the personal avowals, just short of their climax in the next verse, with a corporate plea for the king.[1] This could well be the mark left on the psalm by a national tragedy, such as the deportation of the king (*cf.* the poignant words of Je. 22:10f., or La. 4:20), for whom the congregation seizes this appropriate moment to intercede, echoing the psalmist's prayer so as to make it the vehicle of their own.

10. Now the psalmist's individual voice returns, with a declaration comparable to Paul's 'all things but loss' (Phil. 3:8, AV), or to Asaph's 'Whom have I in heaven but thee?' (Ps. 73:25). This is eloquence, certainly, but not extravagance, as the next verse will demonstrate.

On a point of detail, some such word as *elsewhere* (which is not in the text) is needed to round off the first line of verse 10, and in fact the Hebrew for *I would rather* (lit. 'I have chosen') looks as if it may be a copyist's error for such an expression; perhaps for 'at home' (NEB). Then the next line will continue with '(Better) to . . .'. In that line the word *doorkeeper* is not the same as that of 1 Chronicles 26:1, 12, which speaks of a fairly exalted office. The term here is a verb, and the line should run '(Better) to stand at the threshold . . .'. It is a contrast of status, or apparent security, as well as of company.

11. This rich verse, 'a box where sweets compacted lie',[2] silences any misgivings over the enthusiasm of verse 10 by its

---

[1] *Cf.* Ps. 89:18 ('our shield . . . our king') and the subsequent intercessions there, especially in verses 38ff. On the Messianic significance of such terms as 'shield', 'anointed', *etc.*, see Introduction, pp. 18f. (On Dahood's alternative translation of 'shield', see footnote at 89:18.)

[2] George Herbert, 'Sweet day, so cool, so calm, so bright'.

vision of what God is, and of what He gives and withholds. The two figures for what He can be to His followers, both *sun and shield*, picture vividly all that is outgoing and positive (light, joy, heat, energy . . . ; *cf.* Mal. 4:2) and all that is protective; the answer to fear and defeat—but a soldier's answer. As for His gifts, *favour and honour* are translated still better as 'grace and glory' (AV, RV), since both these words were due to unfold their meaning as the Bible proceeded. Already grace meant something like the smile of God; but by the time of the Epistles 'all the benefits of His passion' have come to light. Glory, too, was already glimpsed in terms that were far from earthbound (see on 73:23, 24); but quite new aspects would emerge with the gospel (*e.g.* 1 Pet. 4:14). The final line of the verse, too, contained even more than was yet evident. It may seem a truism that what God will *withhold* is not 'nothing', but *no good thing* (*cf.* 34:10); yet the gospel showed the unimagined length and breadth of this (Rom. 8:32; Phil. 4:6–19). The limiting phrase, *from those who walk uprightly* (*i.e.*, with an undivided heart), is not an arbitrary condition but as logical as the one in the promise 'Open your mouth wide, and I will fill it' (81:10). Jeremiah uses the language of our verse to express the converse of it: 'your sins have withholden good things from you' (Je. 5:25, AV).

12. The last of the three beatitudes, like its predecessors, sums up the thought of its stanza (see the end of the opening remarks on the psalm). By his disciplined response to nostalgia the psalmist has found the blessing of 'those who have not seen and yet believe' (Jn. 20:29), and can teach us to treat our present state of glimpses and longings as he treated his: not only as a spur to pilgrimage but as a chance to respond to God already in delighted trust.

Psalm 85

Revival

Out of a bleak situation this psalm leads up to a point at which a gloriously fertile stretch of country comes into view. The first half of the poem is mainly a chastened prayer (4–7), nourished by recollection (1–3); the second half mainly promise, or vision (10–13), the outcome of a resolve to listen (8, 9). The climax is one of the most satisfying descriptions of concord—spiritual, moral and material—to be found anywhere in Scripture.

Title
On *the choirmaster*, see Introduction, p. 40. On *the Sons of Korah*, see p. 35.

85:1–3. Former mercies
The simple past tenses of rsv (*cf.* Gelineau: 'O Lord, you once favoured your land'), which look back to a scene very different from the present, make good sense of the prayers which will follow in verses 4–7. To interpret the verbs of 1–3 as perfects ('thou hast been . . .'), as do most translations, is to miss the point and to bring, *e.g.*, verses 3 and 5 into needless collision.

Favourable (1) is more than a kindly word: it speaks of deeming someone or something to be acceptable, often in a context of atonement (*e.g.* Je. 14:10, 12). For the phrase, *restore the fortunes*, see on 14:7.

These phrases, and especially those of verses 2f., show that Israel is not pining for past glories, which are often an optical illusion (*cf.* Ec. 6:10), but remembering past mercies. This is realistic; it is also stimulating: it leads to prayers (4–7) rather than dreams.

85:4–7. Present estrangement
In various forms the verb 'to turn' contributes much to the colouring of the psalm, especially in the first half: as 'restore' (1, 4) and 'turn' (3, 8), and as the basis of the 'again' in verse 6. In verse 4, translations of it are divided between 'Turn us' (so most versions; *cf.* rsv *Restore us*) and 'Turn back to us' (neb, rv mg.); the grammatical evidence is indecisive.[1] It is a versatile word, whose prominence in the Old Testament bears witness to the open situation which prevails there, in which God may turn from His wrath, and men from their rebellion (or their obedience; see on 8b), and situations be revolutionized.

The prayer gradually gathers strength from the remembrance of God's self-consistency. The questions of verse 5

---

[1] A different part of the verb is used at 80:3, *etc.* See comment there and at 80:14.

virtually answer themselves in the light of this (*cf.* the query, '*to all generations?*' with the standing reply of 33:11f.), and the petitions of verses 6 and 7 dare to invoke not only God's covenant (see on 17:7 for *steadfast love*, 7) but His delight in *salvation* (7); for this is creative work, bringing life out of death, and joy out of gloom (6). Judgment, by contrast, is His 'strange' and 'alien' work, in which He takes no pleasure (Is. 28:21; Ezk. 18:32).

85:8, 9. Pause for reflection

The singular, *Let me hear*, after the collective prayer, may well indicate the entry of a solo voice: the psalmist or a prophet listening for God's answering word, and encouraging the rest to heed it. *Cf.* the first comment on 12:5, 6.

8. *Peace*, which includes the thought of wholeness or well-being, is a standard greeting, and welcome enough even at that level; but what God speaks He also creates: *cf.* Isaiah 57:18ff.—a passage which could be a commentary on these verses, not least in the warning of 'no peace . . . for the wicked' (Is. 57:21). The corresponding warning in 8b, 'but let them not turn back to folly', is relegated to the margin in RSV,[1] but there is no compelling reason to reject it.

9. The promise, 'I will fill this house with glory, . . . and in this place will I give peace' (Hg. 2:7, 9, RV), may illuminate this verse by its similar context—possibly the very context of the psalm—in which the great deliverance from Babylon had been followed by lean times (*cf.* the first two stanzas of the psalm), now coming to an end. The glory that had departed (see on 78:59–64) would return; God would be resident again. The psalm sees this not in token, by the ark in the temple, but in God's own presence throughout the land. The word for *dwell* is the root of the term Shekinah, which in later Judaism became an expression for God's glory dwelling among His people, and so a name for God Himself (see on 26:8).

85:10–13. Harmonious prospect

The prevailing concept in the justly famous verse 10 and its companions is that of concord: vast, unspoilt and rich with life. Verse 10 is discussed below, since the thought is especially

---

[1] NEB emends it without a note. The alternative, adopted by RSV, NEB, is the text of LXX, Vulg.

clear both in verse 11, where heaven and earth reach out towards each other in perfect partnership, no longer at cross purposes,[1] and in verse 12, where the Lord will give the *good*, on which everything depends, while the land (*our* land, for it is no less ours for being His) will give the *increase* which is its proper return. The repetition of the same verb, 'will give', in both lines of the verse (which most if not all translations studiously avoid), seems designed to bring out this simple correspondence.

10. In the light of the verses just discussed (11f.), and of the usual meanings of the nouns of this couplet, it seems that we should see here a settled state of concord rather than the act of resolving a state of discord. But the older translation, 'Mercy and truth', tends to suggest the meeting of opposites; so would the restricted understanding of *peace* as chiefly an absence of hostilities, and *righteousness* as primarily moral perfection, the sinner's condemnation. In those terms the verse would appear to give a graceful picture of atonement, though it runs the risk of presenting atonement as the settling of a conflict within God Himself.

But *steadfast love*[2] *and faithfulness* (as RSV rightly translates them) are partners, not opponents; and *righteousness* can have the welcome role of putting things right,[3] not only of pointing things out, so that it goes likewise hand-in-hand with *peace*, whose fuller meaning is discussed at verse 8. Here, then, are the fruits of atonement rather than the act of it. There may in fact be already in this verse a suggestion that the partnered qualities face each other from heaven and earth respectively, as God's grace and earth's response through grace. Certainly this is so in the remaining verses, with their prospect of mutual joy and unbroken harmony.

11, 12. See the comments at the opening of this stanza.

13. Lest the foregoing picture should seem too static, the final verse is one of movement. The variety of translations confesses that the Hebrew is ambiguous, but most of the variants come from the conjecture that the word *make* has displaced a noun such as 'peace' or 'salvation'. This is attractive but unsupported, and we may be content with RSV, perhaps

---

[1] *Cf.* JB, 'Loyalty reaches up from earth
and Righteousness leans down from heaven.'
[2] See on 17:7; 62:12.
[3] See on 24:5; 65:5.

with RV's explanatory addition: 'his footsteps a way to walk in.' So we are roused from basking to following.

Psalm 86

'In the day of my trouble'

This is, in more senses than one, a lonely prayer of David, the only poem of his in the third book. Its form is simple, with an opening and closing supplication punctuated by a deliberate act of praise—deliberate, because the final verses reveal no abatement of the pressure, and no sign, as yet, of an answer.

Title
On *David*, see Introduction, p. 33.

86:1-7. The suppliant
The first two verses balance the appeal to God's compassion (*for I am poor and needy*) with the appeal to His faithfulness. Verse 2 emphasizes the second of these by its stress on the threefold cord that binds David to God and, by implication, God to David: first the bond of covenant (*godly* is the same word as 'loyal' in 18:25, where see note; it speaks of a steadfast response to the 'steadfast love' of verse 5), and then the tie that binds a *servant* to his master,[1] and the link, no less strong, between one who *trusts* and one who is trusted. Strictly speaking, the interjection *Thou art my God* (2) should come between *save thy servant* and *who trusts in thee*; an urgent aside.

4-7. As so often in the Psalms, the prayer resolutely heads toward clearer skies and firmer ground. *Gladden* (4) is a bold request at such a time, and good reasons are summoned to support it. They are given in the three clauses introduced by 'for'; the single-mindedness of the one who is praying (4b, on which the contrasted uses of the expression 'lift up his/my soul' in 24:4; 25:1 make the perfect comment), the character of the Lord (5), and the conviction that He answers prayer (7b). After this, the 'sunlit uplands' of the next stanza are not wholly a surprise.

[1] The appeal is doubled in verse 16 (*cf.* 116:16), with the reminder that his mother before him was in 'service'. They are old retainers.

86:8-13. The sovereign

The word *Lord, i.e.,* 'Master' or 'Sovereign' (as distinct from
LORD, conventionally printed in capitals in the Bible to
indicate the name Yahweh) occurs seven times in this psalm,
three of them in the present stanza (8, 9, 12). To God in this
capacity David now gives his full attention.

His praise is not at random: he makes comparisons first in
the realm of heaven (8a) and then in those of nature (8b),
mankind (9) and history (10), on all of which see the further
comments below. Finally he exposes his own self to this
sovereignty and its searching implications (11ff.).

8a. *The gods* may be a rhetorical expression, as if to say, 'the
gods, even supposing they existed!' But the downright statement of 10b, *thou alone art God,* makes it more probable that in
verse 8 David is speaking of angels rather than hypothetical
beings: see on 8:5; also the introduction to Psalm 82.

8b. *Works* probably mean here the things God has made,
rather than the deeds He has done (which come later, 10a).
Cf., e.g., 8:3, 6; 19:1.

9. The prospect of the world's homage is often clear and
strong for David; *cf.* especially 22:27ff. Here the logic of it is
brought out by the clause '(whom) *thou hast made*'.

10a. *Wondrous things,* variously translated in the Psalms, is
a frequent term for God's miracles of salvation. *Cf., e.g.,* 78:4,
11, 32; see also on 9:1.

10b. On the uncompromising declaration, *thou alone art God,*
see on 8a. Its proximity to that verse, which otherwise might
have seemed to fall short of monotheism, is a fact to bear in
mind in studying statements about 'gods' in other psalms.

11. This prayer for guidance should be related to the
context, which sings of God's sovereignty. David is now applying that fact to his life, not merely to the world in general as
in 8–10. It is a prayer about forming the right habits (note the
end in view in the middle line), rather than making the right
moves—not that David belittled the importance of these (see,
e.g., 1 Sa. 23:2, 4, 10ff.).

The last line, *unite[1] my heart to fear thy name,* is a penetrating
climax, confessing in a single phrase the disintegrated state of
man which is shown elsewhere in Scripture in many forms,

---

[1] This accurately translates the Hebrew as almost all translations agree.
LXX, Vulg., Syr., however, vocalized the consonants differently, to yield the
sense 'let my heart rejoice (*yiḥad*) to fear thy name'.

from insincerity (see on 12:2) and irresolution (Jas. 1:6ff.) to the tug-of-war which Paul describes in Romans 7:15ff. His concern is not with unifying his personality for its own sake; the lines meet at a point beyond himself, the fear of the Lord.

> 'Direct, control, suggest, this day,
> All I design, or do, or say,
> That all my powers, with all their might,
> In Thy sole glory may unite.'[1]

12. Here is a God-given beginning (and practical means) to the answer of his prayer: his *whole heart* absorbed in praise. He is not going to wait passively for the spiritual maturity he has been seeking in verse 11.

13. Nor is this praise simply an exercise: there is abundant reason for it. As for the rescue *from the depths of Sheol*, it is possible to take this as either past or future, and as either heightened language for a serious crisis (*cf.* 88:6) or sober terms for a state beyond death. Since *my soul* normally means 'my life' or 'myself', this word does not settle the question by itself.

Nevertheless the balance, in my view, is towards a future deliverance from the power of death (taking the verb either as a 'perfect consecutive', as in a prose construction, or as a 'prophetic perfect' which expresses the certainty of future events as though they were already complete). On *Sheol* and its *depths*, see on 6:5; on the prospect of rescue from it, see on 49:15; 73:23, 24.

86:14-17. The scornful

Now at last the immediate threat comes into view. We may admire and learn from the self-discipline which has confined the prayer so far to the priorities: David's relationship to God, and God's own character and sovereign rights. So the temptation to pour out a tirade instead of a petition has been overcome.

14, 15. The schemers are described quite bluntly, but David shows the same openness to correction as when Shimei cursed him (2 Sa. 16:10ff.). Not all their enmity may be undeserved, for all he knows; so it is God's mercy that he invokes, even before God's faithfulness; and he rests his case on Scripture, quoting Exodus 34:6b word for word.

[1] Thomas Ken, 'Awake, my soul'.

16, 17. Among the prayers for pity and comfort, note the plea for *strength*. David is hard-pressed enough to long for some *sign* (and God is good to those who truly need this: Jdg. 6:36ff.; 7:9ff.), but he is spirited enough to want to play the part of a man, not a sick man, in driving back the enemy. Even the comfort he desires is less to ease his lot than to prove his point and clear his name (17b, c). This is a whole world away from self-pity.

Psalm 87

'Glorious things of thee are spoken'

In its enigmatic, staccato phrases this remarkable psalm speaks of Zion as the destined metropolis of Jew and Gentile alike. Nothing is explained with any fullness, yet by the end there remains no doubt of the coming conversion of old enemies and their full incorporation in the city of God. Here (with Is. 54) is the vision behind Paul's phrase, 'The Jerusalem above . . . is our mother' (Gal. 4:26). The most memorable commentary on the psalm is John Newton's masterly hymn whose first line we have borrowed as the general heading, above.

Title
On *the Sons of Korah*, see Introduction, p. 35. On *A Song*, see p. 37.

87:1–3. City of God
It is a constant source of delight in the Psalms that Zion, of all places, has been chosen as God's *holy mount*, to the baffled envy of its rivals (68:15f.). The city owes all its stability and sanctity to Him: the first word of the psalm is literally 'His establishment'—an abrupt and emphatic opening—and its hills are (lit.) 'hills of holiness' because He is there; it is not the other way round. He is there simply because He *loves* the place (2), which is as sufficient and inscrutable a reason as the one which He gave for choosing Israel itself: 'it is because the Lord loves you, and is keeping the oath which he swore to your fathers' (*cf.* Dt. 7:6–8). Since the psalm will make it clear that Zion

gives its name to a community, not only a place, the relevance of this to the church is direct.

3. The word *spoken*[1] introduces an oracle from God, and the *glorious things* indicate not merely a high reputation in general, but the particular things which will be said in the next verses. Zion's splendour will be its King and its roll of citizens.

87:4-6. Mother-city

God's oracle, or declaration, is cast in a somewhat official form, not only in verse 6 but in the first Hebrew word of verse 4: 'I will make mention' (RV)—as if it were a formal proclamation on a state occasion. It is momentous enough. A representative sample of the Gentile world is being enrolled in God's city. Their status is declared in two ways, each of which puts the matter very strongly. Towards God, they are counted as *those who know me*, an even higher designation than 'those who fear me' (*cf.* Je. 31:34). Towards the people of God they are not mere proselytes: they can avow, as Paul said of his Roman status, 'But I was born a citizen' (*cf.* Acts 22:28). This is the gospel age, no less.

The names are well chosen: *Rahab* (*i.e.*, Egypt, the blustering monster, 89:10; Is. 30:7) and *Babylon*, the two great powers and persecutors of Israel's world; nearer home, *Philistia*, the enemy which Israel never dislodged, and *Tyre*, the affluent merchant; finally *Ethiopia* (or 'Cush'; see on 68:31), the symbol of the remoter nations.

The repetition, *This one was born there*, grows gradually clearer. In verse 4 it provokes the question 'Where?'; in verse 5a that question is answered (*Zion*), but the reply lacks authority until verse 6 supplies it with the Lord's endorsement. Here is His 'book of life', written with His own hand (*cf.* the written right of entry to the city, into which the kings of the earth bring their glory, in Rev. 21:24-27).

5. Two further details in this verse call for comment. In 5a, LXX has the additional word 'mother' (a Hebrew word of two letters, which may have dropped out of MT by haplography[2]);

---

[1] On the grammatical point that 'spoken' is a singular verb with a plural noun (not altogether uncommon in Heb.), Delitzsch calls attention to, *e.g.*, Is. 16:8 or, by a different construction, Mal. 1:11. NEB's transference of the verse to follow verse 7 only increases the difficulty.

[2] *I.e.*, by copying only once a combination of letters which appears twice. The same two letters appear in the Heb. word 'it shall be said', nearby.

NEB, hence, freely, 'and Zion shall be called a mother in whom men of every race are born'. This gives the same sense as the MT (preserved in RSV), but makes it more explicit. Paul evidently had the LXX in mind in Galatians 4:26: 'the Jerusalem above is free, and she is our mother'.

In 5b the word *'elyôn, Most High*, is placed a little unusually in the sentence, and suggests the possibility that it should be spelt (so to speak) without capitals, to give the sense 'for he himself will establish her as supreme'. The word is used in this way in 89:27 (28, Heb.) and, more closely, Deuteronomy 28:1.

87:7. City of joy

Here is the response to the prospect of verses 4–6 and to the realities already enjoyed in 1–3. It is praise in two of its most exuberant forms: *cf.* 68:25; 150:4. True to character, this final outburst is as abrupt as the rest of the psalm (even the word *say* is left to be understood), and translations therefore differ among themselves in smoothing its roughness by small changes. RSV, however, fairly represents the Hebrew text as we have it, to show Zion as a place not only of the stability and glory already described, but of joy and freshness. The expression, *in you*, could grammatically refer either to the Lord or to the city; the context points to the latter, somewhat as in 46:4 with its 'river whose streams make glad the city of God', or as developed further still in Ezekiel 47, where the waters that issue from the temple threshold flow out to revive the very desert.

> 'Who can faint while such a river
> Ever flows their thirst to assuage—
> Grace which, like the Lord the Giver,
> Never fails from age to age?'[1]

Psalm 88

The Darkness Deepens

There is no sadder prayer in the Psalter. Here, as with other laments, the reader's part need not be that of spectator, whatever his current mood, but that of companion in prayer

[1] J. Newton, 'Glorious things of thee are spoken'.

to the depressed or outcast people whose state of mind the
psalm puts into words: words which are for use.

If there is hardly a spark of hope in the psalm itself, however,
the title (see below) supplies it, for this supposedly God-
forsaken author seems to have been one of the pioneers of the
singing guilds set up by David, to which we owe the Korahite
psalms (42-49; 84f.; 87f.), one of the richest veins in the
Psalter. Burdened and despondent as he was, his existence was
far from pointless. If it was a living death, in God's hands it
was to bear much fruit.

Title
This is a double title. One view of it is that the first two
sentences, which are a mirror of the title to Psalm 87, belong
to that psalm, signing it off. It seems possible, however, that
these sentences identify the collection to which our psalm
belongs, *i.e.*, the Korahite group, while the rest of the title
gives the usual details, which here include the author's name.
If *Heman the Ezrahite* was the Heman named as leader of the
Korahite guild (1 Ch. 6:33, 37; see also Introduction, p. 35),
there is no contradiction between the two parts of the title.

On *the choirmaster*, see p. 40; on *Mahalath Leannoth*, p. 42;
on *Maskil*, p. 38.

88:1, 2. Sleepless entreaty
If this is the last of the Korahite psalms, its story of mourning
day and *night* echoes the first of the group (42:3). More closely,
however, see 22:2, a psalm which our Lord knew well; and
note His comment in Luke 18:7f., which reveals God's
sensitivity to these ceaseless cries, for all His apparent in-
difference.

There is more faith expressed in verse 1 than is allowed in
RSV, NEB, *etc.*, since the words *my God, I call for help* emend the
Hebrew, which runs, 'God of my salvation, I cry out'. It is the
only positive note in the psalm, apart from the qualities that
are subjected to the questions of 10-12, and apart from the
crucial fact that he continues to pray.

88:3-9. Encroaching shadows
On *Sheol*, and the sense in which the dead are viewed as
unremembered, cut off (5) and silenced (11), see the discussion
at Psalm 6:5. Here there may be a darker shadow still: a sense

of being treated like the wicked (*cf.* the references to *the Pit*
given at 28:1), for whom death is indeed the end. This doom
is stated clearly enough in another Korahite psalm, 49,
especially verses 13–15. Already the psalmist feels he is tasting
a banishment like theirs. Even more telling than the metaphors
of dungeons and deep waters (6f.) is the remembered look on
the faces of his fellow men, a revulsion which isolates him in
the narrow prison of himself (8); and in this, he feels, they are
God's agents. 'Thou hast caused . . . ; thou hast made . . .' (8).
Yet he refuses to be silenced. The *every day* of verse 9 reinforces
the 'day' and 'night' of verse 1 and the 'morning' of 13. He is
as dogged as the wrestling Jacob.

5. *Forsaken* is literally 'free', which may be an allusion to the
dissolving of earthly ties in Sheol, as in Job 3:19, here in the
bad sense of 'cut adrift' (*cf.* BDB).[1]

88:10–12. Death's alien land

From the standpoint of God's congregation and His glory in
the world, all that is said here is true. It is among the living
that His miracles are performed, His praises sung, His constancy and acts of deliverance exhibited. Death is no exponent
of His glory. Its whole character is negative: it is the last word
in inactivity, silence (10), the severing of ties, corruption
(*Abaddon*,[2] 11), gloom, oblivion (12). The New Testament
concurs, calling it the last enemy. Not death but resurrection
is His goal; the psalmist's indignant queries allow no satisfying
answer short of this.

88:13–18. Unanswered cry

We have already noted the singer's persistence in prayer
(verses 1, 9, 13); now the psalm will end with bewildered
questions (the repeated *Why?* of verse 14) to which the only
response appears to be a rain of blows, as unremitting as his
cries ('all day long', 17). Looking back, this man can remember
nothing but ill health and ill fortune (15); looking Godward

---

[1] RP's emendation, 'I am become like' (*cf.* NEB) sits very loose to the
Hebrew, while Dahood's alternative, from an Ugaritic root, ['In Death is
my cot', is hardly a compelling suggestion.
[2] *Abaddon* is a noun from the root 'to perish', hence 'Destruction' or
'Ruin'. Like 'the Pit', it is a parallel term to Sheol (*e.g.* Pr. 15:11; 27:20),
with a more sinister tone; *cf.* Rev. 9:11.

he is terrified (15b–17); looking for human comfort he can see no-one at all (18).

With *darkness* as its final word, what is the role of this psalm in Scripture? For the beginning of an answer we may note, first, its witness to the possibility of unrelieved suffering as a believer's earthly lot. The happy ending of most psalms of this kind is seen to be a bonus, not a due; its withholding is not a proof of either God's displeasure or His defeat. Secondly, the psalm adds its voice to the 'groaning in travail' which forbids us to accept the present order as final. It is a sharp reminder that 'we wait for adoption as sons, the redemption of our bodies' (Rom. 8:22f.). Thirdly, this author, like Job, does not give up. He completes his prayer, still in the dark and totally unrewarded. The taunt, 'Does Job fear God for naught?', is answered yet again. Fourthly, the author's name allows us, with hindsight, to see that his rejection was only apparent (see the opening comments on the psalm). His existence was no mistake; there was a divine plan bigger than he knew, and a place in it reserved most carefully for him.

Psalm 89

Sure Mercies of David?

The foundation to this psalm is the great prophecy of 2 Samuel 7:4–17, at the heart of which is the promise of a throne for David's dynasty for ever, and of unique honours for its occupant. 'I will establish the throne of his kingdom for ever. I will be his father, and he shall be my son' (2 Sa. 7:13f.). Other scriptures explore the Father-Son relationship more fully (see on 2:7–9); this psalm seizes chiefly on the clause 'for ever', which the turn of events seemed to have flatly contradicted.

So there is painful tension here, yet the spirit of the psalm is humble, never bitter. Instead of railing at the promise or explaining it away, it faces the full clash of word and event in an appeal to God to show His hand. Like an unresolved discord it therefore impels us towards the New Testament, where we find that the fulfilment will altogether outstrip the expectation.

Title

On *Maskil*, see Introduction, p. 38. On *Ethan the Ezrahite*, see p. 35. As with certain of the psalms of Asaph, this is evidently a product of the choir, rather than of the founder himself (since no disaster befell the throne of David for several centuries after his time), unless indeed the psalm originally ended at verse 37. On this possibility *cf.* the comment on 51:18, 19.

89:1-4. A throne for ever

The theme of the psalm is quickly established by the repetition of *for ever* (1, 2, 4). The confrontation between this robust motif of verses 1-37, and the plaintive cry, 'But now—' and 'How long—?' of verses 38-51, gives the psalm its distinctive character. The whole poem is a commentary on Nathan's prophecy to David in 2 Samuel 7:12ff., summarized here in verses 3f.[1]

2. This verse should open with the words 'For I say . . .';[2] it is well paraphrased in TEV, 'I know that your love will last for ever'. It rounds off the sequence 'I will sing . . . I will proclaim . . .'. Incidentally, the word *established* ('will last', TEV) is literally 'built', which was another of the key words in 2 Samuel 7, with its play on the theme of the house David would have built for God, and the living house God would build instead for David (2 Sa. 7:5, 7, 13, 27).

3. The *covenant* with David, which some commentators regard as almost a rival to the Sinai covenant, is given loving attention in verses 19-37, and God's apparent repudiation of it will be the lament of verse 39 and of the whole section in which it stands.

89:5-18. The Throne above the throne

The psalm rises magnificently above the temptation to focus on the immediate scene and make God incidental to it. It reaches up to heaven, exulting in the majesty (5-8), mastery (9-13) and moral grandeur (14-18) of God. Against that blaze of glory it reveals the grace that allows Israel and its king to know and belong to such a Lord.

---

[1] These verses are transferred in NEB to follow verse 19.

[2] LXX and Jerome introduce verse 2 with 'For thou hast said'; but this goes less well with the 'thy . . . thy' which follow it. There is no warrant for transferring it, with RSV, to verse 3.

5-8. Majesty. The biblical universe is not empty, but peopled with myriads[1] of angels, here called *holy ones* (5, 7) and *heavenly beings* (6, lit. 'sons of '*ēlîm*'; *cf.* on 29:1; 82, opening). The word 'holy' is used of them in what is probably its primary sense, namely 'belonging to God's realm, not man's' (*cf.* Ex. 3:5); its ethical sense of 'morally perfect' follows from this, taking its colour from God's character,[2] just as 'sons of God' can be used with or without its ethical implications (*cf.* Jb. 1:6; Mt. 5:45). Here the angels are seen as a company called together (*assembly*, 5, is a frequent term for Israel as God's church: *e.g.* Dt. 23:1-3, 8), and as a *council* (7),[3] but this great host only throws into relief the majesty of God before whom the mightiest tremble (7) and with whom none begins to compare either in greatness or (5b, 8b) in goodness.

9-13. Mastery. As the most formidable and unpredictable part of man's environment, *the sea* portrays in Scripture what only God can tame (see on 24:2). With verse 9 as background to Mark 4:39, the disciples were rightly awed as they asked one another, 'Who then is this?'

10. After the general example from nature, the particular one from history; after the sea, the monster. *Rahab*, the blusterer, is the nickname for Egypt (*cf.* Is. 51:9f.; see on Ps. 87:4). This victory is as central to the Old Testament as Calvary to the New.

12. NEB and some commentators find four mountains here, since Zaphon (*ṣāp̄ôn*), the Hebrew for *north*, is also the name of a mountain, north of Succoth in Transjordan. But the word for *south* does not easily yield another mountain name. NEB's 'Amanus' is too remote, as a word and as a place, to be convincing.[4] *Tabor and Hermon* are possibly paired as works of God which praise Him in different ways: the lowly Tabor (1,900 ft.) by its history, as the scene of Deborah's victory, and the giant Hermon (9,000 ft.) by its physical majesty. The Creator's hand is both *strong* and *high* (13).

---

[1] *E.g.* Dt. 33:2; Dn. 7:10.

[2] The very different colour it would take from a false god is shown by the word *qāḏēš*, 'holy one', for a male temple-prostitute, and the feminine of it for a female one (translated as 'dog' and 'harlot' in Dt. 23:18), as persons consecrated to Canaanite and other deities.

[3] See on 25:14; *cf.* Micaiah's picture of the celestial council of war (1 Ki. 22:19-23).

[4] The consonants *ymn* (south) have to be changed to '*mn* for Mt. Amanus in southern Turkey. For documentation see Dahood, *ad loc.*

14–18. Moral grandeur. The might which is praised in verse 13, summing up the previous stanza, would be tyranny without the right which underlies it as *foundation* (14a) and which marks out the way it is to take (14b). God's *faithfulness* has been prominent already (1, 2, 5, 8); now at least four other facets of His goodness (14, 16, 17) add their lustre to it.

15. *The festal shout* is the cry of joyful homage, such as greeted the ark in 1 Samuel 4:5f. (*cf.* Pss. 33:3; 47:5). NEB puts it well: 'Happy the people who have learnt to acclaim thee.' The *walk* of verse 15 may picture a procession in the first place, but this is to make vivid the reality it symbolizes: a constant, joyful progress (*all the day*, 16) with Him and with one's fellows. A New Testament equivalent is in 1 John 1:4–7.

18. *Our shield*[1] and *our king* are parallel terms—a revealing touch: *cf.* Introduction, IV. The Messianic Hope, pp. 18f. So this verse leads on to the burning topic of the rest of the psalm.

89: 19–37. The covenant with David

The 'covenant' which came briefly into view in verses 3f. was the promise made to David in 2 Samuel 7:4ff. The psalm now clothes it in rich poetry, dwelling on it at length and expounding it from other scriptures. Then the final section (38–51), all unannounced, will expose the quite different face of present experience, to make these promises the basis of an urgent prayer.

19–27. The peerless prince. All the emphasis now falls on God's initiative in choosing (19–21) and exalting David (22–27). Here was no self-made king and empire-builder, carving out a career for himself. And with God behind it, such a story as his could not simply break off unfinished.

19a. *Of old* (lit. 'Then') sets the scene in the now distant days of David.[2] *Thy faithful one* should be plural, according to most texts, and in fact the words that follow are a summary of messages to two prophets, Samuel and Nathan, and of assurances to David himself, attested in his psalms.

---

[1] Dahood argues for the sense 'Suzerain', here and elsewhere, on the basis of Ugaritic and Phoenician. But this involves reinterpreting 'belongs to' as a formula of emphasis: 'Truly Yahweh is our Suzerain'. It is a forced and improbable translation of a straightforward text.

[2] A. Bentzen, *King and Messiah* (Lutterworth, 1955), p. 19, would make this *Then* allude to a primeval decree before Creation. But this ignores the 'faithful ones' who were addressed with this oracle.

19b, 20. This is, in essence, what God revealed to Samuel, recorded in the famous saying of 1 Samuel 13:14, 'the Lord has sought out a man after his own heart' and in the story of David's anointing in his father's house (1 Sa. 16:1–13). *The crown* (*nēzer, cf.* verse 39 [40, Heb.]) is a conjectural emendation of '*ēzer*, 'help' (*cf.* AV, RV); it certainly makes easier sense than the latter. But more important than any crown was the fact of being *anointed*, and so set apart for a sacred office; it was this that gave rise, in due course, to the title Messiah or Christ.[1]

21. *Abide* is rather colourless; the word means 'be firm' or 'be well prepared'. NEB gives both aspects of it with 'My hand shall be ready to help him'.

22–24. Various psalms of David record promises such as these, revealed to him as oracles of God, *e.g.*, 2:7–9; 21:8–12; 110:1ff., to mention a few. The present psalm, written in very different circumstances, draws on this store of truth.

25. Psalm 72:8 shows that the old promise in Exodus 23:31 of a land stretching from the Red Sea to the Euphrates was stirring new hopes in the early days of the monarchy, with David's empire approximating to this pattern. Still more directly, there was the 'decree' of Psalm 2:7–9, which seems to be in mind in the next two verses.

26, 27. While the exalted terms of these verses could each be interpreted at a moderate level (*e.g.*, Israel could corporately address God as *My Father*, Je. 3:19, and be called His *first-born* and *the highest*,[2] Ex. 4:22, RV; Dt. 28:1), they become overwhelming when they are heaped together, as here, and directed to an individual. If God could push language so near to its limits in addressing David, the psalm is right to seize on the fact and, in the end (38ff.), to ask what has become of it. On its fulfilment, see the Introduction, p. 20.

28–37. The endless dynasty. The oracle of Nathan (esp. 2 Sa. 7:13ff.) has already coloured verse 26 with its promise of kingly sonship. Now its pledge of the throne *for ever* becomes the dominant theme.

It could have been played down, to mean that unlike Saul

---

[1] See Introduction, pp. 18f.

[2] This word is '*elyôn*, the term translated 'Most High' when applied to God. *Cf.* JB, more literally than most: 'I shall make him . . . the Most High for kings on earth'. This could be understood to mean that what God is to the powers of heaven, David is appointed to be to those of earth. David himself could never have attained to this.

(2 Sa. 7:15), who lost the kingship for his descendants, David would keep it in the family as long as the kingdom lasted. 'For ever', like our term 'a permanent appointment', need mean no more than this. But this passage expounds it for us at full strength, by a succession of parallel phrases in 29b, 36b, 37.[1] So it keeps alive a question which remains unanswered up to the first chapter of the New Testament. That question is the pressing concern of the final section of the psalm.

89:38–51. The covenant in eclipse
This is the first hint of the disaster which has overtaken the singers. Either the unclouded praise of verses 1–37 was a miracle of self-discipline, if it was composed in this situation, or else it was drawn from an existing psalm to strike a positive note (by a different exercise of self-discipline) before the unburdening of grief which now ensues.

38–45. But now . . . Although the *now* of RSV makes a good contrast to verse 19 ('Of old'), verse 38 should begin with '*But thou . . .*', a pointed reminder that the God who made the promises has unmade the king. He is the subject of almost every verb that follows (*cf.* on 60:1–4).

38. On *anointed*, see on verse 20.

39. *Renounced* may be too decisive a word for this rare verb, whose meaning has to be guessed from its parallel terms, *i.e.* 'defiled' (39b) and 'scorned' (La. 2:7a). Perhaps 'disdained' or 'held cheap' would be more accurate. It is in any case the language of experience, not an accusation of bad faith.

The word for *crown* (*nēzer*) emphasizes its aspect as a symbol of consecration for both king and (Ex. 29:6) high priest. It is related to the term Nazirite, 'consecrated one'. So the word *defiled* is doubly humiliating.

40ff. Rather than a ritual drama,[2] as some hold, these verses more readily reflect the fall of Jerusalem, in terms akin to Lamentations: *cf.* the broken walls (La. 2:8) and the looting and gloating of *all that pass by* (41; La. 1:10, 12). Note, too, the *youth* (45) of king Jehoiachin, deported to Babylon at

---

[1] There is no compelling need to emend 37b (38b, Heb.), which runs 'even the faithful witness in the sky', or 'and the witness in the sky is faithful'. But its interpretation is uncertain, with 'the witness' variously identified as 'the moon' (our faithful calendar keeper, Gn. 1:14), 'the rainbow' (Gn. 9:13ff.), and God Himself (Jb. 16:19).

[2] See Introduction, pp. 10ff.

eighteen, after three months on the throne (2 Ki. 24:8), to be *covered with shame* (45) all too literally (Kirkpatrick), clothed in prison garments for the next thirty-seven years (2 Ki. 25:27, 29).

44. *Sceptre* is not in the Hebrew text, which has 'Thou hast deprived (him) of his lustre'.[1]

45. See above, on 40ff.

46-51. How long . . . ? This question can be as fruitful as it is painful. In terms of personal fulfilment it made the shortness of earthly life seem tantalizing, as it should be. The problems of verses 47f. cry out for the gospel's answer. In terms of the empty throne of David (49ff.) it invited fresh thinking about the Lord's anointed and His reign.

Finally, the prayer which the psalm prays in the exiled king's name (*cf.* 50f.) begins to accustom our eyes to the combination of *servant* (50) and Messiah (*anointed,* 51), the recipient of God's promises and man's *insults*.[2] The outline is fragmentary, but it is beginning to appear (*cf.* 69:9; Rom. 15:3). The unanswerable questions, like our own, were to have undreamt of and unquestionable answers.

89:52. Doxology

The blessing and the double *Amen,* like those of 41:13 and 72:19, end this Third Book of the Psalter, in which national suffering has played a large part, on a firm note of praise.

---

[1] Or 'his purity' (*cf.* 39b). The Heb. is awkward, but is supported by LXX, *etc.*

[2] The word *insults* is an emendation, but the context supplies it (*scorned . . . taunt . . . mock*). 50b (51b, Heb.) reads lit. '. . . all of many (or mighty) peoples'. As the consonants of 'all' are the opening consonants of 'insults', a copying error seems possible.

Book IV: Psalms 90–106

Although the psalms of this collection are not linked by name with the temple choirs, as were most of those in Books II and III, most of them are psalms for public worship (note the titles of 92 and 100: 'A Song for the Sabbath'; 'A Psalm for the thank offering'), and they have given the Christian church a number of its canticles (95, 98, 100) and hymns (based on, *e.g.*, 90, 92, 100, 103, 104). Unless one assigns a cultic origin to everything in the Psalter, one can say with Kirkpatrick[1] that in general the psalms of Book I (1–41) tend to be *personal*, those of Books II and III (42–89) to be *national*, and those of Books IV and V (90–150) *liturgical*, *i.e.*, concerned with the regular corporate praise of God.

In Book IV God is predominantly named Yahweh (the Lord).[2] Most of these psalms are anonymous; but Psalm 90 is attributed to Moses, and Psalms 101 and 103 to David.

Psalm 90

'O God our Help'

Only Isaiah 40 can compare with this psalm for its presentation of God's grandeur and eternity over against the frailty of man. But while Isaiah is comforting, the psalm is chastened and sobering, even though the clouds disperse in the final prayer. A closer companion to the poem in some respects is Genesis 1–3, on which the psalmist evidently meditates; and this is appropriate, since the title names him *Moses, the man of God*. (For a discussion of his authorship see Introduction, p. 36.)

In an age which was readier than our own to reflect on mortality and judgment, this psalm was an appointed reading (with 1 Cor. 15) at the burial of the dead: a rehearsal of the facts of death and life which, if it was harsh at such a moment,

---

[1] Kirkpatrick, p. lviii.
[2] In most Bibles the word 'Lord' is printed wholly in capitals (LORD) when it represents the name Yahweh rather than the Heb. for 'master'.

wounded to heal. In the paraphrase by Isaac Watts, 'O God, our help in ages past', it has established itself as a prayer supremely matched to times of crisis.

90:1, 2. God the Eternal

This opening of the psalm corresponds to the close, in that God is seen here as *our* God, whose eternity is the answer, not simply the antithesis, to our homelessness and our brevity of life. The middle stanzas will display the darker side of the picture, revealing our membership of a race under judgment; but that fact is not given the first word or the last.

1. *Lord*, in this verse, is a title, not a substitute for the name Yahweh (see on 86:8). So God is addressed as our sovereign as well as our shelter: we are His to command, though He is also ours to enjoy. For *dwelling place* (*mā'ôn*), LXX and Vulg. read 'refuge' (*mā'ôz*). Either would be true, but 'dwelling place' is specially relevant to this psalm's emphasis on human rootlessness, and is a metaphor found also in the Blessing of Moses: 'the eternal God is your dwelling place' (Dt. 33:27). The personal prayer of 71:3 (AV, not RSV) makes it a truth to live by: 'Be thou my strong habitation, whereunto I may continually resort.'

2. Two translations of the middle line of this verse are possible, as it stands. The first is, literally, 'or ever thou hadst travailed in birth with the earth and the world'—a vivid metaphor but more in line with non-Israelite thought than with the biblical insistence on the Creator's distinctness from His work.[1] The second (*cf.* Anderson) is 'or ever the earth and the world travailed in birth (with them)', *i.e.*, to produce the mountains (*cf.* 104:8; and *cf.* the sea issuing as if from the womb of earth, Jb. 38:8). But God's immemorial majesty, which is the theme of the verse, has disturbing as well as reassuring implications, as the psalm goes on to show.

90:3–6. Man the ephemeral

Although *dust* is a different word from that of Genesis 3:19 ('you are dust, and to dust you shall return'), the idea of returning to it (*Turn back*) almost certainly alludes to the curse of Adam, and uses the same verb.[2] This accounts for the stress

[1] In Pr. 8:24f. it is the divine Wisdom that is 'brought forth' as God's offspring, before the material world is made.

[2] Also *children of men* could be translated 'sons of Adam', but the allusion, if it is there, is not emphasized.

on God's wrath as the reason for man's transience; but that theme will not emerge until verse 7. For the moment it is the transience itself that occupies us, in a series of devastating comparisons.

4. Some Jews and Christians have attempted to map out the ages as a 'week' of thousand-year days because of this verse. But this is to overlook the last phrase, *or* (lit. 'and') *as a watch in the night*, which rules out any such woodenness of inter-pretation. The comparison is like that of Isaiah 40:15ff., where the nations are 'like a drop from a bucket, and . . . as the dust on the scales'. It puts our world into its context, which is God, and our time-span into its huge setting of eternity. This is humbling to human pride (the point of this verse), but heartening with regard to God's interventions and their timing (the point of 2 Pet. 3:8f.).

5. The swift changes of metaphor add to the sense of in-security and flux; there is no compelling need to tidy them out of the text, with some modern versions, though the text has its difficulties. *Sweep . . . away* is more literally 'flood . . . away', as if by a rainstorm or a swollen river. The word used here for *dream* is 'sleep', which could be an expression for death (*cf.* 76:5 (6, Heb.); Jb. 14:12) but is probably rightly understood by RSV, *etc.*; *cf.* Psalm 73:20, though the latter uses the normal word for dream.

5b, 6. It is tempting to link the phrase *in the morning* (5b) to the vanished dream or sleep of 5a (*cf.* NEB, 'like a dream at daybreak'); but verse 5b, as it stands, reinforces the next verse with the repeated picture of early promise; one which will make its failure all the more frustrating. The reiterated word *renewed* points to a landscape reclothed in morning freshness, and so to the human scene as a whole, ever renewed but ever fading. It is a favourite biblical figure: *cf.* 37:2; Isaiah 40:6ff.; 1 Peter 1:23–25; but note our Lord's unusual handling of it in Matthew 6:28–30.

90:7–12. Man under wrath
At the heart of these verses lies the truth of, *e.g.*, Psalm 30:5 (AV, RV, NEB): 'in his favour is life', of which we now explore the converse. As verse 3 has shown (see above), the setting is the Fall, which reveals death as our sentence, not our intended lot. Its universal shadow is a standing reminder of our human solidarity in sin, and of the seriousness with which God views this.

7, 8. We are shown God's wrath as doubly irresistible, by its vigour and by its justice, leaving us with no resource (7) and no excuse (8). *Consumed* is literally 'finished', 'spent': there is nothing left. *Overwhelmed* is the word used of an army facing disaster (Jdg. 20:41) and of Joseph's brothers in their dismay at the moment of truth (Gn. 45:3). As for *our secret sins*, they must include those that we would disguise even from ourselves. On *the light of thy countenance*, in such a context, see the quotation from C. S. Lewis in the comment on Psalm 14:5a.

9. Both lines of this verse speak of anticlimax, and see it as further evidence that man is under judgment. The first line uses the figure of the day that passes its zenith: the verb *pass away* is that of Jeremiah 6:4, 'Woe to us, for the day declines . . .'. The closing *sigh* or murmur (rather than 'tale', AV, *etc.*) is even more expressive,[1] and its effect is, if anything, heightened in the unaltered form of the verse with its sense of prolonged effort that comes to nothing: 'we bring our years to an end . . .' (RSV mg., RV, PBV).

10. The decline and fall of the previous verse are painfully predictable and scarcely worth postponing. Perhaps the seventy or eighty years[2] are also tacitly contrasted to the life-span of the patriarchs, to which the thousand years of verse 4 may incidentally allude (*cf.* Anderson).

11, 12. In spite of all these signs of God's displeasure, the message never registers until God brings it home to us. As Weiser points out, 'the poet observes that part of the nature of sin is that men hardly ever realize the ultimate relationship between mortality and sin, because they live for the moment . . .'. The psalmist includes himself among those who need this lesson. But he has learnt it well. Perhaps nowhere outside the book of Ecclesiastes is the fact of death so resolutely faced, or the fear of God[3] so explicitly related to it (*cf.* Ec. 12).

---

[1] T. S. Eliot ends his poem 'The Hollow Men' on a not dissimilar note, though it is no guide to eschatology!

> *This is the way the world ends*
> *Not with a bang but a whimper.*

[2] The sonorous expressions *threescore and ten, . . . fourscore* are a relic of old English; the Heb. simply has 'seventy, . . . eighty'.

[3] The difficult line 11b is probably to be understood as in RV: 'And thy wrath according to the fear that is due unto thee'. *I.e.*, the measure of the homage we owe is the measure of our judgment if we withhold it. But the fear that God desires is filial: see the paradoxical duplication of the word in Ex. 20:20.

90:13–17. God of grace

With the boldness of verse 1, which claimed relationship with God, the remainder of the prayer largely begs for a reversal of what has gone before.

13. God had rebuked man with His 'Turn back!' (3); now man returns this cry to God: 'Turn back' (*Return*)—for mercy. The second line of the verse is closely echoed in the Song of Moses (Dt. 32:36, Heb.), in God's intention to do the very thing for which this pleads.

14, 15.[1] The contrasts continue. Whereas 'all our days' are, by our deserts, 'under thy wrath' (9), within the covenant *all our days* can be joyful. And here is a longer-lived *morning* than that of verse 6. The New Testament, incidentally, will outrun verse 15's modest prayer for joys to balance sorrows, by its promise of 'an eternal weight of glory beyond all comparison' (2 Cor. 4:17).

16, 17. The crowning contrast is between what was seen as perishable in verses 3–12 and the abiding glory of what God does. Here is a heritage for our *children* in a transitory world; here is delight (17a; *favour* is too colourless a word); here, too, the possibility of labour that is 'not in vain' (*cf.* 1 Cor. 15:58). Not only God's work (*thy work*) will endure, but, with His blessing, *the work of our hands* as well. It has been worth facing the unwelcome facts of time, wrath and death, to have been moved to such a prayer and such assurance.

Psalm 91

Under His Wings

This is a psalm for danger: for times of exposure and encirclement or of challenging the power of evil. Some of its language, of strongholds and shields, reminds us of David, to whom the LXX ascribes it; other phrases echo the Song of Moses in Deuteronomy 32, as did Psalm 90; but it is in fact anonymous and timeless, perhaps all the more accessible for that.

---

[1] Briggs draws attention to a linguistic link between verse 15 and the Song of Moses, in the parallelism of *yᵉmôṯ*, *šᵉnôṯ* (Dt. 32:7). Both forms are unusual, and the former is found only in these two places.

The changes of person (obscured in some modern versions), from 'I' to 'you' and on to the divine 'I', mark the divisions of the psalm and are indicated in the three main headings suggested here.

91:1, 2. My refuge

There is no need to alter the flow of these two verses, which, as in AV, RV, read well as a self-contained statement (1) followed by a vow of trust (2). *I.e.*, 'He who dwells . . . will abide in the shadow of the Almighty. I[1] will say to the Lord, "My refuge . . .".' So the psalmist declares his own faith before applying it to us. It is an eloquent opening, enriched not only by the four metaphors for security but by the four divine names. *Most High* is a title which cuts every threat down to size; *Almighty* (Shaddai) is the name which sustained the homeless patriarchs (Ex. 6:3). By the further appellation, *The Lord* (Yahweh), Moses was assured that 'I am' and 'I am with you' (Ex. 3:14, 12, NEB); while even the general term 'God' is made intimate by the possessive, as *my God*.

91:3–13. Your refuge

Now the psalmist spells out for each of us (the *you* is singular throughout) some aspects of the truth he has just outlined.

3–6. Versatile protection. Most of these dangers are of a kind which strike unseen, against which the strong are as helpless as the weak. Some, like *the snare of the fowler* (3), are obviously metaphors for the plots[2] which would entangle our affairs (140:1–5) or compromise our loyalty (119:110). Others are ills that attack the mind (5a) or the body, by human or non-human agency (5b, 6). The pictures of *pestilence that stalks* . . . and *destruction that wastes* (*i.e.* devastates) are poetic personifications; there is no reason to interpret them as demons, as did LXX and later Judaism.[3]

As for God's care, it combines the warm protectiveness of a

[1] This is the Heb. text. In recent versions the consonants are re-vocalized in various ways, but they already make excellent sense.

[2] Perhaps 3b is a parallel to this, if *deḇer*, 'pestilence' is vocalized as *deḇar*, 'word' (LXX *et al.*), since 'pestilence' occurs again in verse 6. The 'deadly word', if so, might be slander, curse or spell.

[3] The Midrash on Lam. 1:3 alludes to this verse, quoting lurid descriptions of the demon *qeṭeḇ* (destruction): *e.g.* 'full of eyes, scales and hair'; 'whoever looks at it falls down dead'. *Midrash Rabbah*, VII (Soncino, 1939), pp. 98f.

parent bird (4; *cf.* Dt. 32:11; Mt. 23:37) with the hard, unyielding strength of armour (4b). *Shield and buckler* gave respectively the cover that was large and static, and small and mobile.

7–10. Individual protection. *You* is emphatic: 'to you it will not draw near'. This is, of course, a statement of exact, minute providence, not a charm against adversity. The no less sweeping promise of Romans 8:28 ('. . . . everything . . . for good with those who love him') does not exclude 'nakedness, or peril, or sword' (8:35); *cf.* again the paradox of Luke 21:16, 18. What it does assure us is that nothing can touch God's servant but by God's leave;[1] equally (8) that no rebel can escape His retribution.

11–13. Miraculous protection. This brings the promise doubly to a climax, by revealing the unseen host 'sent forth to minister for them who shall be heirs of salvation' (Heb. 1:14, AV) and by depicting God's servants not merely as survivors but as victors, who *trample* deadly enemies *under foot*.

11f. It was characteristic of the devil to read this promise as an invitation to arrogance (Mt. 4:6). It was characteristic of God, Father and Son, that angelic help was sent when it was most needed (Mt. 4:11; Lk. 22:43), accepted as strength for service and sacrifice, and refused for self-advantage (Mt. 26:53f.).

13. These creatures are even more formidable than they seem from RSV, since *adder* should probably be 'cobra' (*peten*; see on 58:4). Such terms are frequently symbols for evil men and powers; *cf., e.g.,* 58:3–6; Deuteronomy 32:33. Our Lord, in giving His envoys a similar promise of the upper hand, warned them against the pride it could induce (Lk. 10:19f.).

91:14–16. God's pledge

Now comes the confirming oracle of God: a change of voice such as can be heard in several psalms (*e.g.* 60:6–8; 81:6–16; 95:8–12).

The trust that invites the Lord's protection has already been

---

[1] The text of 9a seems to have suffered: see RSV mg. for the abrupt changes of person. AV ('Because thou hast made the Lord, [which is] my refuge, [even] the most High, thy habitation') gives a possible solution without altering the text. RSV and others make small adjustments: *viz.*, *maḥsekā* (RSV, NEB, TEV) for MT *maḥsî*; or *'āmartā* (JB, Gelineau, RP) for MT *'attâ*.

compared to our taking shelter under His roof (1, 2, 9). Now this trust is analysed into three of its constituents, and God's safe keeping into as many as eight.

The word for *he cleaves to me in love* is used elsewhere in contexts of setting one's heart on somebody or on some enterprise. As man's commitment to God it comes only here. Deuteronomy (7:7; 10:15) reminds Israel that God's commitment, not man's, came first. *He knows my name* is the second element, since the relationship has rational content, and rests on revelation (*cf.* 76:1; Ex. 34:5–7). The third element asserts the basic simplicity of it: *he calls to me*. At bottom the bond is between helper and helpless, a matter of grace.

On God's side, the eight expressions in 14–16 for what He undertakes are not only eight aspects of the whole. There is perhaps a certain progress traceable from the thought of His initial deliverance to that of His abiding companionship ('with him') and crowning gifts of glory, length of days (1b; see on 23:6, end) and a salvation no longer waited for but seen. For the Christian, these last three gifts (*cf.*, respectively, Rom. 8:18, 11, 23–25) reveal dimensions only occasionally evident to the saints of the Old Testament.

Psalm 92

They that wait on the Lord ...

This *Song for the Sabbath* is proof enough, if such were needed, that the Old Testament sabbath was a day not only for rest but for corporate worship ('a holy convocation', Lv. 23:3), and intended to be a delight rather than a burden. If it was at the same time a test of faith and loyalty against the pull of self-interest ('When will the new moon be over, . . . And the sabbath, that we may offer wheat for sale?' Am. 8:5; *cf.* Is. 58:13f.), the psalm's picture of transient worldlings and, in contrast, of the godly who ever renew their strength, is doubly appropriate.

The hymn, 'Sweet is the work, my God, my King', by Isaac Watts, is a felicitous and illuminating paraphrase of this psalm.

92:1–4. Tireless praise

Clearly enough it is right to give God thanks and sing His praise; but here we go further and call it *good*: good, no doubt, in the sense that, in love, He values it, as He valued His creation; but also in the sense that it uplifts and liberates us. We are *made . . . glad* by the works of God (4) and by His ways (2) in proportion as we give our minds and voices (4b) to expressing the wonder of them. The converse of this will come out at the opening of the next section, in verses 5 and 6.

To return to some details of verses 1–4: *to sing praises* (1) is a single verb, the root of the Hebrew word for 'psalm', meaning to play an instrument or to sing with an accompaniment. See further the Introduction, p. 37, subsection 2. *The lute* (3) is in Hebrew 'the ten', *i.e.*, presumably a ten-stringed instrument (*cf.* LXX). JB calls it a zither. In the same verse, *melody* is 'higgaion' (see p. 37) and *lyre* is the instrument which David used to play to Saul; most versions now agree with AV in calling it a harp.

92:5–9. Heedless arrogance

5, 6. To look up, in true worship as in verses 1–4, is to be made not only 'glad' (4) but thoughtful, awed by the scale of God's design (5). By contrast, to be blind to all this is to become 'like the beasts that perish' (49:10, 12, 20), which is the literal force of the word *the dull man* (6). It has nothing to do with mental capacity: only with the use of it. *Cf.* Samuel Johnson on those who ask no more of life than to be carefree: 'It is sad stuff; it is brutish. If a bull could speak, he might as well exclaim,—Here am I with this cow and this grass; what being can enjoy better felicity?'[1]

7, 8. RSV and NEB insert the word *that*, at the beginning of verse 7, to indicate that what follows is the matter which the 'dull' and 'stupid' (6) never grasp, *i.e.*, the short life-cycle of the wicked (7). But their crucial disregard is of God's majesty, the theme of verse 5 to which verse 6 more probably looks back.[2]

---

[1] J. Boswell, *The Life of Dr. Johnson* (Everyman Edn.), I, p. 464.

[2] So, among others, Weiser, Gelineau, JB. The interpretation in RSV, *etc.*, rests on the fact that the word *this*, used unqualified as at the end of verse 6, almost invariably points forward: *cf.*, *e.g.*, Gn. 42:18; 43:11; *etc.* But there are exceptions. Ezk. 21:27 mg. (21:32, Heb.) points backwards; and examples of a retrospective 'this' compounded with the preposition *bᵉ* or with *bᵉkol* slightly outnumber those that are prospective: see, *e.g.*, Pss. 27:3; 78:32; Is. 5:25, *etc.*; Je. 3:10; Mal. 3:10; *etc.*

So verse 7 introduces the doom of the wicked and the eternal triumph of God, as a fresh subject which will now be developed with some of its corollaries. The verb translated *sprout* (7) or 'flourish' (12, 13) helps to bind the remaining verses together by the stark contrasts it depicts. TEV puts it boldly here, with 'the wicked may grow like weeds' (*cf.* JB). *Destruction for ever* may simply look forward to their disappearance from the scene, or it may imply a contrast between their end and that of the righteous, as in 49:14f.; 73:17ff.

9. This verse, with its cumulative force, is noticeably similar to certain lines from Ugarit, written some centuries earlier.[1] If these were well known, the present verse could be a pointed assertion that it is the Lord, not Baal, who will triumph, and that His victory will rid the world of evil, rather than relieve a mere nature-god of his rivals.

92:10–15. Endless vitality

Once again, as in verse 4, the singer boldly makes the Lord's exploits his own delight and inheritance. If God is 'on high for ever' (8), He can raise *my head* on high—indeed *my horn* (10), symbol of power; and if His enemies are doomed (9), so are mine (11).

Even something of His changelessness (the *for ever* of verse 8) is shared by His servants, in the form of resurgent life. It is marked in these verses by the repetition of the words 'fresh' (10, 14c ['green']) and 'flourish' (12, 13).

To look at these more closely:

10. *Fresh oil*, in such a context, speaks eloquently of a renewed anointing (*cf.* AV, RV, NEB), or consecration, to serve God. There may be the additional thought of preparing a 'living sacrifice', since the verb is used elsewhere not for anointing but for moistening the meal-offering with oil before presenting it at the altar (Ex. 29:40, *et al.*). In some Christian circles this phrase from the psalm still enriches the prayers offered for ministers and preachers.

12, 13. *Flourish*, in both verses, is the same verb as 'sprout' in verse 7, making a telling contrast to it which is intensified

---

[1] Baal, about to do battle with the personified seas and rivers, is told:
> 'Behold, thine enemies, O Baal,
> Behold, thine enemies shalt thou crush,
> Behold, thou shalt crush thy foes!'

See Introduction, p. 2.

by the further details of the picture. The *palm tree* is the embodiment of graceful erectness; the *cedar*, of strength and majesty. Their natural dignity and stability are enhanced here by the honoured place they are pictured as occupying and the protection they accordingly enjoy (*cf.* 52:8). Setting metaphor aside, the connection between *the house of the Lord* and the flourishing of the righteous is explained in the promise of Isaiah 40:31 (AV): 'They that wait upon the Lord shall renew their strength. . . .'

14. Instead of a static and obstructive permanence, hardly more desirable than the transience of verse 7, this is a satisfying climax. It is not the greenness of perpetual youth, but the freshness[1] of age without sterility, like that of Moses whose 'eye was not dim, nor his natural force abated' (Dt. 34:7); whose wisdom was mature and his memory invaluably rich. It is a picture which bodily and mental ills must often severely limit, but which sets a pattern of spiritual stamina for our encouragement and possibly our rebuke.

15. The final verse returns us to the keynote of the psalm, which is not the contemplation of our prospects but the praise of God. The opening verses called us to declare this (2) with our lips; the conclusion, with our lives. *To show* (or 'declare') *that the Lord is upright* is the crowning phrase to which verses 12–14 lead up; *i.e.*, that by our vitality we may not only sing but '*be*' (in terms of Eph. 1:12, AV) 'to the praise of his glory'.

Psalm 93

The Throne above the Tumult

A group of psalms to God as King begins here, continuing to Psalm 99 or 100 (with the exception of 94). The fact that the cry 'The Lord reigns' (93:1; 96:10; 97:1; 99:1; *cf.* 47:8 [9, Heb.]) has the form of an announcement,[2] rather than a timeless statement like that of 95:3, has suggested to some interpreters that these songs originated in a festival to celebrate the Lord's accession. There is a brief discussion of this view in

[1] *Green* (14) is the same word as 'fresh' in verse 10.
[2] *Cf.* 2 Sa. 15:10; 2 Ki. 9:13; but in the Psalms the word-order is reversed.

the Introduction, pp. 9–16;[1] here it is perhaps enough to say that the objection to anything but a forward-looking interpretation (for this, see on 93:1, 2) is that the Old Testament looks back to no event that invested the Lord, like the Babylonian Marduk, with sovereignty, and makes no provision in its calendar of feasts (Lv. 23) for an enthronement festival. To hear the authentic voice of these psalms we need no cultic expertise: they speak to us directly.

93:1, 2. The King

There is a decisiveness in the Hebrew for *The Lord reigns* which at least calls for an exclamation mark (as in TEV, 'The Lord is king!'). It has the ring of a proclamation, like the phrase 'Jehu is king' (2 Ki. 9:13), for all its unlikeness to that announcement in other ways (see the opening paragraph). A truer parallel is Isaiah's picture of the news of victory reaching a despondent Jerusalem with the runner's shout: 'Your God reigns' (Is. 52:7). It confronts us afresh with a fact whose impact on us may have weakened; and further, its decisive tense[2] points on to the day when the King will come in power—a theme which is prominent in some other psalms of this group, especially 96 to 99, and may be implied in the rest of this verse.

Robed ... robed: every verse of this song, except the last, reverberates with doubled or even trebled expressions, a powerful feature which it shares with some of the earliest biblical and Canaanite poetry.[3] Here the repetition hails a sovereignty that is by no means muted or dormant: God appears in full magnificence, and armed for battle. These verbs are as decisive as the first (see above); they are better translated, with Coverdale, 'hath put on glorious apparel ... and girded himself with strength'. While His kingship, glory and might are ever-present facts, this acclamation of them may well be a leap into the future, anticipating the great Day of the Lord in a series of 'prophetic perfects' (see the final comment in the paragraph above) which display already 'the assurance of things hoped for'.

---

[1] For a closer scrutiny see A. Gelston, 'A note on YHWH MLK', *VT* 16 (1966), pp. 507–512.

[2] On the 'prophetic perfect' see on Ps. 9:5f., or the second paragraph on 86:13. For a particularly clear use of it, see 102:16 (17, Heb.), where the preceding verses put its futurity beyond doubt.

[3] See the victory songs of Moses and Deborah, Ex. 15 and Jdg. 5. See also on Ps. 92:9, and Introduction, p. 2 and footnotes.

The stability envisaged here is not inherent; the physical world is *established* (1) only because *thy throne is established* (2), and the world of men only in so far as that throne is acknowledged. Of itself, humanity is ever in turmoil, as pictured in verse 3 or in Psalm 46 where 'the nations rage, the kingdoms totter'. True to Israel's faith, the psalm reaches back to the Creator Himself for what is everlasting, not to the seeming eternity of the earth. Then it can look confidently and purposefully ahead (5; *cf.* 90:2, 17; 102:25ff.).

93:3, 4. The tumult

There is meanwhile no belittling of 'the surge's angry shock',[1] whose pounding (*cf.* NEB), rather than *roaring*, is expressed in the last word of verse 3 and in the relentless repetitions of these lines. This is, pictorially, the hostile scene familiar to us at ground-level, faced here in its full fury with biblical realism; yet outfaced in verse 4, with equal realism, by the glory of God.[2] *Mighty*, in both its occurrences (see footnote), has the ring of majesty, as in Psalm 8:1 (2, Heb.); and this psalm's presentation of the majesty *on high* can add its own virile tone to our invocation of God, 'who art in heaven'.

93:5. The reign of right

Here is God's true glory, not of mere strength but of character: wholly reassuring, wholly demanding. *Thy decrees* are literally 'thy testimonies' or 'affirmations', a term which emphasizes that Scripture rests on the integrity of God who vouches for its statements, promises, warnings and commands. It is one of the set of words on which Psalm 119 rings the changes.

In the second line NEB brings out the force of the word *befits* with its translation, 'holiness is the beauty of thy temple' (*cf.* Ct. 1:10, 'comely'; Is. 52:7, 'beautiful', its only other occurrences). God's holiness is the temple's inner glory in the first place; man's holiness, by God's gift, is the only fit response. The New Testament relates this to the living temple, the church, with equal rigour: 'If any one destroys God's temple, God will destroy him. For God's temple is holy, and that temple you are' (1 Cor. 3:17).

---

[1] S. Johnson, 'City of God, how broad and far'.

[2] RSV and most modern versions assume a small scribal error in the middle line (proposing '*addîr mimmišberê* for MT '*addîrîm mišberê*); but RV makes good sense of the existing text (MT): 'Above the voices of many waters, The mighty breakers of the sea, The Lord on high is mighty.'

But all the emphases of this psalm are positive, and it ends by opening up a further vista in the last two words. *For evermore* is literally 'to length of days', as in the final phrase of Psalm 23. Here, as there, the length is undefined, and it is left to the New Testament to explore it further and find it as eternal as God Himself (Rev. 21:22 – 22:5).

Psalm 94

A God who Punishes

This title is borrowed from the first line of the TEV translation, since 'punishment', as our language has developed, is a less loaded word than 'vengeance', though still a controversial one. For a discussion of this theme in the Psalms see the Introduction, pp. 25–32. In the present psalm the tone is urgent, but underlying it there is a reflective and basically confident spirit: a conviction of God's self-consistency which is akin to that of Psalm 37 and the book of Proverbs, and an ardent personal faith which knows God's faithfulness at first hand.

94:1–3. A case for the Judge

There is better ground than wishful thinking in the appeal to the *God of vengeance* (or punishment; see above) and the *judge of the earth*, since God Himself uses or accepts the terms in two famous passages in the Law (Dt. 32:35; Gn. 18:25). So the only question about the power of evil is *how long?* (3); there is no room for the crippling suspicion that God, perhaps, is blind (7) or has done a deal with darkness (20). Nothing has changed the Sun or corrupted the Judge: it is simply that the night is long (1b, 2a).

94:4–7. Boastful brutality

These tyrants are not necessarily foreign; they may equally be home-born, like the apostate king Manasseh or the cynics of Isaiah 5:18ff. The taunt of verse 7 has always been plausible in the short run; what escapes the scoffer is the damning display he makes of himself when he fancies he can do as he likes. This is indeed part of God's purpose in keeping silent:

cf. Psalm 50:21. Meanwhile the wording of this lament contains the seed of its own answer in the expressions *thy people* and *thy heritage* (5), which will come to flower in verse 14, where they reappear with their implications now unfolded.

The two verses just mentioned, verses 5 and 14, can add both depth and height to the familiar prayer of Psalm 28:9[1] for God's church, quoted in the *Te Deum* and elsewhere in the Book of Common Prayer.

94:8-11. Brutish stupidity

Counter-attack may prove the right defence in such a battle, where the sceptic grows dogmatic. The psalmist is not impressed: he takes up the attackers' taunt and throws it back at them, as NEB points out in its rendering of 7b and 8: 'they say, "... the God of Jacob pays no heed." Pay heed yourselves, most brutish of the people.' He also takes up part of his own expression, 'how long ... ?' (3), in the *when* of verse 8. But by using a verb rather than an adjective for the word *dullest*, or 'most brutish', he puts the emphasis on behaviour rather than ability. These people are adopting a bovine view of life; they are capable of better things, and the psalmist now appeals to them to use their minds.

9, 10.[2] The logic is inescapable, once the premise is accepted that God is our Maker. What the psalm does not contemplate is the crowning absurdity, reserved for modern man, of rejecting even this. For the biblical view of such a denial in practice, if hardly in theory, see on Psalm 14:1.

11. This verse disparages not the mind, as verses 8–10 show, but the airy opinions and futile schemes (both nouns are aspects of the word *thoughts*) of man on his own. To be awed into exclaiming 'Thy thoughts are very deep!' (92:5), and 'the thoughts of man ... are but a breath', is the beginning of knowledge. See also Isaiah 55:8f.

94:12-15. The blessing of patience

12. This verse would be well at home in Proverbs where, especially, the word *chasten* stresses the role of character-

---

[1] See also the commentary at that point, p. 124.
[2] Verse 10b perhaps invites the emendation of NEB, TEV (*midda'aṭ*, or *ha͏lō' yēḏa'*, for MT *da'aṭ*), to match it to 9, 10a; but the MT makes good sense, as in RSV, JB, granted the possibility of dividing the three verses into two tricola as in, *e.g.*, 93:3, 4.

building in the school of wisdom. But here it is the pupil speaking, not the teacher, and the words are a triumph of faith: a positive reaction to present trouble (1–7), and a personal reception of a general truth which would be easier to apply to 'the nations' (10) than to oneself.

13. *Respite* is hardly the meaning here; in any case the Hebrew word tends to be used of inward quietness in face of outward troubles (*e.g.* Is. 7:4, 'be quiet, do not fear'; *cf.* Is. 30:15). JB paraphrases it, 'His mind is at peace though times are bad'. In God's economy the *pit . . . dug for the wicked* is largely dug *by* the wicked (9:15); and this is not done in a day, nor without general havoc.

14. There is quite solid ground for this statement, since a person goes back on a pledge only for reasons of necessity or of inconstancy, neither of which can apply to God. This is the answer to the distress of verse 5, where see comment. It was on ground similar to this that our Lord found the resurrection of the dead implied in an inconspicuous statement to Moses (Mt. 22:31f.).

15. In a rather cryptic promise, the Hebrew has 'righteousness' rather than *the righteous*. JB is awkward but more accurate than most, with 'for verdict will return to righteousness again, and, in its wake, all upright hearts'; *cf.* the paraphrase in TEV, Gelineau. This straightforwardness in public life is a modest enough ideal, but its blessings are immense, moving the prophets to poetry and the psalmists to song: *e.g.* Isaiah 11:3ff.; 32:1ff.; Psalm 72:1ff.

94:16–19. The only champion
At last the concerns of 'me' and 'my' are given a hearing, and the mood is both sober and thankful. It has been no easy passage, but lonely (16f.; *cf.* 2 Tim. 4:16f.), precarious (18; *cf.* 1 Sa. 20:3b in the physical realm; Ps. 73:2 in the spiritual) and care-ridden (19; *cf.* 2 Cor. 11:28). Yet each of these facts has brought out its own aspect of God's character: staunch (16f.), strong (18) and heartening (19); aspects which otherwise would have been chiefly known by hearsay.

94:20–23. The certain judgment
Yet experience is not all. The question of verse 20 expects the answer 'No' because God has revealed Himself, not because of the way things are going. 'On the side of . . . oppressors

there was power' (Ec. 4:1), and on the side of *mischief* the prestige of law. Together, unopposed, these may well begin to look normal, as if God Himself accepted them as facts of life. Against this the psalmist knows the true facts: see again on verses 1–3.

So the last verse looks forward confidently to what the opening verses pleaded for; and the New Testament has no quarrel with it—always supposing that the sin is unrepented, a proviso which both Testaments take for granted (Je. 18:8; Jn. 12:46–48).

Meanwhile verse 22, in metaphors reminiscent of the psalms of David, rejoices in what is better than justice: the living God who, as *stronghold*, *rock* and *refuge*, has proved Himself equal to anything the enemy can send.

Psalm 95

The Way to Worship

From primitive times the Christian church has widely used this psalm (known as the *Venite*, from the Latin for 'O come') as a call and guide to worship. Its austere conclusion balances the exuberant opening with the same realism as that of the prophets with their call to match fine gestures with fine deeds. This abrupt change of tone led Wellhausen and others to analyse the psalm into two unrelated fragments; but most recent scholars see it as a unity, perhaps composed for the Feast of Tabernacles, when God's people re-lived, in token, their time of encampment in the wilderness. Its closest companion is Psalm 81, where again the voice of God breaks in, presumably through a priestly or prophetic singer, to challenge Israel with the claims of the covenant.

But Hebrews 3:7 – 4:13, expounding our psalm, forbids us to confine its thrust to Israel. The 'Today' of which it speaks is this very moment; the 'you' is none other than ourselves, and the promised 'rest' is not Canaan but salvation.

The LXX ascribes the psalm to David, but here it outruns the Hebrew text, which leaves it anonymous like its immediate companions. Hebrews 4:7 quotes it as the word of God 'in David' (not 'through David', which is RSV's interpretation), but this need mean no more than 'in the Psalter'.[1]

95:1-5. Rejoicing

To come singing into God's presence is not the only way—*cf.* the 'silence' of 62:1; 65:1; or the tears of 56:8—but it is the way that best expresses love. So before making ourselves small before Him (as we must, 6f.), we greet Him here with unashamed enthusiasm as our refuge and rescuer (1). The full-throated cries urged in the verbs of verses 1 and 2 suggest an acclamation fit for a king who is the saviour of his people. Like most of the verbs of this psalm, they are urged upon us as worshippers, indeed we address one another, to make sure that we rise to the occasion, not drifting into His courts preoccupied and apathetic.

3ff. But it is not a forced cheerfulness: the explanatory *For* introduces a reason bigger than the world itself, seen and unseen, a fact whose implications will be spelt out in Paul's catalogues of 'things . . . in heaven and on earth', 'principalities . . . powers . . . height . . . depth', which were created through and for the Son of God; which in the end must bow to Him; which, meanwhile, can do nothing to separate us from His love (*cf.* Col. 1:16; Phil. 2:10; Rom. 8:38f.). Indeed the world itself is ours, while we 'are Christ's; and Christ is God's' (1 Cor. 3:22f.). What the New Testament expounds in detail the psalm conveys by implication with a few graphic strokes, in the repetition of *his . . . his* and the picture of this immense and varied world[2] not only as hand-shaped (5) but as hand-held (4).

To the heathen, incidentally, *the sea* might represent a power even older than the gods, not conquered without a bitter struggle. It is a far cry from this to the simplicity of *The sea is his, for he made it.*

---

[1] For this preposition (*en*) as locating a passage of scripture, *cf.* the Gk. of Rom. 9:25; 11:2. *Cf.* the preposition *epi* in Mk. 2:26; 12:26.
[2] *Depths* contains the idea of something to be searched out; NEB's 'farthest places' transposes two Heb. consonants, after LXX, but this is hardly necessary. *Heights*, or 'peaks', is a rare word; its use in Nu. 23:22 (RSV 'horns') suggests such a meaning, but AV takes it as 'strength' in both places, and NEB finds the idea of curvature in it: hence 'curved horns' in Nu. 23:22, and 'folds of the hills' here. The contrast of *depths* and *heights*, however, seems the most probable.

95:6–7b. Reverence
This is the deep and basic note of worship, without which the 'joyful noise' of the opening will be shrill and self-indulgent. Each of the three main verbs of verse 6 is concerned with getting low before God, since the standard word for *worship* in Scripture means to prostrate oneself: *cf.*, *e.g.*, Abraham in Genesis 18:2. (The idea of worship expressing the 'worthship' of God belongs to the English word, not the Hebrew or the Greek, though it does occur in such expressions as 'Ascribe to the Lord the glory due . . .', in 96:8, *etc.*) A public act of homage is urged on us here as part of the service we owe to God, accepting our own place and acknowledging His. At the same time it is intimate, not the tribute of strangers. The familiar metaphors of verse 7 express His commitment, which is constant (*our God*), and His care, which is all-sufficing (*his pasture*) and personal (*his hand*). He is no hireling.

95:7c–11. Response
'To hear his most holy word' is presented here as one of the prime acts of worship. And 'hear', or *hearken to*, has often the added dimension in Hebrew of 'obey', for which the Old Testament has virtually no other word (*cf.* 'obeying' and 'obey' in 1 Sa. 15:22). So the worshipper singing this psalm is reminded to ask himself *how* he hears—will it be obediently?—and for whose *voice* he listens.[1]

On the crucial word *today*, as expounded in Hebrews 3 and 4, see the comments at verse 11 on God's rest.

8, 9. The *me* and *my*, *etc.*, now show the change of speaker, for which the last line of verse 7 has alerted us. Verses 8–11 should be in quotation marks, like 50:7ff.; 60:6b–8; 81:6–16, for this is God's oracle.

It is a cold douche of realism; and it was doubly so if its setting in the first place was the Feast of Tabernacles, when Israel in holiday mood remembered the wilderness (Lv. 23:40–43), and was doubtless tempted to romanticize it as an idyllic age. So the sober facts of then and now are brought to bear on us.

Meribah and *Massah*, 'dispute' and 'testing', are two place-names which sum up the sour, sceptical spirit of Israel on their

[1] The attractive variant in NEB (*cf.* RP), 'you shall know his power today if you will listen to his voice', is only a network of conjectures.

desert journey, and link the early crisis at Rephidim (Ex. 17:1–7) with the climactic one at Kadesh which cost Moses the promised land (Nu. 20:1–13). But while we might have expected the emphasis to fall on Meribah and the sin of disputing with God, verse 9 picks up the thought of Massah ('testing'), with its pattern of refusal to take God at His word. This is the basic danger, the 'evil, unbelieving heart' of which Hebrews 3 and 4 still find it necessary to warn us.

10. If *loathed* is too impulsive a word, 'indignant' (NEB) is perhaps too distant. 'Disgusted' (TEV) is exactly right, both here and in most other contexts (*e.g.* Ezk. 36:31). It is deeply personal, but has no suggestion of caprice, only an outraged sense of what is fitting and what is shameful.

11. *My rest* is pregnant with more than one meaning, as Hebrews 3 and 4 make clear. In relation to the Exodus it meant God's land to settle in, and peace to enjoy it (*cf.* Gn. 49:15; Ps. 132:14; 1 Ki. 8:56). But Hebrews 4:1–13 argues that the psalm still offers us, by its emphatic *Today*, a rest beyond anything that Joshua won, namely a share in God's own sabbath rest: the enjoyment of His finished work not merely of creation but of redemption. The quitters who turned back to the wilderness (so the Psalm and Epistle warn us) may be but pale shadows of ourselves, if we draw back from our great inheritance.

By ending on this note the psalm sacrifices literary grace to moral urgency. If this is a psalm about worship, it could give no blunter indication that the heart of the matter is severely practical: nothing less than a bending of wills and a renewal of pilgrimage.

Psalm 96

King of the World

In recapturing for us the triumphal entry of the ark into Jerusalem, the Chronicler writes out nearly the whole of this psalm, with parts of two others (105, 106), as the centrepiece of his chapter. The symbolism of the march, in which God crowned His victories by planting His throne in the enemy's former citadel, is matched by the theme of the psalm, although

1 Chronicles 16 does not claim that these were necessarily the very words that were sung on that occasion.[1]

The build-up of repeated words and phrases (*e.g.* 'sing . . .', 'ascribe . . .', 'he comes . . .') gives the psalm an insistent vigour (see on 93:1) and contributes to the air of almost irrepressible excitement at the prospect of God's coming. The creation's 'eager longing', of which Paul speaks in Romans 8:19, breaks out here into singing at the moment of fulfilment.

On the possibly festal origin of this psalm and its companions, see the comments and references at Psalm 93.

96:1-6. The King's glory

Nothing listless or introverted, nothing stale, befits the praise of God. There is a natural crescendo in the threefold 'Sing . . .' and the vision of *all the earth* as God's proper choir will be sustained in every verse. The *new song* (*cf.* on 33:3) is not simply a piece newly composed, though it naturally includes such, but a response that will match the freshness of His mercies, which are 'new every morning' (*cf.* Anderson here).

2, 3. With the word *tell*, the direction of flow changes from Godward to manward, for this is a messenger's word: 'take the news' (*cf.* 68:11; Is. 52:7; 61:1). The LXX, here and elsewhere, translates it by the verb which gave us 'evangelize', used here in almost our modern sense of bringing news of God to the world at large. There may be a lesson hidden in this sequence (first upwards to God, then outwards to man): a corrective to static worship and shallow preaching alike.

4, 5. There are places in the Psalter where *gods* are a term for angels and potentates (see on Psalm 82; also on 8:5; 95:3), but here they are clearly the unreal gods of the heathen. The term *idols* is *'elîlîm*, which the Old Testament treats as a mere parody of *'elōhîm* (God). It is the word translated 'worthless' in Job 13:4 ('worthless physicians') and Jeremiah 14:14 ('worthless divination'). Its robust challenge to the accepted ideas of the day invites the Christian to be equally unimpressed by currently revered nonsense, whatever its pedigree or patronage. The second line of verse 5 is still a valid retort

---

[1] They may have been. Although Ps. 106:47 (1 Ch. 16:35) looks exilic, there were Israelite captives and refugees at all periods. But 1 Ch. 16:7 (accurate in RSV) leaves the exact relation of the psalms to the narrative undefined. AV inserts two words, and NEB a colon, to settle the matter; but the Heb. is non-committal at that point.

to those who would shelve the question of creation, and start their thinking at some secondary point.

6. If we ask whether this *sanctuary* is earthly or heavenly, the probable answer is both. The earthly one was a 'copy and shadow' of the heavenly (Heb. 8:5); but its outward *strength and beauty* (*cf.* Ex. 28:2; 31:3ff.) were to be outshone by the inward glory of Christ, the true earthly sanctuary (Jn. 1:14; 2:21). There is also a telling contrast in Isaiah 28:1–6 between the fading glamour of human display and the abiding beauty and strength with which God crowns the steadfast.

96:7–9. The King's due

The threefold *Ascribe* . . . (lit. 'give'), like the threefold 'Sing . . .' of verses 1 and 2, makes a stirring call which repeats almost exactly the opening of Psalm 29. But this time it is mankind, not the angelic host, which is summoned; hence the bidding, *bring an offering*. The latter word (*minḥâ*) is used both of the gifts which a king expected (*cf.* 45:12 (13, Heb.); 2 Ki. 17:4) and of those which God appointed as a passport, for the time being, to His presence (20:3 (4, Heb.); but 40:6 (7, Heb.); Hebrews 10:5–10).

9. On *holy array*, or 'the splendour of holiness' (NEB), see on 29:2. Notice that the two aspects of *worship* which were discussed at 95:6 are both present in this group of verses. The NEB sees a third here, translating *tremble before him* as 'dance in his honour'; but while this is a valid concept (*cf.* 150:4), it is an unlikely meaning at this point.[1]

96:10–13. The King's coming

So the psalm moves to its climax. If the cry, 'The Lord reigns!' was a message first of all to Israel (*cf.* 93:1, and comment) like that of the lone runner in Isaiah 52:7, here a host of messengers spreads it to the world. The decisiveness of the Hebrew verb and the exultant response in 11–13 point to a new and overwhelming assertion of sovereignty rather than a timeless

---

[1] The verb means to whirl round or writhe, and so gives rise to two groups of nouns, meaning respectively 'dancing' and 'anguish'. But the verb has almost always the darker sense, and Dt. 2:25 (a close parallel to our verse) has 'and be in anguish because of you'. NEB itself has 'writhes in pain' at 97:4. Further, the version in 1 Ch. 16:30 uses a composite preposition which makes the expression 'in his honour' less plausible than here.

theological truth. It announces God's advent, the Day of the Lord.

What it will mean to the world, to be *established* and *never . . . moved* (10), is best seen against the welter of raging nations and collapsing régimes depicted in, *e.g.*, 46:6. The first and last lines of verse 10 make it additionally clear that this is a prophecy of perfect government, not a pronouncement on—of all things!—the earth's rotation, as an old controversy suggested.[1] The disastrous freedom of the Fall will be replaced by the only 'perfect freedom', which is serving God.

11ff. This ecstatic welcome had its human counterpart on Palm Sunday, with a hint, as well, that given half a chance 'the very stones would cry out'. How much more the teeming seas, fields and forests. The belief of fallen man that *righteousness, truth* (*i.e.*, dependability), the rule of justice, and the Lord Himself are the enemies of joy, is scouted by this passage. Where God rules (it implies), His humblest creatures can be themselves; where God is, there is singing. At the creation 'the morning stars sang together'; at His coming, the earth will at last join in again; meanwhile the Psalter itself shows what effect His presence has on those who, even through a glass, darkly, already see His face.

Psalm 97

Formidable Majesty

With its companions, especially its immediate neighbours, this psalm sings of God's coming as universal king. But whereas Psalms 96 and 98 catch the sheer delight that is in store for the world, here the doom of rebels brings out the darker side of that event. If 96:10ff. pictured, as it were, the home-coming of a beloved master, this psalm shows the awesome approach of a conqueror.

---

[1] Another curiosity in the history of this verse is the insertion of the words 'from (the) wood', after 'the Lord reigns', in the bilingual (Greek/Latin) Verona Psalter (6th century?). This has left its mark on various hymns which speak of Christ 'reigning from the Tree'. The insertion may have owed its origin to 'the wood' in verse 12.

97:1-5. The fiery presence

Whatever else God's advent[1] brings, the joy of liberation will be world-wide—a fact made vivid by the mention of *the many coastlands*, or better, 'islands', a favourite term in Isaiah for the remote, innumerable outposts of mankind.[2] Every psalm of this group (93-100) has this theme of universal empire.

2ff. Sinai (Ex. 19:16, 18) and the Song of Deborah (Jdg. 5:5) contribute to this picture of the terrifying impact of God's presence.[3] *Clouds and thick darkness* warn of His unapproachable holiness and hiddenness to presumptuous man (yet the hiddenness owes nothing to caprice: 2b), while the *fire* and *lightnings* reveal a holiness that is also devouring and irresistible (*cf.* Heb. 12:29). There is no escape. To speak of mountains melting is to see the most immemorial landmarks disappear, the most solid of refuges dissolve.

97:6-9. The prostrate gods

There is the same mixture of delight and dismay here as in the New Testament predictions of Christ's coming, when 'all the tribes of the earth will mourn' (Mt. 24:30; *cf.* Rev. 1:7) while His people rejoice. The emphasis now falls on the sole deity of the Lord, over against the fictitious gods of heathendom in the first place (7a, b[4]) and all the angels (*gods*, 7c) in the second. While *gods* in 7c could still refer to false gods, as in 96:5a, it is also a term for supernatural beings (see the references at 96:4, 5); and in Hebrews 1:6 these 'gods' are interpreted as angels, as in the Greek version (LXX) of this line, or of a close companion to it.[5] The Epistle, incidentally, expounds this kingly advent as that of God the Son, 'the firstborn'. It also supports the understanding of verse 7 as a command or exhortation, as most versions agree, rather than a statement as RSV and TEV suggest.

8. This verse is almost identical with 48:11, where see comment. So it brings with it the jubilant spirit of that psalm, where God's final victory has already been tasted in advance,

[1] For this implication of the expression, *The Lord reigns*, see on 93:1.

[2] *E.g.* Is. 24:15f.; 40:15; 41:5; 42:4, *etc.*

[3] *Cf.* other theophanies in Ps. 18:7ff.; Is. 6:4; Ezk. 1:4ff.; Na. 1:5; Hab. 3:3ff.

[4] *Worthless idols* represents the single word translated 'idols' at 96:5, where see note.

[5] For the view that the Epistle is quoting a line of the LXX of Dt. 32:43 which is not in MT, see, *e.g.*, F. F. Bruce, *The Epistle to the Hebrews* (*New London Commentary*, Marshall, Morgan & Scott, 1964), pp. 15f.

it seems, by a great deliverance of the literal city of *Zion*.

9. *Most high* is *'elyôn*, a title of God specially linked with His worship at Jerusalem (*cf.* 'Zion', 8), yet carrying its own reminder, as here, that all earth and heaven are His. The name first meets us with the priest-king Melchizedek, who was well aware of what it meant (Gn. 14:18ff.). The paradox of so great a sovereign acknowledged by so small a circle is one that continues to the present, but the whole psalm looks eagerly beyond it, rebuking our small ideas. The final section will now enlarge on this.

97:10–12. The radiance of the righteous

Encouragement to hold on till daylight and victory come is the note on which the psalm ends. The Hebrew text of 10a is more forthright than RSV and most moderns: simply, 'Lovers of the Lord, hate evil!'[1] Then follows the reassurance, 'he preserves . . .', *etc.*; for such a stand is costly.

But *preserves* would be better rendered 'guards' or 'watches over'; and *lives* is a word that includes the whole person. It is a promise of God's defence and watchful care, not a guarantee against casualties. The last line (10c), similarly, will prove true in a variety of ways: *cf.* the certainty of the words 'he will deliver us out of your hand, O king', which went along with an open mind as to the method God would choose (Dn. 3:17f.).

11. Light *dawns* (rather than 'light is sown', AV, RV) is surely the right reading here, following one Hebrew MS and all the ancient versions.[2] The thought is parallel to the classic couplet in 30:5 (AV), 'Weeping may endure for a night, but joy cometh in the morning'. It is factual, not wishful, being the goal of all history.

12. But we are not to wait for 'the morning' (see above). The whole spirit of the psalm has been to view the final victory as if it were already an accomplished fact. The imperative, *Rejoice*, picks up the noun 'joy' from 11b, as something not to contemplate but to exercise. On the practicability of such advice we may compare Habakkuk 3:17f. On its value, 2 Chronicles 20:21f.

---

[1] RSV's alterations (*'ōhēḇ* and *śōn'ê* for MT *'ōhªḇê* and *śin'û*) make a smoother sentence by matching 'loves' and 'preserves'. But the textual support is scanty, and smoothness is not a safe criterion.

[2] In the consonantal text it is the difference between *z-r-ʿ* (sown) and *z-r-h* (rises, appears). The latter is used regularly of the sun's appearing.

Psalm 98

King and Saviour

Known as the *Cantate Domino* ('O sing to the Lord'), this psalm was interposed in the Book of Common Prayer between the evening Old Testament reading and its New Testament fulfilment. It is a close companion to Psalm 96, but is wholly given up to praise. Here there are no comparisons with the heathen, no instructions in right worship: all is joy and exhilaration.

98:1-3. The victory of God

Victory, the word which dominates this stanza (1, 2, 3) and calls for *a new song* (for this, see on 96:1; 144:9), is a richer word in Scripture than with us. Its chief aspect is 'salvation', as in the name 'Jesus'; so it looks at both friend (with salvation) and foe (with victory), and is big enough to combine the hard decisiveness of the latter with the compassion and constructiveness of the former. This salvation/victory is wholly supernatural, a single-handed exploit of the Lord. The supernatural aspect is expressed in the term *marvellous things*, which is more than a superlative, a standard term for the miraculous interventions of God, such as those at the Exodus (106:7), to save His people. The single-handed aspect is stirringly presented in Isaiah 59:15ff.; 63:1-6; it is one of several links between Isaiah and this group of psalms (see on verses 4 and 8). The New Testament will show with sharper definition both the Saviour and the saving, and both the initial victory (Heb. 10:14) and its consummation (Rev. 19:11ff.).

2, 3. The meaning of *victory* (see on verse 1) now leans towards the 'salvation' side of its content in both these verses, for *the nations* and the whole *earth* see it with joy, as the remainder of the psalm makes clear. Likewise *vindication* should be rendered 'righteousness' (NEB, JB), which is its primary meaning; and this is righteousness in its positive sense of putting right what is wrong.[1]

98:4-6. The victory-song of man

The *joyful noise* of verses 4 and 6 meets us elsewhere as the spontaneous shout that might greet a king or a moment of

[1] See on Ps. 24:5.

victory. It is the word translated 'shout aloud' in Zechariah 9:9, the prophecy that was fulfilled on Palm Sunday. The unaffected joy of that hour gives us some idea of this greater welcome; so too does this cluster of verbs and catalogue of instruments. *Break forth* is a favourite expression in Isaiah (*e.g.* Is. 14:7; 44:23; 55:12) for such an outburst of delight, too great to be contained. Yet, as human praise, it is articulate and enriched with contributory skills and associations. The verb, *sing praises*, is the source of the word 'psalm' (see Introduction, p. 37, and the second paragraph on Ps. 92:1-4); and the instruments are among those that regularly enlivened the temple worship (*lyre, trumpets,* 1 Ch. 16:5f.) or announced some great occasion (*the horn* proclaimed such events as the year of jubilee, or the accession of a king: Lv. 25:9ff.; 1 Ki. 1:39).

So there are two levels to the scene: one, God's day of power, at His coming; the other, its anticipation in every act of worship. The psalms we sing now are a rehearsal, and God's presence among His worshippers is a prelude to His appearing to the world.

98:7-9. The chorus of nature

This praise is artless and inarticulate, unlike the praise of man. But it too can be heard already, since the whole earth even now is full of God's glory. This passage is not only delightful as poetry. With its companion pieces (Ps. 96:11ff.; Is. 55:12f.) it makes the point which Romans 8:19ff. expounds: that nature will not come into its own until man himself, its proper master, is ruled in *righteousness* and *equity*. It is a truth which modern man is learning by default and with alarm. The same truth is the spring of this psalm's happiness, and the reason is found in the phrase of verse 9 which sums up the Christian hope: *for he comes.*

Psalm 99

Holy is He!

In this group of psalms, 93–100, on the kingship and advent of the Lord, the mood alternates between high festivity and a chastened awe—for God is all that stirs us and all that shames us. Here, after the carefree delight of Psalm 98, we recollect how exalted and holy He is, and how profound is the reverence we owe Him.

99:1–5. Holiness enthroned

While every line of this kingly portrait is true eternally, the form of the opening statement makes it primarily a proclamation, it seems, of God's final advent (see on 93:1). His living throne of *cherubim*—not the weaponless cupids of religious art but the mighty beings whose forms summed up for Ezekiel the whole kingdom of earthly creatures—this living throne is a flying chariot, fiery with judgment and salvation. It is magnificently pictured by David in Psalm 18: 6–19 and by Ezekiel in his opening vision (Ezk. 1:4ff.; *cf.* 10:1ff.).

2, 3. But He reigns *in Zion*, which meant initially the earthly city but ultimately the whole company of those who love Him (Heb. 12:22f.). His grandeur is not solitary. Although He is *great and terrible*, He is above all *great in Zion*, in the midst of His covenanted people, from whom His kingdom reaches out to the world.

Holy is a word to emphasize the distance between God and man: not only morally, as between the pure and the polluted, but in the realm of being, between the eternal and the creaturely. If the gulf has been bridged, as the paragraph above assures us that it has, it was done from the far side. The repeated cry, *Holy is he!* forbids us to take it casually.

4, 5. After the greatness of God's being and grace, we praise His integrity, in every phrase of verse 4. Only in Him are holiness and grace, power and justice, perfectly at one.[1]

99:6–9. Holiness encountered

The sudden impact of God's holiness on the worshipper himself is not unlike that of Psalm 95; and again the wilderness provides the main object-lesson (another indication, perhaps, that this group of psalms arose from the Feast of Tabernacles, which commemorated the wilderness: see on 95:8, 9).

---

[1] In the standard Heb. text, 4a reads 'And the king's strength loves justice' (*cf.* AV, RV)—an abrupt but intelligible statement of the union of might and right. But RSV and most modern versions revocalize '*ōz* (strength) as '*āz* (strong, mighty), and either append it to 3b ('He is holy and mighty', *cf.* JB, NEB) or make it qualify 'king' by changing the Heb. word-order ('Mighty King', RSV, TEV).

That lesson is first positive, with its heartening example of prayers heard and revelation given. By naming the great men of verse 6 as *among* the priests and *among* the men of prayer, it refuses to place them in a class apart. We can be in their company.

What is more, while these were at heart obedient men (7b), verse 8 reminds us that they had 'human frailties like our own' (to borrow from a similar context, Jas. 5:17, NEB). Moses and Aaron are chiefly in mind here, with their tragic lapse which could be forgiven but not undone (Nu. 20:12). Note the distinction between the healing of relationships (*forgiving . . . to them*) and the punishment of actions (*an avenger*, or retributor, *of their wrongdoings*). So the negative lesson reinforces the positive, and is twofold: neither to despair of mercy nor to trade on it.[1]

9. So the theme of holiness, enriched by its unfolding in the two stanzas of the psalm, returns in a refrain which is a partner to verse 5. It is not without point that the motto phrase, *Holy is he!* (3, 5), is now expanded and given warmth, to read (in its actual word-order) *For holy is the Lord our God!* The majesty is undiminished, but the last word is now given to intimacy. He is holy; He is also, against all our deserving, not ashamed to be called ours. Well may we worship.

Psalm 100

Into His Courts

A song of thankful praise brings this group of homage-psalms (see on Ps. 93) up to an unclouded summit after their alternations of exuberance and awe. The title may link the psalm to the *thank offering* (so RSV), but since the word means in the first place thanksgiving, and is so used in verse 4, it is perhaps better to take it in its primary sense (*cf.* the introduction to Ps. 38).

---

[1] NEB and some commentators find the conjunction of forgiving and punishing too abrupt here, and revocalize *an avenger* (*nōqēm*) to read 'holding them innocent' (*nōqām*, from the root n-q-h). But a transitive sense of this part of the suggested verb is most unlikely. The ancient versions and most modern ones support the sense given in RSV.

Known as the *Jubilate* ('O be joyful'), it is a psalm much used in liturgical worship; but William Kethe's fine paraphrase, 'All people that on earth do dwell', has even wider currency wherever English is spoken. Finer still, but somewhat freer, is Isaac Watts' version, 'Before Jehovah's aweful throne'.

1. The *joyful noise* is not the special contribution of the tone-deaf, still less of the convivial, but the equivalent in worship to the homage-shout or fanfare (98:6) to a king, as in 95:1 or the almost identical 66:1. This verse claims the world for God: it should be thought-provoking to sing. As a matter of accuracy, there is no special emphasis on diversity in the word translated *the lands* (as there is in, *e.g.*, 96:7; 97:1b); here it is simply 'the earth', a single entity.

2. The command, *Serve the Lord*, is paralleled by *Come into his presence*, which is a reminder that an act of worship is well named a 'service'. It is the first response we owe Him—and not, in either sense of the word, the last. How far it reaches is shown in Romans 12:1, where nothing short of a living sacrifice counts as 'worship'. This is the word which the Greek Old Testament used for a 'service' in the formal sense, in, *e.g.*, Exodus 12:25f.; 13:5. But in Hebrew as in English, service is indivisible; it is a word which leaves no gap or choice between worship and work. (We find this confirmed, incidentally, in practice, in that praise and prayer go stale in isolation, and activity goes sterile.)

On worshipping with *gladness* and *singing* (the word implies singing out with no uncertain voice), see on 95:1; compare also the outbursts of delight in Isaiah 40ff. (*e.g.* 51:11), where these words or their Hebrew roots repeatedly convey the thrill of liberation. Along with this, however, there are perennial sources of praise, which the psalm now draws upon.

3. To *know* is to have firm ground underfoot, the prerequisite of praise (*cf.* 40:2f.), and this knowledge is ours by gift; indeed by command. In the brief space of this verse we are first reminded who God is (revealed by name, Yahweh (*the Lord*), a name richly annotated by His words and works); then whence and whose we are; and finally in how favoured a relation we stand to Him.

The middle line of the verse, in the written text and the oldest versions, runs '. . . and not we ourselves'. Almost all modern translations, however, supported by Massoretic tradition and some MSS and versions, take it in the sense '*and we are his*'. The ambiguity arises from the Hebrew words for 'not' and 'his' (*lō* and *lô*), which sound alike. Either of them would be appropriate here.[1] But the Hebrew sentence continues more smoothly with the second option (*his*), as the AV's need of two extra words in italics confesses. The RSV could have dispensed with these, letting the sentence run: 'and we are his; his people, and the sheep. . .'.

4. The simplicity of this invitation may conceal the wonder of it, for the *courts* are truly *his*, not ours (as Is. 1:12 had to remind the triflers), and His *gates* are shut to the unclean (Rev. 21:27). Yet not only His outer courts but the Holy of Holies itself are thrown open 'by the new and living way', and we are welcome. This in itself is cause enough for praise, and the final verse will have more to add.

5. If the psalm began by broadening our horizon, it ends by lengthening our view and expectation. (On the pairing of *goodness* and *steadfast love*, see on 23:6.) Breadth is nobly expressed in the first line of Watts' verse quoted below,[2] and length in the remaining lines, where 'truth' should be understood in its sense of *faithfulness*, as in RSV.

> 'Wide as the world is Thy command,
>   Vast as eternity Thy love;
> Firm as a rock Thy truth shall stand,
>   When rolling years shall cease to move.'

Psalm 101

A King's Resolve

David's name reappears with this psalm, whose only Davidic companion in this Fourth Book is Psalm 103. It should hardly need saying that the resolve made here to have no truck with evil men does not spring from pharisaic pride but from a king's concern for a clean administration, honest from the top down.

---

[1] The same word in Is. 9:3 (2, Heb.) leaves no doubt in that context that 'not' should be read as 'his' or 'its'. *Cf.* AV with later translations of that verse.

[2] From the hymn, 'Before Jehovah's aweful throne'.

How far he was to fall short of this in his own acts and in his appointments is told in 2 Samuel. But it was an inspired pattern, remaining to challenge him and his successors,[1] among whom can be counted (with due adjustments) all who have the running of any enterprise and the choice of its officials. For its perfect fulfilment we are forced to look beyond our approximations, to the Messiah Himself. On His relation to the kingly portraits in the Psalter, see the Introduction, pp. 18f.

101:1–4. Truth in the ruler

Loyalty and justice define the chief concerns of a king, since *loyalty* (Heb. *ḥeseḏ*) draws attention to the covenant (see on 'steadfast love', at 17:7) by which king and people were bound first to God and then to one another; while *justice* speaks of a ruler's prime duty to his people ('to punish those who do wrong and to praise those who do right', as in 1 Pet. 2:14). With these two priorities in place, the one chiefly 'vertical', between God and man, and the other chiefly 'horizontal', between a man and his fellows, other blessings will have room to flourish. It would be, perhaps, illuminating to consider how this verse would be currently rewritten by various politicians.

2. The emphasis on what is positive continues, dwelling next on the theme of wholeness. Both *blameless* and *integrity* contain this root idea, as of something which no corruption or compromise is allowed to eat into. The interjection, *Oh when . . .?*[2], gives a sudden glimpse of the prolonged and lonely struggle, and of a faith which is ardently personal.[3] But the phrase, *within my house*, is tragically ironic. Here is where godliness begins, as David could see; but here in fact would be its

---

[1] Those who trace the origin of most psalms to recurrent cultic occasions see this psalm either as a declaration drawn up for each Davidic king to make at his enthronement, or as part of an annual ritual in which the king was symbolically humiliated and then reinstated. This cultic approach is discussed in the Introduction, pp. 7–18.

[2] NEB emends *māṯay* ('when') to *mah* ('whatever'), to produce the clause 'whatever may befall me', somewhat after the manner of Jb. 13:13b (which uses a different vocabulary). This has no textual support.

[3] On the purely cultic view of this psalm, however (see footnote to the introductory comments, above), this would be a ritual plea, in the context of the king's humiliation.

worst betrayal, to the poisoning of his whole kingdom.

3, 4. Now come the repudiations, still in the realm of personal standards. Verse 3b is no exception, since 'disloyalty' (NEB) or 'the doing of unfaithfulness' (RV mg.) is nearer to the original text than *the work of those who fall away*. The affirming of values, not the choice of colleagues (until verses 5ff.), is the issue, and the negative picture is that of swerving from the right course (*cf.* 2 Tim. 2:18), yielding to the pull of another influence or another outlook. If this is a sin of weakness, the *perverseness* of verse 4 is more deliberate: a twisted mind and will which hate the plain truth and the straight path.

101:5-8. Truth in the ranks

Now the king speaks as head of the political machine and as the guardian of justice. Verses 5-7 show what he looks for in his appointments, and what he disapproves of as men jockey for position, smearing their rivals (5a) and adopting impressive airs (5b) and devious ways (7). It is not only kings who need this perception. But his good judgment springs from his character. On the one hand he 'cannot' stand self-importance (5; the disclaimer is stronger than *will not*, like God's 'cannot' in Is. 1:13), and on the other hand he warms to people whose spiritual attitude he shares: those who follow *the way that is blameless* (6), as he aspires to do (*cf.* 2a).

8. The final picture shows the king dispensing justice (*cf.* verse 1). This is the context of *morning by morning*: he will be no dilatory judge, whose citizens despair of a hearing; he will be another Moses, whom Jethro had had to dissuade from hearing cases 'from morning till evening' (Ex. 18:13ff.). Yet once more it is ironic that, in the end, Absalom 'stole the hearts of the men of Israel' by intercepting them, morning by morning, with the tale that no court was in session (2 Sa. 15:1–6). False as the tale may well have been (why else did Absalom not waylay them as they left in disappointment?), it at least appeared plausible to them at that stage of David's reign, when something of his early fire had cooled.

The psalm is doubly moving: both for the ideals it discloses and for the shadow of failure which history throws across it. Happily the last word is not with David nor with his faithful historians, but with his Son. There, there is no shadow.

Psalm 102

'My days' and 'Thy years'

Traditionally miscalled a penitential psalm (the fifth of the seven; see the introduction to Ps. 6), this is in fact the cry of one whose sufferings are unexplained, like Job's. As the title implies, it is a prayer which others who are near the end of their endurance can echo, finding words here that lead them 'into a large place'.

The troubles, to begin with, are private griefs, but later they are transcended by concern for Zion, whose destiny is glorious yet painfully slow in coming to fulfilment. A final passage draws out the contrast between the human time-scale and the Lord's eternity, bringing the psalm to a majestic conclusion which is quoted in praise of Christ in the opening chapter of Hebrews.

So the psalm, we learn, is Messianic; and in the light of that, the sufferings and the world-embracing vision of the speaker lead the mind to Psalm 22. For the ground on which Hebrews 1:10-12 discerns the Son of God here, see the comments on the final verses of the psalm.

102:1-11. The day of my distress

A glance at a reference Bible will show that the lament of verses 1-11 has a detailed background of many other cries to God in the Psalter and in Job. The opening plea itself, *Hear my prayer*, echoes that of 39:12; 54:2; *cf.* 61:1; 64:1, *etc.*; and with its matching second line it has since found its way into constant Christian use in shared intercessions. The singer was not as isolated as he felt. Nor are any of his successors, who belong together despite time and space:

> 'The several vessels of Thy fleet,
> Though parted now, by tempests tost,
> Shall safely in the haven meet.'[1]

Like other laments, too, this gives words not only to sufferers themselves, but to their joint-petitioners. The vivid evocations of fever, frailty, wasting, pain, sleeplessness, melancholy, rejection and despair, offer the healthy and the happily placed

[1] Richard Baxter, 'He wants not friends that hath Thy love'.

the means of sharing part of a burden which is otherwise hard to grasp. The psalm is for use, and use by no minority. Its Messianic aspect[1] incidentally underlines this obligation, by its reminder to the Christian of suffering that was voluntary and vicarious.

102:12-22. The appointed time for Zion

The emphatic words, *But thou, O Lord*, mark a turning-point in the psalm, as they often do elsewhere (*e.g.* Ps. 22:3, 9, 19). They could have been said bitterly, enviously contrasting the changeless with the rootless; instead, the true conclusion is drawn from God's eternity, which is His mastery of *time* (13) and the long reach of His purpose (18). These are explored in verses 12-17 and 18-22.

12-17. The appointed time has come. Like the plea, 'It is time to act, O Lord; for men have broken thy law' (119:126, NEB), verse 13 discerns a crying scandal (*cf.* 14) and pleads for haste. It may give earth's perspective rather than heaven's (see on verses 23f.), for God looks beyond the skirmishing to the final victory; yet man's urgency and God's measured pace are both insisting, in their different ways, that there is no time to waste, and that the fullness of time is approaching.

In a wonderful sequel to the lament over Zion's *stones* and *dust* (14)—a potential fixation on past glories and past wrongs which would be paralysing—verses 15-17 turn to a prospect far richer than either revenge or recovery. The New Testament tells of its beginnings (the light to the *nations*; the flourishing of *Zion, i.e.,* of Zion's true citizens;[2] the *glory* of God in our midst; the love shown to the *destitute*), and looks forward to its consummation, when in the fullest sense *he will appear in his glory*.[3]

18-22. A generation to come. This group of verses echoes and expands some aspects of 12-17, but gazes now into the distant future, when *this* deliverance will be the one that people sing about (no longer the song of Moses alone, but also, as Rev. 15:3 will put it, 'the song of the Lamb'). And the singers

---

[1] See on verses 23-28.
[2] Gal. 4:26f.; Heb. 12:22.
[3] Verse 16 is of interest as a clear example of the 'prophetic perfect' (see on 93:1, 2), since the preceding three verses leave no doubt of its reference to the future. The two perfects of this verse add their note of inevitability to the foregoing predictions. (Verse 17 also uses the perfect, but could be translated as either past or future.)

are *a people*, one which is to be 'created' (*cf.* RV). This verb points to a great act of God, either in renewing a dead Israel or in making the gentiles 'God's own people', who were 'once ... no people' (1 Pet. 2:9f.). The translation, 'a people *yet unborn*', does less than justice to this.

The theme of *prisoners* released and of *peoples* and *kingdoms* flocking to *Zion*, is radiantly presented in Isaiah 60–62, and further interpreted in Revelation 21.

102:23–28. Thy years have no end

In the Hebrew text, as translated here, verses 23f. renew the piteous lament of 1–11, drawing the same contrast between man's frailty and God's eternity (24b) as emerged in verse 12. (On the quite different sense of the LXX here, see the additional note, below.) This temporary darkening of the scene after the exultant spirit of verses 12–22 allows the last four verses to stand out in their full magnificence.

25–28. This is not only eloquence surpassing even that of Psalm 90: the range of thought leaves all our space-time landmarks far behind, yet diminishes nothing of the significance of the present. This significance derives from God, who is committed eternally to His *servants* and *their posterity*—and to nothing else in creation, not even the universe itself.

Hebrews 1:10–12 quotes verses 25–27 word for word (as LXX, including the added 'Lord' in 25a), with one minor change of word-order; and verse 27 (*thou art the same*) may also underlie the great saying of Hebrews 13:8, 'Jesus Christ ... the same ...'. The Epistle opens our eyes to what would otherwise be brought out only by the LXX of verses 23f. (see below), namely that the Father is here replying to the Son, 'through whom all things were made'; and this implies that the sufferer throughout the psalm is also the Son incarnate. (See Introduction, p. 21.)

Additional note on 102:23f.

Two different ways of reading verses 23 and 24 are found in respectively the Hebrew (MT) and Greek (LXX) texts. They presuppose the same Hebrew consonants, but differ over the vowels and verse-division (which were not indicated in the original text of Scripture). The Hebrew way of reading it is found in our translations; it renews the plea of verses 11 and 12. The Greek, reading the Hebrew consonants with different vowels, runs as follows: 'He answered him in the way of his strength, "Declare to me the fewness of my days. Do not bring me up[1] in the middle of my days: your years are for generations on end. In the beginning you, Lord, laid the foundation of the earth. . ." ' (*etc.*).

This is obscure, while the Hebrew text (as translated in our Bibles) is plain. But a significant feature of the Greek is that it makes the whole passage, including the tremendous words of verses 25–28, the words of God to the psalmist, whom God addresses as the Lord and Creator; and this is how Hebrews 1:10–12 quotes verses 25–27, in proof of the Son's deity.

On this understanding, the whole psalm is Messianic, showing first the Messiah's sufferings and dereliction (1–11), then his eager anticipation of the kingdom in its world-wide glory (12–22); finally in verses 23–28 God replies that so far this is only half the story, only a few days of His work, which must run its full term, measured by the Messiah's own endless years. This full course will see the universe itself grown old and superseded; but the Son and the generations of his servants will be for ever.[2]

The LXX performs a service in pointing to the Messianic character of the psalm, and its rendering of verses 23 and 24 is a possible interpretation of the Hebrew consonants. But the familiar translation from the Massoretic Text also allows verses 25ff. to be Messianic, and needs no ingenuity to make verses 23f. intelligible.

Psalm 103

So Great is His Love

Admiring gratitude shines through every line of this hymn to the God of all grace, for which the next psalm, 104, seems to have been written as a companion (to judge from its matching

---

[1] *I.e.*, 'Do not summon me to action'. This, rather than *take . . . hence* (24, RSV), is the more usual sense of the Heb. verb; *cf.* Je. 50:9; Ezk. 16:40. Only Jb. 36:20 appears to tell against this, and it is a verse of uncertain meaning.

[2] See the discussion of the LXX form of these verses in F. F. Bruce, *The Epistle to the Hebrews* (*New London Commentary*, Marshall, Morgan & Scott, 1964), pp. 21–23.

opening and close). Together the two psalms praise God as Saviour and Creator, Father and Sustainer, 'merciful and mighty'. In the galaxy of the Psalter these are twin stars of the first magnitude.

Among the psalms attributed to David, Psalm 103 stands a little apart: it is less intensely personal than most of his; less harassed, if at all, by enemies or private guilt. The personal note is there, but David is soon speaking for us all. It is a hymn rather than a private thanksgiving, and we are reminded that David was the founder of the great choirs of Israel.

The closest of his psalms to this is Psalm 145, but there are others in which he similarly gives himself to some broad theme from the start: *e.g.* Psalms 8, 14, 19, 29, to look no further.

Echoes of the psalm are heard in Isaiah and Jeremiah,[1] and it draws on earlier scriptures itself, as the comments will point out. It has inspired one of the best-known hymns in our language, H. F. Lyte's 'Praise, my soul, the King of heaven'.

103:1–5. Personal praise

It is more than eloquence that has shaped this stanza in the form of inward dialogue. It is not the only instance of a psalmist's rousing of himself to shake off apathy or gloom (*e.g.* 108:1; 42:5; 77:6ff., 11ff.), using his mind and memory to kindle his emotions. And there is fuel enough in verses 2–5 for more than kindling.

2. *Benefits* is the noun that corresponds to the fervent phrase in 13:6, 'he has dealt bountifully with me'. The fact that to *forget* such things may have a deeper and subtler cause than absent-mindedness is brought out in the Chronicler's comment on Hezekiah, who 'did not make return according to the benefit done to him, for his heart was proud' (2 Ch. 32:25). A similar point is made in Deuteronomy 8:12–14.

3. For all the similarity of these two phrases, there is a difference between God's handling of *iniquity* and of *diseases*, which was made plain in David's own case when he repented of his sin with Bathsheba. Forgiveness was immediate; but healing was denied, in spite of seven days of prayer and fasting

---

[1] Je. 3:5, 12 has the same terse Heb. idiom as Ps. 103:9 for storing up anger, though indeed this was a standard expression, found also in Lv. 19:18 (and Na. 1:2). Commentators who take this psalm to be post-exilic naturally regard it as the borrower rather than the source of the similarities in Isaiah.

(2 Sa. 12:13–23). If relationship with God is paramount, this makes good sense, for sin destroys it, while suffering may deepen it (Heb. 5:8; 12:11). Yet 'we wait for ... the redemption of our bodies' (Rom. 8:23), and enjoy already many foretastes of it.

4. At one level, to be redeemed from *the Pit* could be an expression simply for rescue from a premature decease (see on 6:5; 28:1). But the larger question of man's ransom from death, 'that he should continue to live on for ever', is seriously explored in the Psalter (see, *e.g.*, 49:7–9, 13–15), and makes it possible, even probable, that we should take 4a in its strongest sense, as resurrection to eternal life. On this hope, Psalm 16:9–11, which is also Davidic, is even more explicit.

5. *As long as you live* is a slight emendation of a puzzling word.[1] Most modern versions adopt this solution; NEB, however, keeps the Hebrew unaltered, but translates it as 'in the prime of life', on the strength of an Arabic root connected with daybreak.[2] Both solutions are somewhat precarious.

The second line is not implying (as RSV's apostrophe suggests, and as some ancient commentators believed) that eagles have the power of self-renewal; only that God renews us to be 'young and lusty as an eagle' (PBV)—the very picture of buoyant, tireless strength which Isaiah 40:30f. takes up. As Weiser comments: 'The poet realizes that the opportunities which life offers lie before him just as they did in the sunny days of his youth.' In different terms, see on 92:14, with its serene prospect of 'fruit in old age'.

103:6–14. Wayward family, gentle Father

No story surpasses the Exodus for a record of human unworthiness: of grace abounding and 'benefits forgot'. Its mention here (7) reminds us of the sullen ingratitude which God encounters in reply to the forgiving, healing and redeeming of which the opening verses sang.

6, 7. 'Righteousness' (as in verse 17) is a better and more basic word than RSV's overworked term *vindication* (see on 24:5). Vindication is only one part of what God does for us, for He puts straight not only the record (as this term would

---

[1] MT has *'edyêk̲*, 'thy ornament', which has been taken to mean 'thy mouth' (AV, RV) or 'thy soul' (the latter by analogy with the term 'my glory'; see on 30:12). RSV emends this to *'ôdek̲ā*, 'thy continuing'; *cf.* *bᵉ'ôd̲î*, 104:33.

[2] See G. R. Driver, *JTS* 36 (1935), pp. 154f.

imply by itself) but the whole situation and the people concerned. How far-reaching this is, begins to be seen in verse 7, since God's *ways* and *acts* were not only displayed in the Exodus miracles, but brought home to Israel intimately and tirelessly in the wilderness and at Mount Sinai—'that he might humble you, testing you . . . ; that he might make you know . . .' (Dt. 8:2f.). This was not bare information. It was the training of sons.

8. This verse quotes, almost word for word, the self-portrait of God in Exodus 34:6, when He passed before Moses in the mount. So it has the background of Israel's golden calf and subsequent reprieve, a classic example of the human inconstancy and divine mercy which are the warp and woof of the next verses.

9, 10. These very human terms point the contrast between God's generosity and the heavy-handed wrath of man, who loves to keep his quarrels going (*chide* translates a term much used for disputes, especially at law) and to nurse his grievances. God, infinitely wronged, not only tempers wrath but tempers justice (10)—though at what cost to Himself, only the New Testament would reveal.

11-14. If immeasurable distances are one way of expressing immeasurable love and mercy (*cf.* Eph. 3:18f.; Is. 55:6-9), the intimacy of a family is another. By the first, we are led out into 'a large place', to walk at liberty; by the second we are brought home. In a family context there is affection as well as compassion in the word for *pities*: it is a warmly emotional word and the mark of a true parent, as Isaiah 49:15 points out in its saying about the heartless mother. But verse 14 adds that this father *knows* as deeply as He cares. *Cf.* NEB, 'For he knows how we were made'—and the *he* is emphatic. He knows us even better than we know ourselves.

103:15-18. Fading life, eternal love

Grass and wild flowers, so brief in their glory, are a favourite theme, sometimes for comparison, sometimes for contrast; rebuking our worldly fears and follies in Psalms 37:2, 20; 90:5ff., or throwing into relief the massive certainty of God's word in Isaiah 40:6-8, and of His covenant-love in the present passage. Our Lord gave a new turn to this analogy from nature, arguing from God's care for things as fragile as flowers to His far greater care for us.

From everlasting to everlasting (17) is another link, whether conscious or unconscious, with Psalm 90, using a phrase which spoke there of eternal being (90:2), to speak now of eternal grace. While its meaning here may be no more than 'from age to age' (*cf.* the parallel, 'to children's children'), it has the seeds of the New Testament assurance that we were chosen in Christ before the foundation of the world, to reign with Him for ever.

103:19–22. Praise from all creation

The youthful David knew the Lord of hosts as 'the God of the armies of Israel' (1 Sa. 17:45), and conquered in that faith. Here his vision takes in the armies of heaven. Here, too, he reminds us that God's realm is the totality of things; he puts the definite article before the *all* of verse 19, as he did in his prayer of 1 Chronicles 29:12, to make it the equivalent of our term 'the universe'.

But the final line is as personal as the first. His song is no solo, for all creation is singing—or will sing—with him; but his voice, like every other, has its own part to add, its own 'benefits' (2ff.) to celebrate, and its own access (*cf.* Ps. 5:3) to the attentive ear of God.

Psalm 104

'How manifold are thy works!'

Variety and breadth, sharpness of detail and sustained vigour of thought, put this psalm of praise among the giants. By its exordium and conclusion, calling on the singer's 'soul', or whole being, to bless the Lord, it links itself to Psalm 103, on which see the opening comments. But unlike its companion, it names no author (except in LXX, which claims it for David).

There are some striking resemblances to the Egyptian Akhenaten's great Hymn to the Sun (14th century BC; text in *ANET*, pp. 370f.), especially in the depicting of creatures of night and day (20–23), of the provision for beasts and birds (10ff.), of the sea with its ships (25f.), and of the life-and-death dependence of all creatures on their creator (27–30). But elsewhere the two poems go their separate ways (*e.g.*, the

Egyptian hymn dwells on the mystery of birth and on the diversity of lands and races), and for its over-all sequence the psalm looks to Genesis 1, as the next paragraph will show. Theologically it displays the incalculable difference between worshipping the sun and worshipping its Maker; indeed the psalm's apparent allusions to this famous hymn seem designed to call attention to this very point.

The structure of the psalm is modelled fairly closely on that of Genesis 1, taking the stages of creation as starting-points for praise. But as each theme is developed it tends to anticipate the later scenes of the creation drama, so that the days described in Genesis overlap and mingle here. We can trace the following correspondences (marking with a plus sign the verses that develop a theme further):

Day 1 (Gn. 1:3-5)	light; Psalm 104:2a
Day 2 (Gn. 1:6-8)	the 'firmament' divides the waters; 104:2b-4
Day 3 (Gn. 1:9, 10)	land and water distinct; 104:5-9 (+10-13?)
,, ,, (Gn. 1:11-13)	vegetation and trees; 104:14-17 (+18?)
Day 4 (Gn. 1:14-19)	luminaries as timekeepers; 104:19-23 (+24)
Day 5 (Gn. 1:20-23)	creatures of sea and air; 104:25, 26 (sea only)
Day 6 (Gn. 1:24-28)	animals and man (anticipated in 104:21-24)
,, ,, (Gn. 1:29-31)	food appointed for all creatures; 104:27, 28 (+29, 30).

One of our finest hymns, Sir Robert Grant's 'O worship the King', takes its origin from this psalm, deriving its metre (but little else) from William Kethe's 16th-century paraphrase, 'My soul, praise the Lord' (the Old 104th).

104:1-4. Pavilioned in splendour

These verses magnificently convey the intimate yet regal relationship of God to His world. He is distinct from His universe (whereas pantheism would have merged Him with it), but He is anything but remote from it, as though He had merely set it going or given it orders. The metaphor of His taking up its parts and powers as His robe, tent, palace and chariot invites us to see the world as something He delights in, which is charged with His energy and alive with His presence. The nature miracles of Christ show that this is no fantasy.

3. The word for *chambers* is translated 'thy lofty abode' in verse 13 (*cf.* a similar word, 'upper chambers', in Am. 9:6), for it contains the idea of height, as with the roof-chamber on an eastern house (2 Ki. 4:10). The dizzy height of 'the waters above the firmament', or the clouds, is pictured as but the base of God's abode, and this insubstantial support as quite sufficient for the ethereal lightness of His palace. This is as poetic a figure as that of the flying *chariot*,[1] no more in conflict with the knowledge that 'the heaven of heavens cannot contain thee' than with the assurance that God dwells in Zion. All these kinds of language are needed to express the relation of God to our familiar world, to the universe and to ourselves.

4. This verse, according to RSV and most modern versions, continues to glory in nature as God's instrument. But LXX takes the sentence the other way round, looking beyond the natural order to the heavenly host: 'who makes his messengers (or, angels) winds, and his ministers a flaming fire'. This suits the Hebrew word-order better,[2] and Hebrews 1:7 quotes it with this meaning. Briggs comments: 'As God Himself is conceived as really present in nature, wrapping Himself in light, setting up His tent in the heavens . . . ; so His angels . . . are made to assume the form of winds and lightnings.' Not that this is always their form; but see 18:10, and *cf.* the storm-wind and flashing fire in which the cherubim were manifested to Ezekiel (Ezk. 1:4ff.; 10:15). The argument in Hebrews 1:7f. is that while angels can be described in these lowly terms, the Son is addressed as God.

104:5-9. The waters in flight
Now we dwell on the third day of Genesis 1, whose quiet statement that the waters were gathered into one place, for the dry land to appear, is now presented with exhilarating vigour,

---

[1] *Cf., e.g.*, Ps. 18:7-10; 68:33; Ezk. 1:4ff.
[2] Perowne, however (4th edn), cites Is. 37:26; 60:18, to show that a departure from the usual order of subject and predicate is not impossible in Hebrew. He therefore abandons in that edition his reluctant agreement with LXX. Yet it remains true that the normal usage favours LXX, and that Heb. 1:7f. bases its argument on it.

but also with a strong emphasis on the Creator's control and 'changeless decree'. Any thought of *the deep* as a threat to His sovereignty (as in some heathen mythologies) is precluded by verse 6. It was He who wrapped the earth in such a mantle. The vivid rhetoric of verses 7 and 9 finely dramatizes the rise of continents and the formation of ocean depths which their companion verse 8 presents in more sober terms. It is a rhetoric we still need, at a time when the accepted model of reality is all mechanism and no Maker.

So the twin emphases of the passage are on the personal Creator (the theme of the whole psalm) and the good order of His creation. The world, while not eternal (*cf.* 102:26), is of reassuring solidity and purposeful design (5, 8, 9). It is a world to rejoice in.

104:10–13. The waters of life

Outrunning the stately progress of the creation story, the psalm surveys the hospitable earth that was the end-product of this separation of seas and dry land. No longer submerged, nor on the other hand turned into a desert, it was to become a place of friendly streams, where God's creatures are perfectly at home, needing no human provision. The expression, *beast of the field*, stands for the non-domesticated animals (*cf.* Gn. 2:20, where it is distinct from 'cattle'); and the *wild asses* are proverbially independent creatures (Gn. 16:12; Jb. 39:5–8), like the *birds*, from which our Lord drew a similar lesson of God's 'bountiful care', and indeed took it further (Mt. 6:26).

104:14–18. 'With verdure clad . . .'

The third day in Genesis 1 went on to speak of the earth's living carpet of vegetation and trees. The psalm enlarges on this, and turns now from the wildlife of the last stanza to the farm beasts (14a) and the cultivable[1] plants and fruit trees, since *wine*, *oil* (from the olive) and *bread* are all partly products of human skill, and are evidence equally of the Creator's varied gifts and of the possibilities He has stored up in man's intelligence and earth's modifiable products. Then, by way of

---

[1] *To cultivate* (14) translates a Heb. noun from a root meaning to serve or (Gn. 2:15) to till. The link with Genesis makes 'cultivate' the most likely meaning here, rather than that of RSV mg. and NEB.

the forest giants[1] (16f.), it reverts to the theme of the homes and coverts that shelter creatures of vastly different kinds. The names add vividness to the scene, with the *stork* and its huge nest, in contrast to the smaller birds and theirs, and with the *wild goats* silhouetted, so to speak, on their native crags. The *badger* is a misnomer for the hyrax, a small and shy rock-dweller (*cf.* Pr. 30:26). To the modern reader, this planet, with the almost infinite variety of life which it supports, stands out in all the more brilliant contrast to its starkly inhospitable neighbours.

104:19–24. Rhythm of dark and light

The fourth day of creation emphasized the role of sun and moon in setting the time-pattern of our existence. Here it mingles with the theme of the sixth day, to show both night and day teeming with life and exerting the gentle pull of their rhythm on man and beast.[2] It is another subtle shade in the Creator's design; a regularity that brings no monotony but only enrichment (*cf.* on 19:2), and (as the phrase *until the evening* may imply) a built-in safeguard of the balance of work and rest which is one of His best gifts.

24. This pause for reflection and adoration saves us from turning the psalm into a poetic catalogue, but also from misreading the almost frightening fertility of the living world. What the sceptic sees as a meaningless swarm of life, the psalmist teaches us to view as giving some inkling of the Creator's wealth,[3] and of the range and precision of His thought. And because all is shaped by His wisdom, the creation is a unity, not only stirring us to wonder but (as Ps. 111:2 will observe) inviting us to explore it.

104:25, 26. The great, immeasurable sea

The psalm has already leapt ahead of the Genesis account, to tell of birds, beasts and man. Here it returns to the fifth day

---

[1] The word for *fir trees* (17) is very similar to the Heb. for 'in their tops' (NEB). The latter, with its built-in preposition, is a somewhat easier expression, and was evidently in the Heb. text translated by the LXX.

[2] This stanza has some evident resemblances to Akhenaten's Hymn to the Sun, on which see the second introductory paragraph to this psalm. Note in this connection the emphasis on the sun's obedient time-keeping (19b), and on God's action to bring about darkness, as if to make doubly plain the subordinate role of the thing which Akhenaten revered as the creator. Even the moon takes precedence over it in 19a.

[3] 'Possessions' is the usual sense of the word translated *creatures* here; see 105:21b. *Cf.* AV, RV. here: 'full of thy riches'.

of creation, in which 'God created the great sea monsters and every living creature that moves, with which the waters swarm' (Gn. 1:21). The winged creatures of the fifth day have been mentioned already; but the psalm, as ever, brings the present scene before us, showing us *the ships* which have turned the oceans into highways instead of barriers. As for *Leviathan*, a name which can have a sinister ring (see on 74:13–15), he makes his appearance simply as some large and sportive creature, whose very existence glorifies and delights its Maker.[1]

104:27–30. In Him we live

In what may be a deliberate contrast to Akhenaten's extravagant praise of the sun—'When thou hast risen they live, When thou settest they die'[2]—the psalm speaks the sober truth of God's maintenance of all life. It gives a rounded view of this by pointing to its visible and invisible operation: that is, at one level, the natural order with its regular bounty of *food in due season*, matched to the abilities of the various creatures to *gather* their supply of it (28a, which opens up a vast area of study); and behind all this, the outflowing energy of God which holds all things in being. The *breath*, or spirit, of every living thing depends on His *Spirit*, or breath; the same word is used in 29 and 30 for both. (This, so far from implicating Him in our misdeeds, deepens our accountability, since we handle only what is His. *Cf.* Dn. 5:23: 'The God in whose hand is your breath . . . you have not honoured.')

104:31–35. O measureless might!

A secularist's unspoken prayer might run: 'May the earth endure for ever; may man rejoice in his works!' The psalm, from first to last, hallows the name of God. The point of verse 32 may be more than simply to assert God's majesty; it may reinforce the prayer of 31b that the Lord may have cause only for joy, not judgment, as He surveys His works.

33, 34. But it was love rather than fear that motivated 31f.

---

[1] Verse 26 can be translated either as in RSV (*cf.* AV, RV, TEV, NEB mg.), 'to sport in it', or as in NEB (*cf.* JB, RV mg.), 'whom thou hast made thy plaything'. In the latter case, Jb. 41:5 brings out a telling contrast between man's and God's ability to handle so huge a monster.

[2] *ANET*, p. 371a. On this hymn, see the second introductory paragraph to the psalm, above.

This is brought out, not only by the glowing phrases of verse 33 but, consciously or not, by the response of 34b to 31b: 'May the Lord rejoice in his works' . . . 'I rejoice in the Lord'.

Such language incidentally chimes in with the climax of Genesis 1, which announced the image of God in man. Up to this point in the psalm, the creation has glorified God simply by what it is. But man's response is personal: he alone on earth can *sing* to Him. There was singing, delightful in its way, in verse 12; but here the song has content, and is meant for Him, offered for His delight.

35. Meanwhile, as this verse abruptly reminds us, the creation is not so much a choir as a battlefield, and there is a time to fight as well as a time to sing. If man's proper response to his Creator is conscious and ardent, as verses 33f. emphasized, it is also exclusive: a dedication to His victory and the reclaiming of His world.

So the final *Bless the Lord, O my soul*, echoing the first words of the psalm, responds not only to the glory that already is, but to the prospect of its consummation.

Praise the Lord is, in Hebrew, 'Hallelujah'. In the LXX it opens the next psalm instead of closing this one. If that is its right position, as it may well be, each of Psalms 103–106 will have a final phrase that exactly matches its beginning.

Psalm 105

Not One Thing Has Failed

A matching pair of psalms, this and the next, rounds off the Fourth Book of the Psalter. They represent, broadly speaking, the two contrasted strands of sacred history: the acts of God the unfailing, and of man the intractable. Here we are shown the former, in the great sweep of events that led from Abraham to the promised land. The recital of them ends and perhaps begins with Hallelujah (see the last comment on Ps. 104), as does the companion piece, Psalm 106.

The first fifteen verses of this psalm, the last two verses of 106, and, in between, the greater part of Psalm 96 (where see comment) are quoted in the account of David's procession with the ark to Jerusalem in 1 Chronicles 16.

105:1–7. Remember His miracles

Like a jewel turned this way and that, the worship of God displays some of its many facets here, with its concern to proclaim Him to the world (1b); to delight in what He has done and said (2, 5) and in what He is (1a, 3a—for the *name* is His self-revelation); and to show gratitude for past mercies by coming back for more (4: *Seek . . . seek . . . continually*).

On *wonderful works* (2, 5) see on Psalm 9:1. On the basic meaning of *judgments* (5, 7) see on 36:6. For some suggested implications of the word *remember* (5), see the discussion of the concept of actualization, in the Introduction, pp. 14f.

6. Galatians 3:6ff. and 4:28ff. show that every Christian belongs to this family, whose history and calling we now inherit. Here are the early chapters of our own story: we can sing of its miraculous beginnings with more than a spectator's interest.

7. The first line is our answering echo to God's 'I am the Lord your God', which opens the Ten Commandments; and while this reaffirms the covenant between us, the second line shows that *all* men, covenant or no covenant, are answerable to Him. The *judgments* here are the dark side of His saving miracles, exhibited at every turn of the story that follows.

105:8–11. The promise of a country

8. The phrase, *for ever*, goes with *He is mindful*; and the latter always implies that He acts on what He has promised, not merely that He calls it to mind. *Cf.* Exodus 2:24; Luke 1:72; and see on Psalm 8:4.

Notice the expression, *the word that he commanded*, as a parallel term to *his covenant*. It puts the stress on God's initiative and authority in the covenant-making, which means that this bond with men is by grace, not mutual bargaining, and serves the interests of God's kingdom, not the selfish ends of men.

10, 11. While in verse 8 the equivalent of *everlasting* described God's remembering, here it describes the covenant, and in particular the promise of Canaan to Israel. Yet we must note from Scripture the relativity of such a pledge: first, in that the earth itself will perish (102:25f.), and secondly, that even God's 'for ever' can be forfeited by man's apostasy (1 Sa. 2:30; Mt. 21:43). It would be a mistake to understand it in a purely political sense, as a territorial title-deed on its own.

105:12-15. Protection for the patriarchs

The book of Genesis fills out this picture with the indiscretions of each generation of the patriarchs, repeatedly imperilling the enterprise they were called to. See chapters 12, 20, 26, 31, 34. The reference of verse 15 is particularly to Genesis 20:6f., where God says of Abraham, 'he is a prophet'. Nothing could make it clearer that it was God, not man, who saw the whole matter through.

105:16-22. Joseph paves the way

It is again God who makes the running; so the *famine*, which was destined to be the pivot of all events, is introduced at the outset as the point to which God had been already working when *he had sent a man ahead*.[1] Joseph himself saw it eventually in this light, and expressed it in two classic statements about Providence: Genesis 45:4-8; 50:20.

18b. Coverdale's haunting expression, 'the iron entered into his soul' (PBV), comes from the Vulgate, not the Hebrew. The latter has it the other way round: 'his *nepeš* entered into iron', where *nepeš* can mean 'soul', 'life', 'self', or possibly (it has been suggested on the basis of Akkadian and Ugaritic) 'throat'— hence the 'iron collar' of most modern translations. This last suggestion *may* be right; but the choice of this word rather than a more obvious one for 'throat' must have aroused at least some thought of the word's more fundamental meaning, *i.e.*, that it was more than Joseph's flesh that felt the iron: his whole being came into its embrace. While Genesis highlights his undaunted spirit of service in prison, the psalm poetically emphasizes the other side: the cruel fact of being caged.

19a. The most literal translation is that of AV, 'Until the time that his word came', which RSV rightly interprets as *... came to pass* (as in, *e.g.*, Jos. 23:14c). This might be *His* word, *i.e.*, the Lord's, as in the second line, but is more likely to be Joseph's own: either his interpretation of his fellow-prisoners' dreams, whose fulfilment led to his release, or perhaps the boyhood dreams which he had told to his brothers.

19b. Here, too, there are alternative possibilities, since *the word of the Lord* could mean either God's decree that he should

---

[1] This pluperfect (RSV, NEB), for which Heb. has no separate tense, is inferred by common sense from the context. It is a curiosity of biblical criticism that the same principle is seldom applied to, *e.g.*, Gn. 2:8a, 9, 19, where common sense equally requires the pluperfect.

suffer as he did (*cf.* NEB, 19a[1]), or else His promise of future greatness. The second is the likelier meaning, since God had held out this prospect to Joseph in his dreams. He was *tested*,[2] in fact, very much as Hebrews 11 shows his fellow patriarchs being tested, by 'hope deferred' and by the need to go on counting Him 'faithful who had promised'.

22. *To instruct* is the reading of the ancient versions, whereas MT has 'to bind' (AV, RV). The two words are easily confused. The former, as a close parallel to 'teach' in the next line, seems slightly the more probable, and it too has a note of discipline about it: *cf.* NEB 'to correct'.

105:23-25. Israel in Egypt

Once more, the bare events recorded in the Pentateuch (Ex. 1:7ff.) are presented theologically, as the Lord's doing: *cf.* the opening remarks on verses 16-22, above. By the same token, our Lord viewed even the treachery of Judas as 'the cup which the Father has given me'. To throw into relief this aspect of all events is one of the concerns of this psalm.

105:26-36. Moses and the plagues

While the Bible uses the word 'plagues' for the troubles that befell Egypt (*e.g.* Ex. 11:1), it prefers to call them *signs* and *miracles* (27; *cf.* Ex. 7:3), since their role was to convince and warn, not only to chastise. They reinforced the command of God,[3] as our Lord's signs reinforced the gospel (Jn. 12:37).

28ff. By singing of the ninth plague first, the psalm prepares us for a free treatment of the theme (it will also reverse the order of the *gnats*[4] and *flies* in verse 31, and leave out the cattle plague and the boils). Kirkpatrick suggests that the plague of *darkness* (28) is put first because it was decisive for the Egyptian people (though not as yet for Pharaoh), who thereupon gave the Israelites all that they asked, and treated Moses with unqualified respect (Ex. 11:3). This is supported by the

---

[1] NEB reverses the order of 19a and b.

[2] The word is primarily used of refining metals by fire. JB, TEV, however, render it 'proved him right'—*cf.* our use of the adjective 'tested' as equivalent to 'verified'. But this would be the only Old Testament occurrence of the word in such a sense: *cf.* BDB, p. 864a.

[3] The strange form of 27a (lit. 'they set among them the words of his signs'—*i.e.*, His words that consisted of signs?- *cf.* G-K 130e) seems intended to make this point, that the miracles were messages from God.

[4] 'Gnats' (RSV, TEV) are rendered 'maggots' in NEB, 'mosquitoes' in JB.

Hebrew text of 28b, namely 'they rebelled *not* against his words', which seems to be an allusion to Exodus 11:3.

So the plagues are presented here not to trace the progress of Pharaoh's hardening—he is not mentioned—but to praise the decisive and versatile power of God. Note the terse simplicity of the verbs: *e.g.* 'He sent ... he spoke ... he gave ... he smote ...', *etc.*

105:37-42. The Exodus

What God does, He does handsomely—such is the burden of the passage. And what He promises, He keeps: *For he remembered* ... (42), as verse 8 has already pointed out. The main passages referred to are as follows:

37, 38. Exodus 12:33-36; Deuteronomy 8:4.
39. Exodus 13:21f.; 14:19f.
40. Exodus 16:2-4, 13f. See also on Psalm 78:23-25.
41. Exodus 17:1-7; *cf.* Numbers 20:11.
42. Genesis 15:12-16 (a very specific promise).

105:43-45. The conquest

So the psalm ends on the positive note which it has sustained from the first, dwelling wholly on the grace of God in these events, ignoring the sins of the redeemed which challenged it at every turn. These will be the theme of the next psalm. Meanwhile the final verse shows why grace abounded: not that sin might also abound, but (to quote a New Testament equivalent of verse 45) 'that the righteousness of the law might be fulfilled in us, who walk not after the flesh, but after the Spirit' (Rom. 8:4, av).

Psalm 106

Not One Lesson Was Learnt

This psalm is the dark counterpart of its predecessor, a shadow cast by human self-will in its long struggle against the light. The span of this history overlaps that of Psalm 105, starting at the Exodus and going on to what appears to be the Babylonian exile. But the last two verses are quoted in the account of a much earlier event, David's procession with the ark to Jerusalem (1 Ch. 16:35f.). Whether this means that the psalm refers to the captives of earlier wars, or that 1 Chronicles 16 borrowed it to illustrate the kind of rejoicing and praying that accompanied the ark, rather than to record it verbatim, is discussed briefly in the introduction to Psalm 96; see also on verses 37ff., 46f., below.

For all its exposure of man's ingratitude, this is a psalm of praise, for it is God's extraordinary longsuffering that emerges as the real theme. This is the basis of the final prayer (47), and this gives reality to the doxology that closes not only the psalm but the Fourth Book of the Psalter (Pss. 90–106).

106:1-3. A God to praise

After the opening Hallelujah (see the last comment on Ps. 104) the first verse is identical with that of the next psalm and of Psalm 136. It may indeed have provided the seed from which the latter psalm originated. On the words *good* and *steadfast love*, see the comments and further references on 'goodness and mercy' at 23:6.

3. This verse, one of the many beatitudes in the Psalms (listed at 1:1), seems to glance back to the question of verse 2 and then on to the long catalogue of failures which will dominate the psalm. That is, 'to show forth all his praise' (2) will take lives as well as lips; and while even our sins throw His grace into relief, as the psalm will show, our obligation to righteousness is total and uninterrupted. The phrase, *righteousness at all times*, was to be outbid, if this is conceivable, by Paul's 'urgent in season and out of season' (2 Tim. 4:2).

106:4, 5. A personal plea

This little prayer beautifully relates the one to the many, refusing to lose the individual in the crowd, yet retreating into no private corner of enjoyment. We are reminded again of Paul, whose joy and crown was the prosperity of God's chosen (*e.g.* Phil. 4:1; 1 Thes. 2:19; 3:8), and whose daily burden was 'the care of all the churches' (2 Cor. 11:28, AV).

106:6-39. A record of failure

It is one thing to condemn an earlier generation; quite another to see oneself mirrored and involved in it.[1] Verse 6 makes this

---

[1] The difficulty is partly that different temptations find out different weaknesses. It took our Lord to see the solidarity between, *e.g.*, the generation that killed the prophets and the one that entombed them; a solidarity which was to be demonstrated all too soon.

crucial admission, binding together the recurrent 'they' of 7–39 with its own 'we', turning an indictment into a confession. The modern singer of the psalm has to do the same. The Israelites are our ecclesiastical forbears; their sins are our own writ large.

7–12. Unbelief. The ingredients of unbelief throw light, by contrast, on the ingredients of faith. Beginning in the mind, with reasoning that took no account of God's revealed acts (7a) and character (7b), it found its outlet in the will. If *rebelled* (7c)[1] seems an extreme expression, it is one of only two possible responses to God's call, though it has many degrees of seriousness. What this passage shows is that their eventual faith (Heb. 11:29) owed everything to God, nothing to their initial reaction, which can be read in Exodus 14:10–12.

13–15. Discontent. Of Israel's many demands for a more comfortable pilgrimage, this example from Numbers 11 is picked out as the most revealing. At two points where our Lord was to triumph in the wilderness, Israel utterly failed: in relation to the body (where her *wanton craving*, commemorated in the place-name of Nu. 11:34, contrasts with His self-mastery), and in relation to God, whom He, unlike them, refused to *put . . . to the test* by a foolish challenge.

15. This classic statement of God's accommodation to man's self-will, and of the unhappy sequel, refers initially to the disenchantment and disaster of Numbers 11:18–20, 33. But it reveals a pattern which is memorably expressed in the AV: 'He gave them their request; but sent leanness into their soul'. The prodigal son illustrates it; still more, the history of Lot. Conversely, our Lord's readiness to *wait for (God's) counsel* (13) bore fruit in His return from the wilderness 'in the power of the Spirit'.

16–18. Jealousy. The self-righteous attacks on Moses' spiritual and temporal leadership in Numbers 16:3, 13 are unmasked in the simple words, *men . . . were jealous*. Such directness is as characteristic of Scripture as are the elaborate self-justifications of men. There is a close parallel in another brief summary, 'it was out of envy', in Matthew 27:18.

18. This mention of the men who perished by *fire* (*cf.* Nu. 16:35) shows that the party of Korah, the religious wing

---

[1] The phrase, *against the Most High* ('*elyôn*), is a small emendation of the Hebrew. The latter has '*at the sea* ('*al-yām*), at the Red Sea', which makes adequate sense as it stands, and is indirectly supported by LXX.

of the revolt, is included in the reckoning here, although their leader is not mentioned.

19-23. Idolatry. In Romans 1:23 Paul quotes from the LXX of verse 20, *They (ex)changed the glory . . .* , in his great indictment of heathen man. Neither he nor this psalm, nor again the recorded wrath of God and Moses (Ex. 32:10, 19), leaves any room for the view that the idol was a mere focus for worship of the true God. It was an exchange. There is withering contempt in the aside, *that eats grass*; and there is irony in the fact that in this choice they parted with *their* glory (lit.; *cf.* RV, NEB; and see Je. 2:11), for they had no other, only the God they served.

23. The bold expression, *Moses . . . stood in the breach before him*, accepts the risk of our misunderstanding God's part in the matter, in case we should miss the importance of intercession. So does the narrative itself (Ex. 32:7-14). It is left to other scriptures to point out that God longs to see such a concern as Moses showed. See especially Ezekiel 22:30f., which uses the same expression as this, but states both sides of the paradox, while emphasizing that such prayer is no mere exercise. The issue does hang on this: there is a '*Therefore*' and a '*had not*'(23) which are wholly disquieting (*cf.* Ezk. 22:31).

24-27. Drawing back. This was the 'moment of truth', when the challenge to march into Canaan was flatly refused ('Let us . . . go back to Egypt'), and the only dissentients were threatened with stoning (Nu. 14:4, 10). What Israel *despised* and disbelieved was not only 'the pleasant land' and the promise (24), but the Lord, as He Himself put it (Nu. 14:11).[1] The symbolism of His oath-taking (26; *cf.* Nu. 14:28, 'As I live') marked this moment as the turning-point for a whole generation, which would now wander and die in the wilderness.

27. The threat of scattering belongs to an earlier speech (Lv. 26:33ff.), reaffirmed in Moses' parting charge (Dt. 28:64ff.).

28-31. Apostasy. When Numbers 25:1 tells of Israel beginning 'to play the harlot with the daughters of Moab', it sees the spiritual harlotry of it as the most damning factor: 'So Israel yoked himself to Baal of Peor' (25:3). The psalm makes the same point, and adds the detail of *sacrifices to the dead*,

---

[1] A different but parallel verb is used here for 'despised'.

which is not found in the Numbers account (unless *the dead* is a scornful reference to idols). But various prohibitions of rites connected with the dead show that these held a strong temptation for Israel and presumably for her neighbours. See especially Deuteronomy 26:14.

The swift intervention of Phinehas 'made atonement for the people of Israel' by satisfying the claims of judgment (Nu. 25:13), which is one facet of atonement (*cf.* Rom. 8:3b). In another crisis Aaron 'made atonement for the people' by standing between the dead and the living, as High Priest, with the symbols of sacrifice and intercession (Nu. 16:46ff.; *cf.* Lv. 16:11-13), which is another facet, expounded in the Epistle to the Hebrews. God's accolade for Phinehas, summarized in verse 31, is given in full in Numbers 25:11-13. The phrase, *reckoned to him as righteousness*, is reminiscent of Abram's justification and ours (Gn. 15:6; Rom. 4:3, 23-25); happily it is Abram's faith we are to follow, not Phinehas's zeal! But this is because sentence has been executed (on the just, for the unjust) and atonement made, not in token but in full.

32, 33. Provocation. This is the incident of Numbers 20:1-13, when Moses struck the rock in anger. The balance of blame is restored here, for it was Moses who bore the brunt of it at the time, paying the price of leadership; but God has no illusions.

34-39. Paganization. This stanza has common ground with Deuteronomy 32:15-18, which Paul uses in 1 Corinthians 10:19-22 in discussing the Christian's dealings with a pagan culture. All three passages are agreed that while idols are fraudulent (the psalm does not even call them gods), yet behind them there are demons. So they are not simply a delusion but a snare (36).

37ff. There are warnings against human sacrifice to Molech in the law of Moses (*e.g.* Lv. 18:21); but the recorded examples of it, and the expression *innocent blood*, are a feature of the declining monarchy (*e.g.* 2 Ki. 16:3; 21:16; Je. 19:4f.), which makes the psalm look late. But there is no reason to think that it did not happen in the dark days of the judges, when we know of one such sacrifice offered even to the Lord (Jdg. 11:31).

106:40-46. A tempered judgment

Judgment had to begin only a generation after the death of Joshua, and to recur with tragic regularity. The book of

Judges amply illustrates the tale of verses 40–45 with its recurrent cycle of apostasy, a cry for help, liberation and renewed apostasy. But verse 46 is harder to place in that early period: examples of this clemency (for which Solomon prayed in his Temple prayer, 1 Ki. 8:50) are recorded for us only from a later age (*e.g.* 2 Ki. 25:27–30; Ezr. 1:2–4).

106:47, 48. Cause for prayer and praise

The prayer of verse 47 has behind it the frank confession of national sin on the one hand, and of divine forbearance on the other, which have dominated the psalm. It is the kind of praying which God delights to answer. Its inclusion, with the next verse, in the psalmody which the Chronicler incorporates in the account of David's procession with the ark (1 Ch. 16:35f.)[1] underlines the fact that penitence is never out of place in praise, nor praise in an act of penitence.

Verse 48 therefore makes a fitting crown to a psalm whose theme has been God's steadfastness even more than man's perversity, and a doxology to conclude Book IV of the Psalter.

[1] See the opening comments on the psalm.

Book V: Psalms 107–150

Apart from the doxology at the end of Psalm 106 there is little if anything to mark off this final book from its predecessor. Within it, however, there are certain obvious groupings: two collections of Davidic psalms (108–110; 138–145); the fifteen Songs of Ascents (120–134), four of which bear David's name (122, 124, 131, 133) and one Solomon's (127); and a burst of praise to bring the Psalter to its climax in the five 'Hallel' psalms, 146–150, each of which begins and ends with 'Hallelu-jah' ('Praise the Lord'). Jewish tradition also groups together Psalms 113–118, known as the 'Egyptian Hallel', for use at the Passover. The 'hymn' sung at the Last Supper (Mk. 14:26) is likely to have been part of that Hallel.

Psalm 107

God to the Rescue

The centre-piece of this striking psalm is the set of four word-pictures of human predicaments and divine interventions. In themselves the adventures are not characteristically Israelite situations; yet the fact that this is a piece to celebrate the return of exiles raises the possibility that these episodes are four different ways of depicting the plight from which the nation had been delivered. 'The scenes are at once fact and figure; scenes from life, yet intended to represent Israel's experience. This is especially clear in verses 10–16, where some touches are obviously national and personal' (Kirk-patrick).

A final section (33–43) enlarges on the great reversals of fortune which God delights to bring about in the affairs of men.

107:1–3. Joy of reunion

This opening call gives the psalm its setting in the great deliverance of Israel from exile, the theme on which the rest of the psalm rings the changes (see the introductory remarks,

383

above). The word *redeemed* brings echoes of the custom which obliged a kinsman to step in to rescue his close relative from debt or slavery (see the references at 69:18). God had done just that; and the word *gathered* answers the very prayer of 106:47. This matching of petition and answer has persuaded some expositors that Psalms 105–107 are a trilogy, despite the traditional boundary between Books IV and V, telling the story of God's grace in His choice and nurture of Israel (105), His forbearance and chastisement (106) and finally His reclamation of her (107). Kirkpatrick points out the link between the three in the expression *the lands*, crystallizing the promise (105:44), the punishment (106:27) and the rescue (107:3).

107:4-9. Wanderers retrieved
In most modern versions, each of the next four stanzas has the same kind of opening ('Some wandered . . .', 'Some sat in darkness . . .', *etc.*), as though we were following the fortunes of different groups. This is inaccurate,[1] and obscures the probability that the four scenes are four ways of looking at the same reality, namely the disastrous situation from which Israel has now been rescued. As that situation is analogous to the plight of all sinners, the psalm can be appreciated directly, not only through the eyes of Israel.

Lostness, hunger, thirst and exhaustion are all figures which our Lord was to employ in relation to His self-offer as the Way, the Bread and Water of life and the Giver of rest. The scene in this stanza unites all these aspects of salvation and crowns them with that of *a city to dwell in*: a climax without which the rescue, at either level of meaning, would be little more than first aid. The New Testament is full of it: *cf.*, *e.g.*, Ephesians 2:11ff.; Hebrews 12:22ff.; Revelation 21 and 22.

107:10-16. Prisoners released
Guilt (*cf.* 11), darkness, grinding toil, and the constriction of *bonds*, *doors* and *bars*, create another dimension of distress, distinct from the first scene; yet as a metaphor, whether of the exile or of the fallen state of man, it makes an apt companion

---

[1] The opening phrases are, respectively, 'They wandered' (4); 'Those that sat' (10); 'Fools' (17); 'Those that go down' (23).

to it. Until rescued, man is not simply lost in too wide a world, like the travellers of 4ff., or trapped in too small a one, like these prisoners; he is both.

The last verse of the *Benedictus* (Lk. 1:79), which combines both metaphors, quotes our verse 10, in which *gloom* is literally 'the shadow of death' (see on Ps. 23:4). Our Lord's manifesto of Luke 4:18f. can be read with livelier understanding against the background of this stanza, especially of its portraits of prisoners, in their postures now of cramped inactivity (10), now of exhaustion and collapse (12).

> 'Long my imprisoned spirit lay
>> Fast bound in sin and nature's night;
> Thine eye diffused a quickening ray,—
>> I woke, the dungeon flamed with light;
> My chains fell off, my heart was free,
> I rose, went forth, and followed Thee.'[1]

107:17–22. The sick restored

Sickness is certainly the plight described here, but not the kind of sickness that carries no blame.[2] The opening of verse 17 is not, as in RSV, TEV, *Some were sick*, but, bluntly, 'Fools, through their sinful ways . . .'; and fools in Scripture are the perverse, not the unintelligent. What is more, the verb as well as its supporting phrases points to their trouble as self-inflicted. In such a context, verse 18 could well call to mind in modern times the drug-addict, but only as one example of man's perennial determination to get hurt.

So the wages of sin, or at least its interim payment, must be added to the composite picture. With the previous stanza, this emphasizes guilt; in both cases man's fundamental guilt of spurning God's counsel, which is stated in verse 11 and now implied in the term 'fools' (17, see above). But guilt shows up God's rescuing activity as grace: 'love to the loveless', not merely to the hapless (as in the rescue of the lost or the overwhelmed in verses 4–9 or 23–32).

22. For two fine examples of the *songs of joy* that accompanied and reflected deeply on the *sacrifice of thanksgiving*, see Psalms 40 and 116.

---

[1] Charles Wesley, 'And can it be . . . ?'
[2] *Cf.* the implications of, *e.g.*, Jn. 5:14, as against Jn. 9:1–3.

107:23-32. The storm-tossed rescued[1]

This fourth parable of Israel's former plight (and, by extension, humanity's as well) speaks not of our guilt but of our littleness. The hurricane shakes us into seeing that in a world of gigantic forces we live by permission, not by good management. The point is made explicitly in verse 27, where *wits* could be translated 'seamanship' (NEB). *Cf.* TEV, 'all their skill was useless'. There are *wondrous works* to humble men as well as to save them (24, 31, using the same word).

If this is initially a figure of Israel's exile and deliverance, as the pattern of the psalm suggests (see above), it finds support (as Kissane points out) in the epithet 'storm-tossed' which Isaiah 54:11 uses of Jerusalem in the same connection. But the stilling of the lake-storm by our Lord as a sign for disciples ensures that we read this stanza as relevant to others besides Israelites and sailors.

107:33-42. Disposer supreme

The psalm now drops the pattern of calamity—cry—salvation —thanksgiving, for a conclusion which draws out the lesson of God's sovereignty from experiences like these. A final verse, as an epilogue, makes sure that the lesson is not missed.

33-38. This recalls the desert scene of verses 4-9, but now it is not man who gets lost and found, but his habitat which dies on him or presents him with abundance—so far is he from being master of his fate. Verse 34 is underlined by the doom of Sodom and by the warnings of the Law, 'lest the land vomit you out, when you defile it' (Lv. 18:28). Verses 35-38 recall the idyllic prophecy of Isaiah 35:6f. and the blessing of Deuteronomy 28:1-5, to make it doubly clear that with God poor resources become fertility and wealth.

These verses are, we may suppose, not merely about deserts and farmland, but pointers to other kinds of poverty and riches, not least those of the mind and spirit. *Cf.*, *e.g.*, the contrasts of outward and inward poverty in Revelation 2:9 and 3:17.

39-42. It is hardly a coincidence that those who sing of the

---

[1] Verses 23-27 (and verse 40) were marked by the Massoretes with a sign indicating a parenthesis. But the verses are well attested, and there seems to be no sufficient reason for this annotation. *BH* adds to the confusion by placing the sign at 21-26.

great reversals of human fortunes tend to be the newly reprieved or promoted. Here it is the restored Israel that takes up the theme; elsewhere most memorably Hannah and Mary. But their songs belong to all the redeemed.

107:43. Epilogue

The book of Hosea closes on just such a note as this: a sober reminder not to be carried away by eloquence, in shallow response to what God has done in depth, or in purely imaginative participation in a chapter of history. It is himself that the reader is to recognize in the fourfold picture of plight and salvation, and it is the steadfastness of God that he is now to praise with new insight.

Psalm 108

We Shall Do Valiantly

Two psalm-endings of David, 57:7–11 and 60:5–12, have been joined to make this single piece. Each had begun under stress, with David hunted in Psalm 57 and defeated in Psalm 60; but each had ended strongly. The new psalm starts at this more positive point in each of them, and so provides for a situation which is certainly chastening (11), but whose challenge is that of an inheritance not yet seized (10ff.; *cf.* 9), rather than a defeat not yet avenged (*cf.* Ps. 60:1–3, 9ff.). For our use, the earlier psalms may well provide for times of personal or corporate peril, but the present one for times which call for new initiatives and ventures of faith.

There are a few minor variations from Psalms 57 and 60, one of which is discussed at 60:8. The fact that the term *God* is used by itself frequently in this psalm, but in only one other place in this Fifth Book of the Psalter (144:9), makes it clear that the present psalm is the borrower from the other two, not the lender, since Book II, in which they occur, strongly prefers this title to 'the Lord'. See the footnote to page 5 of the Introduction.

The details of this psalm are discussed in the comments on Psalms 57:7–11 and 60:5–12.

Psalm 109

The Character-Assassin

This psalm spares us nothing. What such outbursts are doing in Scripture is discussed in the Introduction, pp. 25–30 ('Cries for Vengeance'). Here, our main task is to consider what the psalm is saying, and what has provoked it.

Title

On *the choirmaster* and *David*, see Introduction, pp. 40, 33.

109:1–5. The complaint

The words, *O God of my praise*, are, to be exact, the opening phrase of the psalm (*cf.* NEB, *etc.*): a resolute stand taken before the troubled thoughts surge in. The psalm will feel its way back to this vantage-point, but only regain it in the last two verses.

David is under an all-out attack on his character, which has already reduced him to a shadow (23). It is no longer a whispering campaign but brazen and open: 'to my face' (2a, NEB).[1] He feels himself encircled ('ringed ... round with words of hate', NEB).

4, 5. The depth of the wound shows itself in the repeated phrase, *in return for my love* (identical in 4a, 5b) and in the halting words which RSV expands (rightly, it would seem) to *even as I make prayer for them* (4b).[2] It was a betrayal almost worthy of Judas. Indeed by applying verse 8 to him (see the comment there), the New Testament throws light on the problem raised by the psalm as a whole. On the one hand our Lord's unbroken love to His betrayer rebukes any personal vindictiveness which may have motivated David; on the other hand the fearful end of Judas showed that at least one clause of the imprecation had God's endorsement in at least one case.

---

[1] This seems to be the force of the expression 'with me' (2a, lit.), which is variously rendered 'against me' or 'about me' in other versions.

[2] The Heb. has simply 'but as for me—prayer'. This is similar to 120:7, 'as for me—peace'. It could mean 'but I give myself unto prayer' (AV, RV), but the three surrounding expressions of kindnesses betrayed suggest that the prayer was for them. (NEB, without textual support, loses the reference to prayer by emending 'as for me' (*'ănî*) to 'nothing' (*'ên*), and 'prayer' (*t^ep̄illâ*) to 'unseemly' (*tip̄lâ*).)

109:6-20. The imprecation

The sudden change from plural to singular, until the plural returns in verse 20, has prompted several interpretations. The simplest is that the 'him' and 'he' are a way of saying 'each one of them'; a not uncommon Hebrew idiom which verse 20 seems to support if it is summarizing the passage. A second way is to begin verse 6 with 'They say' (which can be left unexpressed), making David, not his enemies, the target of what follows. NEB confines this enemy speech to verse 6 (making David's reply run from 7 to 20) but JB carries it on to the end of verse 15, and some commentators have taken it to the end of 19.

To make the enemy the speaker of this appalling curse is to rid the psalm of its chief affront to our sensibilities, while accounting quite naturally for the long passage in the singular. But it makes Peter's reference to Judas very forced[1] (and he stated that it was a prophecy 'which the Holy Spirit spoke ... by the mouth of David, concerning Judas', Acts 1:16). It also does nothing to draw the sting of other passages of almost equal violence, *e.g.* Jeremiah 18:19-23, which might be called a miniature of this psalm.

We therefore take these words to be David's own, and while giving due weight to the element of righteous anger and of rhetorical hyperbole,[2] we see them as comparable to the outbursts of Jeremiah and Job: recorded for our learning, not for our imitation; yet voicing the cry of innocent blood which God is pledged to hear (Mt. 23:35; Lk. 18:8), and thereby becoming God's mouth-piece in pronouncing judgment on the unrepentant. This is not our function under the gospel, for we are to 'bless, and curse not'. The psalm may even shock us into more fervent compliance with our instructions, as ministers of reconciliation.

6. The word *accuser*, or adversary (*śāṭān*), is prominent in the psalm, coming again in verses 20 and 29, while the corresponding verb has already appeared in verse 4. In those verses he is the enemy's man; so this prayer wishes the enemy a taste of his own medicine. It is the word, incidentally, from which Satan derives his title and name, since he presses the

---

[1] This objection can perhaps be answered by pointing out that in verse 20 David returns the curse to those who deserve it. But this is somewhat circuitous.

[2] This is discussed further in the Introduction, pp. 26f.

case against the righteous with relish and with every artifice (*cf.* Jb. 1:6ff.; 2:1ff.; Rev. 12:10). In Zechariah 3:1 he is seen standing at the right hand of the man on trial, as the accuser does here (see mg.); it was evidently the customary position in a court of law.

7. *His prayer*, in this trial scene, might appear to mean 'his plea to the court'; but, as Kirkpatrick points out, the word everywhere else implies prayer to God. There are many parallels to God's emphatic rejection of such praying: *e.g.* Proverbs 28:9; Isaiah 1:15.

8. *His goods* is a possible but perverse translation, since the word also means 'his office', and is quoted in that sense in Acts 1:20. Verse 11 will deal sufficiently with his goods. On the shadow of Judas in this verse see on verses 4f., above.

9–16. The plight of the man's *children* and *wife* is desired mainly, it seems, for the disgrace it will bring to his memory in the short time that he is remembered at all (*cf.* the variations on the theme of memory in verses 13–16). It makes the imprecation no less cruel, but that is where the emphasis falls. It is reminiscent of David's horrific curse on the house of Joab in 2 Samuel 3:29. At the same time it is not fantasy: such judgments are shown elsewhere to be the dark side of human solidarity, and David's curse, however ugly its motivation, could still have been the vehicle of God's judgment, like the curse of Jotham (Jdg. 9:57). The Law, the Prophets and the Gospel all give warnings, though not with relish, of what the fathers' sins can bring upon the children (Ex. 20:5; 1 Sa. 2:31ff.; Lk. 19:41ff.).

17–20. The terrible logic of judgment, whereby what a man chooses he ultimately and totally receives, and indeed absorbs and is enfolded in, is expressed nowhere else with quite this vivid intensity. To be precise, the Hebrew text puts 17–19 in narrative form ('He loved to curse, and curses came . . .'), and allows verse 20 to be a statement ('This [is] the reward . . .'), as in RV. The difference is one of vowels, which were originally unwritten; but it seems unreasonable to add further curses to the psalm by emendation when the text is content with statements. The LXX confirms the Massoretic Text (with statements rather than curses), understanding the announcements as prophetic.[1]

---

[1] On the 'prophetic perfect' see on 9:5, or on 93:1, 2, where the footnote gives further references.

109:21-29. The prayer

Once more, as so often in the Psalms, the whole mood changes with the pivot-phrase *But thou . . . (cf.* especially Ps. 22:3, 9, 19). The appeal is on the surest basis of all: *for thy name's sake;* see the second paragraph on 23:3. NEB puts this perfectly: 'deal with me as befits thy honour' (21).

23. *Shaken off,* rather than 'tossed up and down' (AV, RV), seems to be the right meaning, as of shaking an unwelcome insect off a garment *(cf.* BDB). The psalistm feels himself doubly humiliated: a puny and a repulsive creature—so withering is the effect of contempt. It is small wonder that our Lord saw this attitude as virtually murder (Mt. 5:21f.).

27. *This is thy hand* means 'my restoration is no accident'.

28. The first line, which may sound like returning blessing for cursing, is of course a plea that when the enemy calls down the worst on David, God will, instead, rain down the best, as the subsequent lines make clear. It is a good prayer with which to turn the edge of an attack: *cf.* Romans 8:31ff.

109:30, 31. The vow of praise

The psalms often emphasize the rightness, indeed the duty, of giving public thanks for personal blessings: *cf.* especially 40:10.

The final verse puts the matter in a nutshell, picking up a phrase from verse 6 (which RSV has relegated to the margin) and replacing the figure of the accuser, who stands at the right hand of his victim, by the figure of God who *stands at the right hand of the needy* in a very different sense. It is the complete answer.

Psalm 110

David's Lord

Nowhere in the Psalter does so much hang on the familiar title *A Psalm of David* as it does here; nor is the authorship of any other psalm quite so emphatically endorsed in other parts of Scripture. To amputate this opening phrase,[1] or to allow it

[1] In the Heb. text there is no break between these words and those which we normally print as the first line. Our custom of placing the title above the psalm, rather than as part of verse 1, is a matter of convenience, which does not alter its status as part of the text. See Introduction, pp. 32ff.

no reference to the authorship of the psalm, is to be at odds with the New Testament, which finds King David's acknowledgment of his 'Lord' highly significant.[1] For while other psalms share with this one the exalted language which points beyond the reigning king to the Messiah, here alone the king himself does homage to this personage—thereby settling two important questions: whether the perfect king was someone to come, or simply the present ruler idealized; and whether the one to come would be merely man at his best, or more than this.

Our Lord gave full weight to David's authorship and David's words, stressing the former twice by the expression 'David himself', and the latter by the comment that he was speaking 'in the Holy Spirit' (Mk. 12:36f.) and by insisting that his terms presented a challenge to accepted ideas of the Messiah, which must be taken seriously. Peter, too, on the Day of Pentecost, stressed the contrast in the psalm between David 'himself' and his 'Lord', who 'ascended into the heavens' to be 'exalted at the right hand of God' (Acts 2:33–35).

So King David speaks in the psalm as the prophet who declaims the enthronement oracle to the Messianic King, corresponding to the oracle given to other kings at their anointing or crowning (cf. 1 Sa. 10:1f.; 2 Ki. 11:12). Therefore those who deny David's authorship of the psalm on the ground that the psalm reads like an enthronement oracle, curiously miss the point. It is just such an oracle. What is unique is the royal speaker, addressing this more-than-royal person.

What the oracle declares was destined to form the basis of the apostles' teaching on the exaltation, heavenly session and royal priesthood of Christ. It is one of the most quoted of all the psalms.

[1] Among early critics, prior to the Qumran discoveries, there was some tendency to date the psalm in the Maccabaean era (2nd century BC), and even to find the name of Simon, the Maccabaean High Priest and political leader, in the initial letters of the verses, with a little rearrangement. With comparable ingenuity H. H. Rowley (*Festschrift für Alfred Bertholet*, J. C. B. Mohr, 1950, pp. 464ff.) saw in verse 4 David's oracle to a Jebusite Zadok, adopting him as Israel's High Priest, while in the rest of the psalm Zadok addressed David, newly enthroned at Jerusalem. The majority of present critics dissent more moderately from the New Testament view of the psalm by seeing it as an enthronement oracle for either David or one of his successors, spoken to him by an anonymous cultic official. Our Lord and the apostles, it is understood, were denied this insight.

110:1–3. The King

The first line, after the title, runs literally, 'The oracle of Yahweh to my lord'.[1] It is an opening which stamps the next words as God's direct message to His King, on which verses 2 and 3 provide the inspired comment. A second message is given in verse 4, but verses 5–7 develop the earlier part of the psalm.

The startling fact that David spoke of a king as *my lord* (*cf.* Knox, freely, 'the Master I serve') was pointed out, as we have seen, by Christ, who left His hearers to think out its implications, and His apostles to spell them out. Like Joshua, who surrendered his command with the words, 'What does *my lord* bid his servant?', David here (so to speak) falls down and worships the Man who stands before him (*cf.* Jos. 5:14). Now follows God's oracle to David's lord.

Sit at my right hand. The authority and power conferred by such an address will be illustrated in the remaining verses of the psalm; but it will take the New Testament to do it justice.

a. He is not only greater than David (Acts 2:34, 'for David did not ascend into the heavens') but greater than the angels (Heb. 1:13, 'to what angel has he ever said, "Sit at my right hand..."?');

b. God exalted Him as emphatically as man rejected Him (Acts 5:30f., 'Jesus whom you killed ... God exalted ... at his right hand');

c. It is as Saviour and Intercessor that He reigns (Acts 5:31; Rom. 8:34, 'Christ ... who is at the right hand of God ... intercedes for us');

d. (*'Sit ...'*): In token of a finished task, He is seated (Heb. 10:11f., 'every priest stands daily ..., offering repeatedly .... But ... Christ ... sat down at the right hand of God');

e. (*'till ...'*): He awaits the last surrender (Heb. 10:13, 'to wait until his enemies should be made a stool for his feet'; *cf.* also 1 Cor. 15:25f.).

So this single verse displays the divine Person of Christ, His power and the prospect before Him. Together with verse 4 it underlies most of the New Testament teaching on His glory as Priest-King.

2. Note how fully at one are the Lord (Yahweh) and this King. It is the Lord who wields the sceptre, it is the King who

---

[1] A kind of parody of such a phrase is found in the Heb. of Ps. 36:2 (1, EV). See on 36:1.

is urged to rule—for human authority is enhanced, not diminished, by such a partnership. The word used for *Rule* has a certain sternness, which suits the contrast between the enforced obedience of enemies in this verse and the glad response of volunteers in the next. There is something of the same contrast in, *e.g.*, Revelation 17:14.

3. Almost every word of this verse is rendered differently in different translations, but the general picture emerges (except when the text is amended) of a host of volunteers rallying to their leader in a holy war. In the first line there is a touch of the Song of Deborah, when 'the people offered themselves willingly' (Jdg. 5:2); but the expression is even bolder here: lit., 'your people (will be) freewill offerings',[1] a way of speaking which anticipates the Pauline pictures of 'a living sacrifice' or of a life poured out 'as a libation' (Rom. 12:1; Phil. 2:17; *cf.* 2 Cor. 8:3, 5).

On the day you lead your host could also mean 'on the day of your power': it is the word used for 'might'[2] or 'force of arms' in Zechariah 4:6, and it corresponds well to 'the day of his wrath' in verse 5.

Upon the holy mountains is the reading of several mss and of Symmachus and Jerome, but the standard Hebrew text has 'in the beauties (or, splendours) of holiness', supported by lxx, Vulg. On the meaning of this expression see on 29:2 (commenting on 'holy array').

Like dew your youth will come to you interprets *youth* collectively (*cf.* TEV), and assumes that the letter *k* (= 'like') has been omitted after a word which ends in *k* ('to you'), which is a common copying error. This gives the picture of a splendid army suddenly and silently mobilized. But the Hebrew makes sense as it stands, *i.e.*, 'You have the dew of your youth' (*cf.* AV, RV). *I.e.*, this king ever keeps the first freshness of the dawn of life, unlike those whose love is 'like a morning cloud, like the dew that goes early away' (Ho. 6:4).[3]

To sum up: this verse (as I see it) pictures the Messiah

---

[1] Reading different vowels (*'immᵉkā nᵉdībôṭ*) lxx has 'with you (will be) sovereignty'. But 'princely gifts' (NEB), or 'noble things' as in Is. 32:8, is a more likely meaning of the postulated word than 'sovereignty'.

[2] NEB here (*cf.* JB) replaces it by a word for 'birth'. This is a conjecture; its only support is in the metaphors of the last two lines of the verse.

[3] lxx and some others read the consonants of *your youth* (*yalḏūṭeykā*) with other vowels, with the sense, 'I gave birth to you' (*yᵉlaḏtîkā*).

going forth in primal vigour, holiness and glory, at the head of a host which is as dedicated as those early Israelites who 'jeoparded their lives to the death' (Jdg. 5:18). The Christian can identify such an army with the overcomers portrayed in Revelation 12:11, little as he may recognize himself and his fellows in either picture.

110:4. The Priest

Here is the second of the two direct oracles from God, which are rightly marked in RSV by inverted commas (*cf.* verse 1) to distinguish them from the third-person statements about God and the Messiah in the rest of the psalm.

If anything is stronger than a divine oracle it is a divine oath (*cf.* Heb. 6:17f.; 7:20ff.), here further strengthened by the pledge that God *will not change his mind*. This may be a glance at the promise which had to be withdrawn from Eli (1 Sa. 2:30). *This* priest will never abuse his office, and this priesthood is both older and more perfect (as the New Testament will show) than that of the whole house of Levi.

The passages which clarify this oracle are Genesis 14:18–20 and Hebrews 5:5–10 with 6:19 – 7:28. It emerges from these that both the name *Melchizedek* (king of righteousness) and his sphere as king of Salem (*i.e.*, of Jerusalem, whose shortened form brings out the meaning, 'Peace') made him a fitting pointer to the one who was to come (Heb. 7:2); that the silence surrounding him in the narrative made him an apt symbol of one who in full reality had 'neither beginning of days nor end of life' (Heb. 7:3); further, that his standing on the Godward side of Abraham, both in the blessing and gifts he gave and in the tithes he received, proved his priority over the whole Abrahamic people, and over the levitical priesthood in particular (Heb. 7:4–19). To this it can be added that, in Melchizedek, priesthood and kingship were united as they were to be in Christ. *Cf.* the emphasis on Christ as King in the early chapters of Hebrews, and on Him as Priest in the later chapters, just as in these verses of the psalm.

The addition of *for ever* is perhaps the most significant clause of all. It is this that clinches our assurance. It is a major theme of the Epistle to the Hebrews after its first appearance in Hebrews 5:6, where the eternal priest is shown to provide eternal salvation (Heb. 5:9), in contrast to the ephemeral priests whose labours were manifestly inconclusive.

110:5-7. The Warrior

Realistically, the psalm ends on the note of fierce battle and strenuous pursuit, since the Priest-King's enthronement is not the final scene but the prelude to world conquest. Psalm 2 showed the same sequence.

Now the Lord (*i.e.*, Yahweh) and His King act as one,[1] and the army of volunteers which was seen in verse 3 is no longer in the picture. The battle is the Lord's, yet He and His King are so united that by verse 7 it is clearly the human partner who is in the foreground. In New Testament terms, we have moved on from Hebrews to Revelation, where the picture of judgment and victory is no less terrible than that of verse 6 (*cf.*, *e.g.*, Rev. 19:11-21).

But the psalm, by its very form, recalls us to a situation still in movement. We are left with the picture of the Warrior following up his victory, like Gideon and his three hundred at the Jordan, 'faint yet pursuing' (Jdg. 8:4), pausing only to renew his strength and press on to complete the rout. Such is the leader, we are to infer, who beckons us to follow.

Psalm 111

God at Work

Psalms 111-113 all begin with Hallelujah, and there is a specially close bond between 111 and 112. These two are acrostics,[2] each having 22 lines beginning with successive letters of the Hebrew alphabet. But they are also a matched pair in their subject-matter, which tells of God in this psalm, and of the man of God in the next, even sharing the same or similar phrases in one or two verses.

As in other acrostic psalms, the alphabet rather than a progress of paragraphs provides the structure, allowing the thought to move back and forth among a few subjects. The main topic is the steady goodness of God displayed in His works. In the RSV the term 'work(s)' occurs in five of the ten

---

[1] There is no need to seek consistency between Yahweh's 'right hand' in verse 1 and the King's in verse 5. The scene has changed from throne to battlefield, to present this new aspect of the partnership.

[2] Other Old Testament acrostics are listed in the first footnote to Ps. 119.

verses; the Hebrew makes this emphasis less obvious by using a number of synonyms, but it is still there. We praise One whose goodness is practical.

1. *Company* is that intimate word *sôḏ*, which has the connotation of a circle of friends or advisers: *cf.* the note on 'friendship' at 25:14. But the wider word, *congregation*, precludes any idea of a narrow clique; the two terms together describe the people of God in their breadth (*cf.* the 'congregation' as a term for all Israel in the wilderness narratives) and in their close ties of fellowship.

2. In the Psalms, the Lord's *works* (*maʿᵃśîm*) are sometimes His deeds, as in verse 6, but more often the things He has made (*e.g.* the heavens, 8:3; 19:1; 102:25; and the populous earth, 104:24). Because these are made 'in wisdom' (104:24 again) they repay research, as recent centuries of rigorous study have shown us abundantly; and this verse was well chosen to grace the entrance of the Cavendish Laboratory in Cambridge, the scene of some fundamental physical discoveries. But while this verse is well taken as God's charter for the scientist and artist, verse 10 must be its partner, lest 'professing to be wise' we become fools, like the men of Romans 1:18-23.

3. Here God's *work* (*pōʿal*) is more likely to mean His providential acts, as in, *e.g.*, Deuteronomy 32:4; but Isaiah 45:9-13 reminds us not to draw too sharp a line between what He has made and what He is doing, which are all of a piece.

The next psalm boldly reproduces part of this verse and of the next two in its portrait of a godly man (see on 112:3ff.)— lest, this time, we draw too sharp a line between what God Himself is like and what He expects of His disciples.

4. The expression *wonderful works* opens up another line of thought. It is a single word, 'wonders', and refers most often to the great saving acts of God. The first line can be rendered, 'He has made a memorial of his wonders', seemingly a reference to the Passover above all (*cf.*, for us, 1 Cor. 11:23-26).[1] TEV links this verse rather effectively with the next by its paraphrase, 'The Lord does not let us forget ...' and 'He never forgets ...'.

5ff. So in quiet conjunction with the resounding acts of

---

[1] It could mean 'he has won a name by his marvellous deeds' (NEB); but the Heb. preposition is a little less suited to this, and the recurrence of the root for 'remember' in verse 5 points to the theme of memory rather than fame, in these adjacent verses.

verse 4 and 6 there is the steady faithfulness of verse 5 which means our daily bread and His daily forbearance. The pattern continues in the rest of the psalm: the reassuring stability of verses 7 and 8 is at one with the awesome activity of verse 9, in which the miracles of the Exodus and the theophany at Sinai are recalled, as Christians recall the greater Exodus and the New Covenant.

Note too the harmony between what God does and what He says: between His *works* and His *precepts* (7f.); *cf.* the other indivisible pairs noted at verse 3. In 8b the reference is to God's workmanship as their Maker and Author: *cf.* NEB, 'strongly based to endure for ever, their fabric goodness and truth'.

10. This verse picks up the theme of reverence from the end of verse 9, where the word *terrible* is part of the Hebrew verb 'to fear'. This famous saying is virtually the motto of the Wisdom writings, where its truth appears in various forms: *cf.* Job 28:28; Proverbs 1:7; 9:10; Ecclesiastes 12:13. At each place the context gives it a particular nuance: here it relates especially to God in His character as Creator, Redeemer and Provider, for whom reverence will be mingled with delight (2), gratitude (4, 9) and trust (5). So men of God have the key to what life is about—that 'from Him, to Him and through Him are all things'—and have the benefit of perfect precepts for its handling.

Note finally the last word: *for ever.* In one or other of its Hebrew synonyms, or in both together (8), it almost dominates the psalm, as is fitting in a song about God. It also reflects the two aspects of His work already noticed: that it is made to last (*e.g.* 8, 9) and that, being His, it is in His constant care (5).

Psalm 112

Godliness at Work

This is the middle psalm of a little group of three which begin with Hallelujah. More significantly, it is the second of a closely-linked pair, both of them acrostics (see on Psalm 111): the first about God and His ways, and the second about the man of God. There are moments when the two portraits coincide completely; and the present psalm can be viewed as a development of the last verse of its predecessor, on the blessedness of fearing the Lord.

1. The opening verses are unclouded: an idyllic picture of piety and prosperity which calls to mind the beginning of the book of Job. The fact that this person is a man of character, not merely of property, will emerge chiefly in the later verses, but already his godliness shows itself as an enthusiasm rather than a burden. There may be an echo of the previous psalm in the word *delights* (1b), which is the verb behind the phrase there, 'all who have pleasure in them' (111:2). To this man God's word is as fascinating as are His works to the naturalist; and the term used for it, *his commandments*, implies that his interest is practical. What grips him is God's will and call.

2, 3. The Old Testament's interest in family continuity corrects our excessive individualism. It could itself be distorted by pride and complacency (Mt. 3:9), but in its healthy form God valued and still uses it (*cf.* Gn. 18:19; 2 Tim. 1:5). The prosperity promised in the present verses may be largely material, but a closer look reveals the moral and spiritual terms which make it an instrument of good. A land needs its *mighty* men, and is fortunate if they are of such stock as this and if wealth is in such hands.

His righteousness (3b), remarkably enough, is tacitly compared to God's, since this line exactly reproduces 111:3b.[1] In both psalms it appears to speak of the right things that these two agents do, which nothing can undo; this is made doubly plain when this line returns yet again in verse 9.

4. It grows steadily clearer that this is a man whose goodness overflows to others. This is obscured in RSV at this point, for the verse is best taken as continuing the portrait, with the righteous man as the subject throughout: *i.e.*, 'He rises in the darkness, a light to the upright; he is gracious, merciful and righteous'.[2] So verse 4b is another bold comparison with the Lord Himself, by its allusion to the corresponding 4b in Psalm 111 (like that of 3b, noted above).

5ff. Now the particular form of this prosperous man's

---

[1] TEV obscures this by translating this word 'prosperity' here, 'kindness' in verse 9, and 'righteousness' in 111:3.

[2] RSV's 'correction' of the text, by inserting '*the Lord*' as the subject of 4b, is unsupported. NEB (apart from transposing the order of 4a and 4b) and JB are truer to the text.

goodness comes into view. It is generosity, the theme of this verse and of verse 9, but already anticipated in 4b. In enlarging on it, the psalm deals realistically with the temptations that go with the possession of money. One of them is the impulse to abuse the power that money brings: hence the commending of both graciousness (5a; *cf.* RV, NEB) and fairness (5b, *justice*) in the lender, who has all too strong an advantage over the borrower.[1] Another snare is fear (7, 8), for there is much that can go wrong for a rich man (*cf.* the *evil tidings* of verse 7), and much malice and rivalry to contend with (8, 10). The answer to it is the Godward stance of 7b: trust, not in a hoped-for turn of events but in the Lord (this is developed more fully in, *e.g.*, Ps. 37). What is promised is not better news (not, at least, for the time being, though it will come: 8b, 10), but a steady heart. More exactly, it is a heart *made* firm: established (7b, lit.) and supported (8a, lit.) by better facts than its own courage.

A third temptation is the miser's. The whole psalm speaks against it, but especially verses 5, 6 and 9, the last of which is quoted by Paul in 2 Corinthians 9:9. There, as here, it is the bold course that is shown as the surest. In the psalm, where the accent is on the things that last, the man who dares to be generous is seen as the one who will be remembered (6), whose good deeds will never lose their value (9; *cf.* 3). In 2 Corinthians, where this generosity has been shown with even greater daring by Christians in 'extreme poverty' (2 Cor. 8:2), it is the idea of scattering which is taken up from our verse 9 (*he has distributed freely*), in the sense of sowing for a harvest; so there the stress is on the abundant yield and widespread joy (2 Cor. 9:9–12) which are its rewards.

10. The companion psalm, whose subject was the Lord, finished with a verse that invited man's response. The present psalm, having expounded that response, clinches the matter by showing how bitter, transient and futile is the only alternative way of life.

---

[1] But 5a may speak of lending without interest (*cf.* JB), and 5b may mean 'who runs his business honestly' (TEV), or 'who can sustain his cause in court' (*cf.* BDB). The Heb. for 'justice' is a word with several shades of meaning.

Psalm 113
Nothing too Great for Him, No-one too Small

A short run of psalms used at the yearly Passover begins here, and is therefore commonly known as the Egyptian Hallel (Hallel means Praise). Only the second of them (114) speaks directly of the Exodus, but the theme of raising the down-trodden (113) and the note of corporate praise (115), personal thanksgiving (116), world vision (117) and festal procession (118) make it an appropriate series to mark the salvation which began in Egypt and will spread to the nations. By custom, the first two psalms are sung before the Passover meal, and the remaining four after it. So these were probably the last psalms our Lord sang before His passion (Mk. 14:26), and Psalm 118 had already made itself heard more than once in the confrontation of the previous few days. There was more relevance in these psalms to the Exodus—the greater Exodus—than could be guessed in Old Testament times.

113:1–4. 'High above . . .'

1. In these calls to praise there is more than mere repetition. There is point in specifying the Lord's *servants* and His *name*, since worship to be acceptable must be more than flattery and more than guess-work. It is the loving homage of the committed to the Revealed. See on 20:1 for some implications of the word 'name'; see also Exodus 34:5–7.

2–4. But the worshippers calling on His name in any one place are but part of a vast company, extending unimaginably in time (2) and space (3), as befits His sovereignty in earth and heaven (4). There is an echo, or else a parallel, of verse 3 in Malachi's vision[1] of world-wide and heartfelt worship—to which the prophet found a painful contrast in the attitudes of his contemporaries.

113:5–9. 'Far down . . .'

The challenge of verse 5, *Who is like the Lord our God?*, meets us, expressed or implied, throughout the Bible. It is put eloquently

---

[1] Mal. 1:11, which (like our verse) contains no finite verb, is best taken as prediction, as in AV, RV mg. See the Tyndale Commentary on *Haggai, Zechariah, Malachi* by J. G. Baldwin (IVP, 1972), at Mal. 1:11.

and at length in Isaiah 40:12 – 41:4, but it has its witnesses everywhere, even in the names of men and angels (Micaiah, 'who is like Yahweh?'; Michael, 'who is like God?'). Here this transcendence is memorably suggested by the perspective of verse 6, where the very heavens are almost out of sight below Him. He is, as JB puts it, 'enthroned so high, he needs to stoop to see the sky and earth!'[1]

7ff. Yet He is anything but aloof. Verses 7 and 8 anticipate the great downward and upward sweep of the gospel, which was to go even deeper and higher than the *dust* and the throne of *princes*: from the grave to the throne of God (Eph. 2:5f.).

Consciously, however, these verses look back to the song of Hannah, which they quote almost exactly (*cf.* 7, 8a with 1 Sa. 2:8). Hence the sudden reference to the childless woman who becomes a mother (9), for this was Hannah's theme. With such a background the psalm not only makes its immediate point, that the Most High cares for the most humiliated, but brings to mind the train of events that can follow from such an intervention. Hannah's joy became all Israel's; Sarah's became the world's. And the song of Hannah was to be outshone one day by the *Magnificat*. The spectacular events of our verses 7 and 8 are not greater than this domestic one; the most important of them have sprung from just such an origin.

But it would distort the psalm, and its values, to make verse 9 simply a means to an end. The psalm finishes with what seems an anticlimax, and it must not be disguised. It is here that God's glory most sharply differs from man's: a glory that is equally at home 'above the heavens' (4) and at the side of one forlorn person.

There is plainly much more than rhetoric in the question of verse 5, 'Who is like the Lord our God?'

Psalm 114

The Earth-Shaking Exodus

A fierce delight and pride in the great march of God gleams through every line of this little poem—a masterpiece whose

---

[1] This is too bold for NEB, which rearranges the lines of verses 5f., to put heaven and earth in a less unusual situation.

flights of verbal fancy would have excluded it from any hymn book but this. Here is the Exodus not as a familiar item in Israel's creed but as an astounding event: as startling as a clap of thunder, as shattering as an earthquake.

1, 2. There is a dramatic change of status between the first verse and the second. The group of aliens, their isolation increased by the *strange language* that surrounded them, is now viewed in relation not to man but to God. They have the dignity of a church and kingdom; they are the visible sign of God's holiness and His rule, little as their character (like that of the church, their successor)[1] matched their calling.

3, 4. So, while the story in Exodus and Joshua recaptures the magnitude of what Israel experienced—the terror of pursuit, the wild elation on the far shore, the trembling at mount Sinai, and the eventual crossing of the Jordan 'in haste' and 'in awe' (Jos. 4:10c, 14)—the psalm takes a totally different view. With a superb flourish it shows us the scurrying and excitement set up by the Creator's arrival with His earthly court: sea and river falling over themselves, so to speak, to make way for Him; mountains and hills no longer aloof and majestic but all animated and agog.

5, 6. The chaffing at all this flurry is another thrust, flaunting the Lord's ascendancy over His world. It has all the light-hearted gusto of Elijah's taunts at the impotent Baal, and it prepares with artistry for the sudden change of mood that will follow.

7, 8. *Tremble, O earth*—as well you may at such a meeting! 'From his presence' (as John would see, before the great white throne) 'earth and sky fled away, and no place was found for them.'[2]

But He is *the God of Jacob*, and His purpose is salvation. The psalm ends, like its predecessor, on the note of His quiet creativity and care: His power directed to the point of need, transforming what is least promising into a place of plenty and a source of joy.

---

[1] Ex. 19:6; 1 Pet. 2:9.
[2] Rev. 20:11. On the other hand, the verb for *tremble*, in our verse, polarizes between agony and delight; hence NEB has 'Dance, O earth'. This is quite possible; but the passages cited in the footnote at 96:9 seem to tip the balance towards 'tremble'.

Psalm 115

Not Unto Us!

In some ancient versions[1] this psalm is joined on to 114—to the detriment of both. The terse vivacity of 114 is all its own: the refrains and catchwords of 115 are a different form of writing. Here we sing of God's unchallengeable glory and the blessings He dispenses to the faithful, rather than of His ancient exploits at the Exodus.

The spirited exchange with the heathen suggests a time when Israel was (or had recently been) exposed to their taunts, perhaps in the Babylonian exile or just after. The mention of 'God-fearers', if they are implied to be a third group alongside Israelites and priests (9–11, 12f.), has led some commentators (*e.g.* Briggs) to date the psalm as late as the Greek period (*i.e.*, post-330 BC), since the term eventually became a standard name for Gentile sympathizers. But its history and its precise reference here are both too uncertain to build on. Further, Psalm 118, which uses the same three terms (118:2–4), is now generally considered to be pre-exilic.

115:1–8. The only God to praise

1. The fine opening verse has the atmosphere of a great deliverance, either present or to come, and has made a place for itself in history. Kirkpatrick quotes, for example, Holinshed's account of the singing of Psalms 114–115 after the battle of Agincourt, when the whole army was ordered to kneel at the words *Non nobis, Domine* . . . (Not to us, O Lord). On a very different occasion, William Wilberforce marked the passing of his bill to abolish the slave trade by meditating on this verse;[2] and many more examples could be given.

2. But the heathen taunt may imply quite another background to the psalm than one of victory. Unless this verse means 'What right have they *now* to say . . .' (*i.e.*, now that God has saved us), it would seem that Israel is at this moment in a sorry state. In that case verse 1 must be taken as a plea for help, though a confident one: that God will save His people,

---

[1] LXX, Theodotion, Jerome, Syr.; also some Heb. MSS.
[2] *Cf.* R. E. Prothero, *The Psalms in Human Life* (J. Murray, 1904), pp. 306f.

not for their sake but for His (*cf.* Ezk. 36:21f.). Verse 2 then has a fine defiance about it, a prelude to the withering retort to the enemy in 3–8.

3–7. The retort wins back the initiative. The pagan's pride in what he can see, and his contempt for what he cannot (which are modern attitudes as well as ancient), are flung back at him. A God too great to tie down to any image or even to earth itself, who is not the prisoner of circumstances but their master, is a God to glory in. And He is *our God*, not in the petty sense in which the heathen have *their idols*—all their own work!—but in the personal bond of 'steadfast love and . . . faithfulness' (*cf.* verse 1).

The caustic catalogue of 4–7, like the work-study on god-making in Isaiah 44:12ff., or on god-transport in Isaiah 46, needs no sermonizing to make its point: the facts are enough. It is one of the places where Scripture, like the child in the story of the Emperor's New Clothes, takes a cool stare at what the world does not care to admit. What the psalm does to the gods, Ecclesiastes will do supremely to man and his ambitions; indeed our next verse already has a hint of it.

8. This is a prediction or a prayer:[1] either 'Their makers will end up like them . . .' (JB, *cf.* RV, NEB), or 'may their makers end up like them . . .' (*cf.* TEV)—in either case, dead. This is truly 'their end', as Psalm 73:17 puts it, in contrast to that of the righteous, whose God is theirs 'for ever' (73:26). See also on verses 17f., and on the hope of seeing and sharing His likeness, in Psalm 17:15.

115:9–11. Help and shield

The refrain, which suggests the way the psalm was sung (cantor and congregation? group and group? *cf.* Ex. 15:1, 20f.; Is. 6:3), also suggests the way the verb *trust* should be taken. In the ancient versions it is a statement,[2] as in NEB: 'But Israel trusts in the Lord . . .', which matches the refrain with its repetition of *their* help and *their* shield. It also fits the

---

[1] For an 'is/are' statement (AV, RSV) the Heb. needs no verb, whereas here it uses the imperfect or jussive ('they will . . .' or 'may they . . .') of a verb whose predominant meaning is 'become'. Strangely enough, RSV translates the same words as an imprecation in 135:18.

[2] The consonants, which constituted the written text originally, can be pronounced either as an imperative (MT) or as a perfect in the 3rd person (LXX, Vulg., Syr.). The 3rd person plural of the refrain points strongly to the latter.

great affirmation of verse 3, and makes a resounding contrast to the misguided trust of 8b.

We have a glimpse of how the congregation saw itself, as made up of lay Israelites, priests (*the house of Aaron*) and God-fearers in general—the latter perhaps a term for both the former groups, but perhaps an acknowledgment of non-Israelite converts, who were an element in Israel from the beginning (*cf.* Gn. 15:2; Ex. 12:48f.; Ru. 1:16). But how soon this expression became virtually a technical term for Gentile sympathizers is not known; nor can we be sure how widely or narrowly it is used here.

115:12–15. Giver of blessing

Here are the same groups of worshippers as in 9–11, and now the thought moves forward from God's power to save (shown in the words *help* and *shield*, 9–11) to His power to enrich. The word *bless* or *blessed* is heard five times in this short section, and its introduction by the words *The Lord has been mindful of us* marks a turning-point from lean times to better things. Such transformations can be the fruit of repentance (*e.g.* Hg. 1:8–11; 2:19) or simply of God's time becoming ripe (*e.g.* Gn. 8:1; Ex. 2:24). But quite apart from these outstanding occasions, the insistent repetition of the word 'bless' drives home the point that all of us alike—every group (12, 13a), every type of person (13b) and every generation (14)—must have the smile and creative touch of God on us if we are to thrive (*cf.* 14 with 1 Cor. 3:6f.). The fullest treatment of this theme is given in Deuteronomy 28, first positively and then by way of warning.

115:16–18. The place and time for praise

The phrase from verse 15, '. . . who made heaven and earth', is now taken up and turned in our direction. All is His, but we are His substantial heirs and trustees. There is generosity in the phrase, 'the earth he has given'; there is responsibility as well, for we are not its makers, nor is it simply 'there' as meaningless matter to exploit. Behind the gift is the Giver, and the psalm's response is altogether positive: praise here and now, in the place and time He has allotted us; praise, moreover (we may take it), in the way we handle this heritage, not only in the way we sing about it.

So the alien realm of death and silence (17) is no business

of ours, only a fresh stimulus to give God the glory which the dead cannot offer. The psalm could have stopped there, content with the practical lesson of buying up the present, which is a valid and important one; *cf.* John 9:4. But in fact it looks ahead to endless praise (18); and while this may mean no more than an undying Israel to offer it, it may well be saying that we who serve the living God will ourselves live on, unlike the worshippers of lifeless objects (see on verse 8). If so, this stanza adds its witness to an after-life to such passages as 73:23ff. and others listed at 11:7; and it has every reason to end, like a number of its neighbours, with a Hallelujah.

Psalm 116

How can I repay Him?

There is an infectious delight and touching gratitude about this psalm, the personal tribute of a man whose prayer has found an overwhelming answer. He has come now to the temple to tell the whole assembly what has happened, and to offer God what he had vowed to Him in his extremity.

Such psalms as this, once written down, would help many another person to find words for his own public thanksgiving.[1] The question whether praises of this kind in the Psalter were all professional compositions for occasions that were likely to arise, or were in some cases at least the direct products of personal experience, is discussed in the Introduction, pp. 7ff., especially pp. 16–18. Perhaps no single answer covers every case, but if ever a psalm had the marks of spontaneity, this is surely such a one. Even where the author quotes another psalm, 'he gives it fresh force from the depths of his own recent experience' (Kirkpatrick).

The Septuagint and Vulgate treat this as two psalms, the second of them beginning at verse 10 (but some Heb. mss make a similar break after verse 11).

116:1-4. Remembered anguish

'I love! For Yahweh listens . . .'—so runs the first line in JB, with complete fidelity to the text. Whether or not the word

---

[1] An example of such a use in our own era is the inclusion of Ps. 116, almost in full, in the 1662 Prayer Book's form of thanksgiving after child birth.

Yahweh (*the Lord*) has changed places with 'for he listens' in the process of copying (which seems likely, as 'love' needs an object), certainly the present tense is right.[1] The singer is not only remembering a past occasion but is drawing a lasting assurance from it ('he hears my voice') and making a lifelong resolve[2] ('I will call . . .', 2). It is a resolve to trust God exclusively (*cf*. Rom. 10:12f.) and worship Him explicitly (*cf*. Gn. 4:26; 12:8).

3. This picture, which draws on the language of Psalm 18:4f., does not portray someone who must pick his way between many dangers (as RSV might imply) but one who is already caught and held ('Death's cords were tightening round me', JB). The rare word translated *pangs* has likewise the idea of constriction or, elsewhere, straits ('Sheol held me in its grip', NEB). In Old Testament poetry *death* and *Sheol* are aggressive,[3] clutching at the living to waste them with sickness or crush them with despondency; so the singer's plight may equally have been a desperate illness or (as verse 11 suggests) a wounding and disillusioning experience. Like Job's, it could well have been both together.

4. Against this onslaught the only refuge is *the name of the Lord*. These words are emphatic, and the verb, too, may indicate the urgency of the prayer: 'I kept on calling' (*cf*. Anderson). This was the turning-point, and the lesson of it was not forgotten: it becomes almost a refrain in 2b, 13b, 17b.

116:5-11. Remembered mercy

The outburst of praise, all unannounced, speaks for itself; it recaptures the delight of finding the prayer answered and the scene transformed. Romans 7:25 has something of the same sudden radiance.

6. *The simple* is a revealing description to use, for in the Old Testament it has no trace of merit. 'The silly' would hardly be too strong a term for these gullible, feckless people who roam the pages of Proverbs drifting into trouble. It is humble of the psalmist to identify with them; it is humble of God to

---

[1] Or else another continuous tense, future or past.

[2] 'Therefore . . . as long as I live' is lit. 'and in my days'. Some modern versions prefer to say 'whenever I call' (*cf*. JB, NEB, TEV); but this gratuitously omits the Heb. for 'and', and revocalizes the consonants of 'days', changing *b^eyāmay* to *bîmê*.

[3] See, further, on Ps. 6:5.

have time for them (if 'them' is the right pronoun for us to use).

7. NEB gives the first line a telling simplicity: 'Be at rest once more, my heart.' Just how *bountifully* God has dealt with the singer will emerge in the next verse.

8. In these phrases salvation is spread before us—here probably on the plane of earthly well-being, but in words that are true at the deepest level (*cf.*, *e.g.*, Rom. 8:10f.; 2 Cor. 6:10; Jude 24). The outer lines of the verse are borrowed from Psalm 56:13a, but the middle line, *my eyes from tears*, is new, adding its own personal note, a grateful counterpart to the remembered gloom of, *e.g.*, verse 11.

9. Prompted again by David's example (56:13b) the author lets the emotions fire the will, giving his delight a practical turn and lasting effect by this fresh resolve.[1] To *walk before the Lord*, like the New Testament expression to 'walk in the light', is both demanding and reassuring, since 'in the presence of the Lord', as TEV translates it, one is wholly exposed but wholly befriended.

10, 11. Most modern versions, apart from NEB,[2] support RSV's understanding of 10a: '*I kept my faith, even when I said . . .*'. Paul quotes the LXX form of the verse: 'I believed, and so I spoke' (2 Cor. 4:13), which is stronger than our Hebrew text. But the latter agrees in making faith the underlying attitude of the speaker, even though it is faith hard-pressed. And the impulse to speak out for God is soon apparent in the remaining verses. As James Denney remarks, 'The open confession of God, as a duty of faith, pervades the psalm from this point to the end.'[3]

So the author makes a point which his fellow psalmists often illustrate: that to feel crushed (10)[4] or disillusioned (11), and

---

[1] While the present tense (RSV, TEV) is a possible translation, the context favours the future, 'I will walk . . .', as in most of our versions. This agrees with the apparent thrust of 56:13, *i.e.*, (lit.) '. . . delivered . . . to walk before God'.

[2] NEB ('I was sure that I should be swept away') revocalizes *'ᵃdabbēr* ('I was saying') as *'eddabbēr*, the presumed hithpaʿel of a second root *dbr*, 'turn back', 'destroy'. *Cf.* L. H. Brockington, *The Hebrew Text of the Old Testament* (CUP, 1973), *ad loc*.

[3] *The Expositor's Bible: 2 Corinthians* (Hodder & Stoughton, 1903), p. 165, n. 3.

[4] This is the basic sense of the word translated *afflicted*; but JB, TEV exaggerate it with the adverb 'completely', which should rather be 'greatly' (RSV) or 'sorely' (Gelineau).

to say so, even in the wild tones of panic (NEB's word for *consternation*, 11; see on 31:22), is no proof that faith is dead; it may even vouch for its survival, as pain betokens life. Indeed, as pain cries out for healing, trouble frankly faced cries out for God. The two exclamations (10b, 11b) have this implied appeal, which we may recognize more easily from the mirror-image of them in H. F. Lyte's lines:

> 'When other helpers fail,[1] and comforts flee,[2]
> Help of the helpless, O abide with me.'[3]

116:12-19. Fervent gratitude

The psalm moves towards the climax of the thanksgiving: a sacrifice offered up to God and given back to men for a feast 'before the Lord' (Lv. 7:11ff.; Dt. 12:17f.).

12-14. The New Testament itself could hardly give a better glimpse than this of heaven's grace and man's response, all in the simplest, most direct of terms. The opening question and unexpected answer show up well in NEB: 'How can I repay the Lord . . . ? I will take in my hands the cup of salvation . .'. (This *cup* could refer to the drink-offering, as TEV conjectures; *cf.* Nu. 15:10. But as a cup *of salvation* it suggests God's gift to man, like that of Ps. 23:5, rather than man's to God.) As the opposite of the 'foaming cup' of wrath which we deserve (*cf.* 75:8), and as something freely offered, it displays the very pattern of the gospel. Man is the suppliant (*cf.* 13b with verses 1, 2) and the recipient, before he has anything to give His only gifts are debts of gratitude (14).

I will lift up (13) is a possibly misleading translation, since although the word is used for lifting up one's eyes, hands, head, *etc.*, it means carrying or picking up when it refers to things external to oneself. Hence NEB, freely, 'I will take in my hands'. (There are other verbs to express the idea of raising something aloft.)

15. *Precious* could mean either 'highly valued' or, in a less happy sense, 'costly'. NEB understands the former here ('A precious thing . . . is the death of those who die faithful to him'); but the singer's rescue from death (3, 8) makes the second meaning more likely. This is well expressed by JB:

[1] *Cf.* 11b.
[2] *Cf.* 10b.
[3] H. F. Lyte, 'Abide with me'.

'The death of the devout costs Yahweh dear' (*cf.* Mt. 10:29–31; and in ultimate terms, Jn. 10:28f.).

16. Here is the living sacrifice to which the ritual offerings were but pointers (*cf.* 40:6–8; 51:17), and here are the voluntary bonds (*thy servant, i.e.,* 'thy slave') which are stronger than the broken bonds of death.

17, 18. So the words of verses 13, 14 are repeated with, it seems, the significant difference that 'I will take' (13, see note) is now replaced by 'I will offer'.

19. We may note finally that the intensely personal faith and love which mark this psalm are not in competition with the public, formal and localized expressions of godliness. This flame is not withdrawn, to burn alone. Placed in the *midst*, it will kindle others, and blaze all the longer and better for it.

Psalm 117

All Nations

This tiny psalm is great in faith, and its reach is enormous. Its message was still too big for some of Paul's readers to have grasped: see Romans 15:7ff., a passage which is clinched by the quoting of this psalm among others.

In singing this, we too are challenged not to measure God's Kingship by His 'little flock', nor to accept the idea that different peoples have a right to different faiths. The very diversity of God's subjects comes out in the expressions *all nations . . . all tribes* (rather than 'all peoples': *cf.* the small units covered by this Hebrew word in Gn. 25:16; Nu. 25:15; its only other occurrences); and this variety reappears in the multitude of Revelation 7:9, 'from every nation, from all tribes and peoples and tongues'.

2. The cause for praise is that His steadfast love 'prevails' (*is great,* RSV). The latter is a vigorous, formidable word, used of the stronger side in battle ('prevailed', Ex. 17:11), or of the waters of the Flood which 'prevailed . . . mightily' (Gn. 7:18–20); or again of our transgressions (Ps. 65:3); but also of God's blessings (Gn. 49:26) and His pledged love (both here and in 103:11). What is more surprising, in this Gentile context, is that the matter for rejoicing is God's goodness toward '*us*', meaning in the first place Israel. Yet in reality it makes excellent sense, for in Abraham all nations were to find blessing, and are indeed finding it (*cf.* Gal. 3:8f.). It may also be that the 'us' of verse 2 has already found room for the 'you' implied in verse 1, by seeing Israelites and Gentiles as one people under God.

If His steadfast love is great, His *faithfulness* is eternal. Not that the two are set in contrast, for they are aspects of the same grace. But the emphasis of the second line can be summed up by saying that God's plans and promises are as fresh and intact now as on the day they were made; and they will remain so.

To revert, in conclusion, to the opening biddings to praise: such exhortations to the whole world have some value even as rhetoric, for they state God's rights over men. But the rhetoric will be largely empty unless the nations and tribes themselves hear it as a genuine and intelligible call. The summons therefore recoils on those who use it, with the obligation to make its invitation heard beyond their walls and their immediate circle.

The shortest psalm proves, in fact, to be one of the most potent and most seminal.

Psalm 118

Hosanna!

The stir of a great occasion lends its excitement to the psalm as it proceeds, and we become aware of a single worshipper at its centre, whose progress to the Temple to offer thanks celebrates no purely private deliverance like that of Psalm 116, but a victory and vindication worthy of a king. Many voices are heard: liturgical (1–4), personal (5–14), popular (15f.); and there are fragments of formal dialogue as the central figure and his procession approach the gates, demand admission (19), and are answered and acclaimed (20, 26), finally to end their pilgrimage at the altar (27).

As the final psalm of the 'Egyptian Hallel', sung to celebrate the Passover (see on Ps. 113), this psalm may have pictured to those who first sang it the rescue of Israel at the Exodus, and the eventual journey's end at Mount Zion. But it was destined to be fulfilled more perfectly, as the echoes of it on Palm Sunday and in the Passion Week make clear to every reader of the Gospels.

118:1–4. Timeless love

The voice of a great congregation can be heard behind the four identical responses to these biddings. The psalm will close with the words with which it opened (verses 1, 29), and other psalms confirm the familiarity of this call to worship (106:1; 136:1), and show the opportunity it gave to cantor and congregation to rehearse the great acts of God together (136:1–26). An authentic glimpse of such a scene is preserved in Jeremiah 33:11, where God promises to restore His people's fortunes, and 'there shall be heard again the voice of mirth and the voice of gladness, . . . the voices of those who sing, as they bring thank offerings to the house of the Lord:

"Give thanks to the Lord of hosts, for the Lord is good,
    for his steadfast love endures for ever!" '

On the word for *steadfast love*, see on 17:7; and on the three groups apparently addressed in verses 2–4, see on 115:9–11. Presumably the response would arise from these different quarters in turn, demonstrating afresh the breadth and variety of the company assembled before God.

118:5–9. Timely help

Now a single voice takes over from the rest; yet this is no ordinary individual. He will soon be speaking as a king (10ff.) and receiving a king's welcome (19–27). For the present, however, his testimony is that of any rescued man; the same word is used by him for *distress* (5) as by the sufferer in 116:3 for the pangs or grip of Sheol; and his defiant cry, *What can man do to me?* was David's in Psalm 56:11, as it is ours in Hebrews 13:6. The memorable motto of verses 8 and 9 is likewise a maxim for everyman, though perhaps especially for those who have access to the powerful (but see on 146:3).

118:10–14. The ring of foes

The true scale of operations now emerges with the words *all nations*. If the speaker includes his people with himself, we are reminded of the world's furious hostility to the city of God in,

413

e.g., Psalms 46 and 48, and of the final gathering of all the nations against Jerusalem in Zechariah 14:2. Many interpreters, however, find a reference here to a ritual humiliation of the king (see Introduction, pp. 10f.) and therefore see the mobbing of an individual rather than the siege of a city. Whether such a ritual existed or not, the events of history were to show that the world's enmity was in fact personal at heart, a straight rejection of 'the Lord and his anointed' (Ps. 2:2); but further, that the conspirators would include Israel itself (Acts 4:27).

The fourfold *surrounded* is menacing enough, and the similes of swarming *bees* and the crackle of *fire* bring out the unnerving closeness and fury of the attack. Our Lord was to experience such venom as this, and not only at His trial: *cf.* Luke 11:53f. But the Hebrew text looks beyond the 'blaze' of this *fire of thorns* to its extinction (see AV, RV, RSV mg., TEV); for such a fire burns out as suddenly as it flares up, and the power of evil will turn out to be as short-lived as it was fierce.

I cut them off (10–12) should probably be translated 'I will drive them back' (*cf.* NEB, *TRP*).

14. This verse is an exact quotation from the victory song at the Red Sea (Ex. 15:2a), and verses 15 and 28 will have further echoes of it. So the Exodus events stamp their likeness on God's acts of redemption throughout history (1 Cor. 10:6, 11, lit. 'as patterns'), consummated in the work of Christ (*cf.* Lk. 9:31: lit., 'his exodus which he was to accomplish at Jerusalem').

118:15–18. The songs of victory

From now on, other voices are heard with that of the king (if such he is). The battle was single-handed; the victory is shared. And that victory (or salvation—it is the same word) was fundamentally the Lord's, as surely as was the deliverance at the Red Sea. Another echo of the Song of Moses draws attention to this, in the reiterated praise of God's *right hand* (*cf.* Ex. 15:6, 12).

118:19–27. A victor's welcome

19, 20. The challenge at the gates. These two verses are a pair: a challenge and counter-challenge like those of Psalm 24. It is the glory of our faith that the King Himself entered *the gates of righteousness* wholly on His merits and perfected through suffering; and a crowning glory that He made this entry 'on our behalf' (Heb. 2:10; 9:24).

21–23. The chief cornerstone.[1] Here is the first hint that in the ring of foes (1off.) were the *builders* themselves, the men of power in Israel. Isaiah shows them rejecting God's corner-stone in his own day for their 'refuge of lies' (Is. 28:15f.), and the New Testament leaves no doubt that this stone fore-shadowed Christ (Mt. 21:42; Rom. 9:32f.; Eph. 2:20; 1 Pet. 2:6ff.). God's *marvellous* vindication of Him was by the resur-rection, as Peter implies in Acts 4:10f.

24–27. Hosanna! Benedictus! What Jesus unmistakably implied (Mt. 21:42, 45), the crowd had intuitively perceived when they greeted Him with words from this context—for verse 25 gave them their 'Hosanna' (*hôšî'ânnā*, 'Save, pray!'), and verse 26 their 'Benedictus' ('Blessed is he who comes . . .').[2]

The occasion which the psalm marked in Old Testament times was evidently a festival (*the day which the Lord has made* (24) could be a sabbath, but the word for *festal procession* (see Additional note on 27, below) points to its being one of the three annual pilgrim feasts, Passover, Pentecost and Taber-nacles), and we can glimpse two companies at this point: one already in the Temple court, greeting another which is arriving with the king. *Blessed be he who enters* is an individual welcome, but *We bless you* is addressed to the many who are with him.

What those who took part in such a ceremony could never have foreseen was that it would one day suddenly enact itself on the road to Jerusalem: unrehearsed, unliturgical and with explosive force. In that week when God's realities broke through His symbols and shadows (*cf.* Heb. 10:1), *the horns of the altar* became the arms of the cross, and the 'festival' itself (see Additional note, below, on *festal procession*) found fulfil-ment in 'Christ our passover' (1 Cor. 5:7, AV).

118:28, 29. Doxology

In verse 28 the single voice is heard again, and it completes (freely) the verse from the Song of Moses which was quoted in verse 14 (*cf.* Ex. 15:2). After it, the congregation's refrain (29)

---

[1] See Introduction, p. 23.

[2] Further, Jesus may have had the next words in mind (*The Lord . . . has given us light*, 27) in His subsequent warning, 'The light is with you for a little longer . . .' (Jn. 12:35f.).

rounds off the psalm as it had introduced it (1)—yet now, for us at least, with new insight into its meaning.

Additional note on verse 27

The festal procession translates a single word meaning 'festival' or 'pilgrim-feast' (*cf.* Ex. 23:14ff.). Here it seems to mean, by extension, some feature of the feast, either the worshippers (*cf.* most recent versions) or the sacrifice, as the parallelism of Exodus 23:18 suggests (*cf.* BDB, AV, RV, RP; also RSV at Mal. 2:3, 'your offerings'. Note also the expression 'Christ our passover', referred to above).

Branches is a rare meaning of a quite common word for 'cords' (*e.g.* Ps. 2:3; Jdg. 15:13; *etc.*); and since 'Bind the sacrifice with cords' makes immediate sense, it has *prima facie* priority over 'Bind the festal procession with branches'.[1] The only objection to it is that the victims were not, as far as we know, bound to the altar horns, although there were tethering rings let into the side of the altar at Herod's temple (*cf.* Delitzsch). But in view of the preposition *up to* (*i.e.*, 'as far as'), the word 'Bind' could be a pregnant expression for 'Bring . . . bound' (somewhat as in verse 5, where the Hebrew leaves the words 'and set me' to be understood. *Cf.* G–K 119 *gg* for further examples). In all, the sense 'Bring the sacrifice, bound, to the horns of the altar' involves the fewest difficulties.

Psalm 119

'The Rich and Precious Jewel' of the Word

This giant among the Psalms shows the full flowering of that 'delight . . . in the law of the Lord' which is described in Psalm 1, and gives its personal witness to the many-sided qualities of Scripture praised in Psalm 19:7ff.

---

[1] In defence of the latter, it has been argued that 'bind' may mean 'begin' or 'join' (see discussion in Anderson, *ad loc.*); but we only know of such senses in the expression 'join battle'. Of more weight is the fact that in Jewish custom (*cf.* Lv. 23:40) willow branches were heaped round the altar at the Feast of Tabernacles, and a procession walked round it reciting verse 25 of our psalm (*Mishnah*, Suk. 4:5)—though it is not known when these rituals were introduced. Also LXX and other ancient versions understood the text in a similar sense to RSV's rendering.

It is an acrostic psalm,[1] an alphabet of prayers and re-flections on the Word of God, giving each Hebrew letter its turn to introduce eight successive verses on the subject. While different thoughts tend to predominate in different stanzas, partly from the stimulus of the alphabetic scheme,[2] they are mingled with others that constantly recur. The mood is meditative; the poet's preoccupations and circumstances come to light in prayers and exclamations, not marshalled in sequence but dispersed throughout the psalm.

So our comments will mainly bring together certain themes, rather than follow the psalm through consecutively. Where the latter is done, in section v, the notes on the successive stanzas will deal mostly with supplementary points of detail.

I. THE MANY-SIDED REVELATION

Like a ring of eight bells, eight synonyms for Scripture dominate the psalm, and the twenty-two stanzas will ring the changes on them. They will do it freely, not with a bell-ringer's elaborate formulae, and they will introduce an occasional extra term. But the synonyms belong together, and we should probably not look for each to show its distinct character at each occurrence, but rather to contribute, by its frequent arrival, to our total understanding of what Scripture is.

Taking them in the order of their first entries we meet the following regular expressions:

a. 'Law' (*tôrâ*)

This is the chief term of all, and is heard most often. Its parent verb means 'teach' (verse 33) or 'direct'; therefore coming from God it means both 'law' and 'revelation'. It can be used of a single command or of a whole body of law, especially the

---

[1] The alphabetic acrostics in the Psalter are Pss. 9–10, 25, 34, 37, 111, 112, 119, 145. Proverbs 31:10–31 is another; also each of the first four chapters of Lamentations, of which ch. 3 is the most elaborate. R. A. Knox's translation of the Old Testament uses twenty-two letters of our alphabet to reproduce this pattern wherever it occurs.

[2] The clearest examples of this stimulus are stanzas 5 and 6 (*hē* and *wāw*), where the former letter lends itself to causative imperatives, and the latter to sequences, each of verses 41–48 being joined to its predecessor by the Heb. for 'and'.

Pentateuch, or again of Scripture as a whole.[1] It reminds us that revelation is not simply for interest but for obedience. *Cf.* James 1:25.

b. 'Testimonies' ('*ēḏôt*)

Israel was told to place the book of the law beside the ark of the covenant, 'that it may be there for a witness ('*ēḏ*) against you' (Dt. 31:26). The outspokenness of Scripture, with its high standards and frank warnings (*e.g.* Dt. 8:19, using this root), is implied in this expression, but so too is its dependability, as the word of the 'faithful and true witness'. Therefore 'thy testimonies are my delight' (24).[2]

c. 'Precepts' (*piqqūḏîm*)

This is a word drawn from the sphere of an officer or overseer, a man who is responsible to look closely into a situation and take action (*cf.* Je. 23:2, where God will 'attend to '(*pōqēḏ*) the shepherds who have not 'attended to' the flock). So the word points to the particular instructions of the Lord, as of one who cares about detail.

d. 'Statutes' (*ḥuqqîm*)

These speak of the binding force and permanence of Scripture, as of laws 'engraved' or inscribed, 'for the time to come as a witness for ever' (*cf.* Is. 30:8).

e. 'Commandments' (*miṣwôt*)

This word emphasizes the straight authority of what is said; not merely the power to convince or persuade, but the right to give orders.

f. 'Ordinances' (*mišpāṭîm*)

These are better known in the Old Testament as 'judgments': the decisions of the all-wise Judge about common human situations (*cf.* Ex. 21:1; Dt. 17:8a, 9b), and hence the revealed

[1] *Cf.* Jn. 15:25; 1 Cor. 14:21, quoting the Psalms and the Prophets as 'Law'.

[2] In the expression 'the ark of' or 'the two tables of the testimony', where the word is '*ēḏūṭ* (Ex. 32:15, *etc.*), 'testimony' is almost synonymous with 'covenant' (*cf.*, *e.g.*, Dt. 9:15). But '*ēḏūṭ* and '*ēḏôt* may not be as closely related as they seem: *cf.* the comment on Ex. 25:16 in the Tyndale Commentary on *Exodus* by R. A. Cole (IVP, 1973); also W. F. Albright, *From the Stone Age to Christianity* (Doubleday, [2]1957), p. 16.

'rights and duties' appropriate to them (as RSV puts it in
1 Sa. 10:25). Scripture, then, as the standard given for fair
dealing between man and man, is a predominant sense of this
term.

g. 'Word' (*dāḇār*)
This is the most general term of all, embracing God's truth in
any form, stated, promised or commanded.

h. 'Promise' or 'Word' ('*imrâ*)
This is very similar to the previous term, and is translated
'word' in AV, RV throughout the psalm. While JB, NEB keep to
'promise' throughout, RSV has 'promise' thirteen times, but
allows it a more general sense (mostly 'word') six times
(verses 11, 67, 103, 158, 162, 172). This probably strikes the
right balance between the general and the particular in this
word, which is derived from the verb 'to say'.

As well as these eight expressions, others too can speak of
God's self-revelation. Verses 3 and 37 have 'thy *ways*', un-
accompanied by any of the above; verse 132 has 'thy *name*';
and perhaps in verse 90 'thy *faithfulness*' refers primarily to the
immutability of what God decrees. Only verses 84, 121 and
122 are without any such expression.[1]
This untiring emphasis has led some to accuse the psalmist
of worshipping the Word rather than the Lord; but it has been
well remarked that every reference here to Scripture, without
exception, relates it explicitly to its Author; indeed every
verse from 4 to the end is a prayer or affirmation addressed to
Him. This is true piety: a love of God not desiccated by study
but refreshed, informed and nourished by it.

II. SOME QUALITIES ASCRIBED TO SCRIPTURE

If the formal titles of Scripture, discussed above, bring their
own implications with them, other facets come to light in the
psalmist's own words as he prays and reflects, so that these
formidable terms unbend and speak to us as potential friends.

---

[1] Verses 84 and 121 contain the word 'judgment' (see on '*Ordinances*',
above), but not as a synonym for Scripture. In verse 91, 'appointment' can
be translated 'ordinances'.

a. A persistent theme is the *delight* these sayings bring. The first references to this, in verses 14 and 16, set the tone of much that will follow, by the words they use for delight[1] and by the comparison of Scripture with the riches it outshines (*cf.* the 'thousands of gold and silver pieces' in verse 72; see also verses 111, 127, 162). This is not merely a scholar's pleasure (though it has this aspect, 97) but a disciple's, whose joy is in obedience: '*in the way* of thy testimonies' (14; *cf.* verse 1 which sets the whole course of the psalm).

b. Deeper than delight is *love*; and Scripture evokes this abundantly.[2] Here verse 132 goes to the heart of the matter in the expression, 'who love thy name'. It is on God's account that we love the writings that reveal Him. The psalmist's longing (20, 40), which he pictures now as pleasurable appetite ('thy words . . ., sweeter than honey', 103), now as gasping urgency ('with open mouth I pant', 131), is for God Himself, as the context shows.[3] *Cf.* the seeking of 'him' in verse 2, the emphatic 'Thou' in verse 4; above all, verse 57: 'You are all I want, Lord' (as TEV paraphrases it).

c. But if Scripture is attractive and gracious, these qualities are combined with strength. As the voice of God, it is *awesome*, a fact conveyed not only by the strong word for 'stands in awe' in 161 but by the startling metaphor of something that makes one's hair stand on end (120; *cf.* NEB: 'the dread of thee makes my flesh creep'. It is the word used of Eliphaz's ghostly vision in Jb. 4:15). Strength of a more reassuring kind is expressed in the fact that the word of God is *righteous* (7, 75, 123, 138, 144, 172), *dependable* (43, 142; note the 'all' in 86, 151, and 'the sum' in 160), and as *unshakable* as heaven and earth (89–91, 152; but our Lord went further, making the 'for ever' absolute for Scripture, relative for heaven and earth: Mt. 24:35). It is also *inexhaustible*, with 'wondrous things' to explore (18, 27, 129) and a breadth which nothing else can approach (96).

[1] 'Delight', in verses 14, 162 (and its noun in 111), is a festive, exultant word, while the parallel word in verse 16 (*cf.* 47, 70, and the nouns in verses 24, 77, 92, 143, 174) has a quieter, more relaxed and homely ring.
[2] See the declarations of verses 47, 48, 97, 113, 119, 127, 132, 140, 159, 163, 165, 167.
[3] Note the emphatic *thou* immediately before 103, and the prayer, 'Turn to me . . .' which follows 131.

III. THE BENEFITS OF SCRIPTURE

a. Liberation

The paradox that where God is master, 'service is perfect freedom', is found not only in verse 96, noted just above (a *commandment*—note the word—which is broader than anything on earth) but equally in verse 45, where 'liberty' is found in God's precepts, not in release from them. Two elements of this freedom are, first, the breaking of sin's 'dominion' as one's steps are steadied by the Word (133), and secondly the mind-stretching encounter with a greater wisdom and vision than one's own. 'At liberty' (45) means 'at large': it is like the 'broad place' that David found in Psalm 18:19 (20, Heb.); but in verse 32 it recalls the 'largeness of mind' which Solomon was given.[1] Moffatt's paraphrase of the verse captures both aspects of this breadth: 'I will obey thee eagerly, as thou dost open up my life'.

b. Light

Two memorable verses speak directly of this. In verse 105 there is a typically practical touch in the mention of 'my feet' and 'my path': it is light to walk by (*cf.* 128), not to bask in. But verse 130 brings out its educative power in creating a discerning mind—for it is little help to have sight without insight. The plea, 'Give me understanding' (or 'insight'), appreciates this; it keeps occurring (34, 73, 125, 144, 169). To this practised eye, what is false (104) loses its appeal. The point is made in other terms in the prayer of verse 66 for good judgment (lit. 'taste', *i.e.*, discrimination; *cf.* 103) and in the testimony of verses 98–100 to a God-taught wisdom that is on a higher plane than man's.

c. Life

This is the theme of many prayers, especially towards the end, where they come thick and fast (five times between 144 and 159). Sometimes the link between Scripture and the gift of life consists of a promise which the singer claims (25, 50, 107, 154); sometimes it is that the very keeping of God's laws is restorative (37) and life-giving (93; *cf.* Ps. 19:7), since they turn one's eyes and steps towards Him. Sometimes, conversely, the psalmist asks for life to enable him to keep these precepts

[1] 1 Kings 4:29 (5:9, Heb.).

(88, and perhaps 40). The various phrases in RSV—'revive me' (25), 'give me life' (37, 40, *etc.*), 'spare my life' (88), 'preserve my life' (149, 159)—reflect the nuances of the context, on the whole; but the Hebrew is the same for all, simply 'cause me to live' (*cf.* AV, RV, 'quicken me'), which acknowledges the direct dependence of vitality on God. This singer is no legalist, content with a round of duties: he will press for nothing short of God's vitalizing touch. Otherwise his religion, he knows, will be dead: see, further, on verse 17.

d. Stability

This is well seen in the threatening situation of verse 23, where Scripture fills and occupies a potentially distracted mind. This is not escapism but attention to the best advice ('thy testimonies are my counsellors', 24) and to the main issue, which is the will and promises of God, more real and more relevant than the plots of men. Verses 49, 50 show the psalmist doing this: basing 'hope' and 'comfort' on a dependable 'word' and 'promise'. Among other examples see verses 76, 89–92, 95, 114–118; above all, the serene testimony of 165: 'Great peace have those who love thy law; nothing can make them stumble'.

IV. THE PSALMIST'S LIFE AND TIMES

a. An alien world

While God, as always, had His loyalists, and the psalmist some kindred spirits (63, 74), the prevailing temper seems to have been a religious scepticism ('they have made void thy law', 126, AV) ranging from the non-committal, the 'men who are half and half' (113, Moffatt), to the thoroughly profane, 'the wicked' who 'lie in wait to destroy me' (95).

The attacks on the psalmist are taking the form of derision (22), slander (described, by a curiously modern touch, as smearing him, 69) and intrigue (23, 85). The fact that the authorities persecute him by devious means suggests that the regime is not openly apostate; but such verses as 87 and 109 show how murderous such pressure can be. And he is young, it seems (the 'young man' of verse 9 is himself, to judge from the context; see also 99f.), and sensitive to scorn ('the reproach which I dread', 39); his isolation makes him low-spirited: 'small and despised' (141), drained of vitality and dried up (25, 28, 83). Like Jeremiah, another thin-skinned personality, he is alternately saddened and infuriated by what he sees, reacting now with tears (136), now with 'hot indignation' and 'disgust' (53, 158).

b. The struggle to survive
All this, however, tightens rather than weakens his grip on God's word. Like Paul and Silas, although their fetters were more literal than his, he rises at midnight to praise God, 'though the cords of the wicked ensnare me' (61f.; cf. 54, 147f., 164); and at many points in the psalm it is impressive to compare the dejection of one line of a couplet with the firmness of the answering line (e.g. in each of verses 81–83). It is also striking to note his humility, for he knows his temptations to worldliness (36f.) and inconstancy, and has exposed his deeds to God (26), conscious that while in principle he does not stray from God's precepts (110), in practice he has 'gone astray like a lost sheep' and needs to be sought and found (176). He is even grateful for the affliction which was needed to bring him to heel (67, 71, 75). As for the rest of his sufferings, they are well outweighed by the 'great spoil' (162) he has found in God's word (see sections II and III, above). So he is eager to witness to it, longing to commend it to high and low (42f., 46) and to his fellow believers (79).

c. The urge to press on
In all, there shines out the quiet steadfastness ('continually, for ever and ever', 44) of one who has chosen to live by God's decisions, refusing false paths, accepting persecution, fighting depression. And for all this doggedness, he is an enthusiast: not plodding but running (32), and, as his two favourite prayers show, still eager to learn ('give me understanding') and to be renewed and kindled ('give me life') by God's creative power.

V. THE TWENTY-TWO STANZAS

These notes supplement the comments in sections I–IV on the main themes of the psalm. The word in italics on the right of each heading is the Hebrew letter which begins each of the eight verses of the stanza.

119:1–8. The undivided heart   *Aleph*
On the terms, *law, testimonies, etc.*, see section I, above.

   1. *Blameless* (Heb. *tāmîn*). See comment on Psalm 18: 30 (p. 95).

2. Note here what is implicit throughout the psalm, that Scripture is revered for being *his* (or 'thy') sayings, and God's servants thereby seek *him*, not the book for its own sake.

3. *Wrong* has the sense of 'wronging' someone, not of faults in general. Better, 'nothing unfair'.

4. *Thou* is emphatic; *cf.* note on verse 2.

119:9–16. Stored treasure   *Beth*
9. From the heartfelt prayers of the surrounding verses it would seem that the *young man* is the psalmist himself in the first place (see IV. *a*, above). He is praying rather than preaching.

11. On this term for *word*, see I.*h*, above (not I.*g*). Proverbs 2:10–12 and Colossians 3:16 show that the mind which stores up Scripture has its taste and judgment educated by God.

16. On *delight*, see II.*a*, above.

119:17–24. Solace in loneliness   *Gimel*
17. *That I may live* is the first of many such prayers (*cf.* III.*c*, above). While some of them could refer simply to surviving an illness or an attack, others are clearly qualitative, speaking of life that is worthy of the name, or in our terms, spiritual life, found in fellowship with God: *e.g.* verses 37, 50, 93, 144, and probably others. It is a familiar Old Testament concept (*cf.*, *e.g.*, Pss. 16:11; 36:9; Dt. 8:3).

18. To feel the force of this request, *cf.* the sight that met the opened eyes of Balaam (Nu. 22:31) or of Elisha's servant (2 Ki. 6:17, using another word). The metaphor here and in the Balaam story is of removing a veil or covering (*cf.* 2 Cor. 3:14–18).

23, 24. See section III.*d*, above.

119:25–32. Revive me!   *Daleth*
25. See on verse 17, and section III.*c*, above.

28. See IV.*a*.

29. *Graciously teach* is a single word, 'be gracious', into which is packed the thought of granting knowledge of this law, and perhaps too 'the grace of living by' it (NEB). It is a happy reminder that God's law is a good gift (*cf.* III.*a*), and is only the antithesis of grace when it is used to try to earn salvation.

30–32. The three opening verbs, of choosing, cleaving and running, make a fine summary of godliness: *cf.*, *e.g.*, Hebrews

11:25; Acts 11:23 (AV); Philippians 3:12–14. On *thou enlargest my understanding*, see the end of section III.*a*.

119:33–40. Teach me!   *Hē*

33. *To the end* is one sense of a word which also means 'consequence' or 'reward', as in Psalm 19:11 (12, Heb.). Hence NEB here has 'I shall find my reward'; and in verse 112 'they are a reward that never fails'. Either sense is possible, and as each has its counterparts elsewhere in the psalm (*e.g.* 44 for constancy, 72 for enrichment) it remains an open question.

38. The strict sense of the second line is 'which is for the fear of thee': a statement about the practical purpose of God's word.

119:41–48. Words for others   *Wāw*

The prayer of Acts 4:29, 'to speak thy word with all boldness', is not only anticipated here (42f., 46) but put in context; for the word spoken is first of all the word appropriated (41), trusted (42b, 43b), obeyed (44), sought (45) and loved (47f.).

48. *I revere* is literally 'I lift my hands to', which is usually a term for praying; here, a bold expression of yearning for God's revelation in Scripture.

119:49–56. Steadying words   *Zayin*

This stanza helps to fill out the picture sketched in section IV.*a*, above.

56. The simplest translation is that of RV: 'This I have had, because[1] I kept thy precepts'—'this' being the cheer and comfort so tellingly described in 54f. Although obedience does not earn these blessings, it turns us round to receive them.

119:57–64. With all my heart   *Ḥeth*

57. On the theme of this verse, and TEV's attractive paraphrase of it, see section II.*b*, above.

60. *Delay* is the word used of Lot as he 'lingered', reluctant to leave Sodom.

61–63. Kindred verses to these are noted in section IV.*a, b,* above.

---

[1] This conjunction can also mean 'when' or 'that'. In the latter case (*cf.* RSV, NEB, TEV), the point will be that obedience is its own reward; *cf.* Ps. 19:11.

64. This makes a good companion to other glimpses of the world as God's handiwork and kingdom: *e.g.* 24:1; 33:5; 104:24; Isaiah 6:3; Habakkuk 2:14; 3:3.

119:65–72. Hard lessons learnt   *Teth*

66. *Judgment*, here, is literally 'taste', not in our sense of artistic judgment, but of spiritual discrimination: 'for the ear tests words as the palate tastes food' (Jb. 34:3). *Cf.* Hebrews 5:14.

67, 71. On the psalmist's gratitude for bitter medicine *cf.* verse 75, and see section IV.*b*, above. But TEV is misleading with its substitution of 'punished' for 'afflicted' in all these verses.

119:73–80. 'They glorified God in me'   *Yod*

73. *Fashioned* is not the potter's word of, *e.g.*, 33:15; 139:16, but one with an emphasis on giving a thing its firm constitution (*cf.* 'established', or 'constituted', in verse 90 or in Ps. 8:3 (4, Heb.); but also Jb. 10:8). Hence NEB, 'made me what I am'; and *cf.* JB, TEV.

75. See verses 67, 71.

78. *Subverted*: *i.e.*, twisted the truth about me (*cf.* La. 3:36).

119:81–88. The brink of ruin   *Kaph*

81. *Languishes* has the idea of coming to the end; *cf.* TEV, 'I am worn out, Lord, waiting . . .'. It is the same verb, but intransitive, as that of 87a.

88. *Spare my life* is too restricted a translation. Better, 'give me life' (*cf.* 93, 107, *etc.*), which is a prayer for more than bare survival: see III.*c*, above.

119:89–96. The great certainties   *Lamed*

A striking feature of these verses is the coupling of God's creative, world-sustaining word with His law for man. Both are the product of the same ordering mind; and not only men but 'all things' are His 'servants' (91). The word for *appointment* (91) is the familiar word 'judgments' or 'ordinances' by which, in a human context, He declares His will for our obedience.

96. This verse could well be a summary of Ecclesiastes, where every earthly enterprise has its day and comes to nothing, and where only in God and His commandments do we get beyond these frustrating limits. On the liberating breadth of this commandment (contrary to our fears of it) see III.*a*, above.

119:97–104. Heavenly wisdom   *Mem*

The New Testament illuminates verses 98–100 by its successive demonstrations that heavenly wisdom begins as a gift 'to babes', hidden from the worldly-wise. This emerges clearly in the ministry of Christ (Lk. 10:21), decisively at the crucifixion (1 Cor. 2:8), and consistently after that in the reactions of the knowledgeable to the gospel (1 Cor. 1:18ff.). On the themes of these verses see also Acts 6:10; 1 John 2:27; but Hebrews 5:11–14; 1 Corinthians 14:20.

102. The word *thou* is emphatic. Here is the guarantor of biblical truth, and the One who alone opens the disciple's eyes to see it.

103, 104. Attraction to the true and revulsion against the false are, for us, acquired tastes. Verse 104 describes the process; 101 reveals the earnest co-operation it requires of us.

119:105–112. Not losing the way   *Nun*

105, 106. Together, these verses show what kind of *light* and *path* are in mind, and verse 104 makes it doubly clear. This is not convenient guidance for one's career, but truth for moral choices: see, for instance, the kind of 'snare' and 'straying' that are implied in 110. The classic example of light from Scripture, well used in a place of many snares, is our Lord's temptation.

112. On the expression, *to the end*, see on verse 33.

119:113–120. No renegade   *Samech*

113. *Double-minded* is akin to the word in Elijah's taunt at those who hobbled 'first on one leg then on the other' (1 Ki. 18:21, JB). Moffatt puts it well here (as noted in section IV.*a*, above): 'the men who are half and half'.

120. On the very strong expression for *my flesh trembles*, see II.*c*, above.

119:121–128. Pressure from the godless   *'Ayin*

122. *Cf.* Job 17:3.

126. For another cry of *It is time* . . . (but addressed to man), see Hosea 10:12.

127, 128. At first sight the *therefore* of verse 127 may seem out of place, and it is emended by some.[1] But it is the logic of loyalty, to be the more devoted the more the pressure grows.

119:129–136. 'The light shines in the darkness'   *Pe*

130. For *the unfolding*, AV has 'the entrance', based on the very similar word for 'door'. 'Unfolding', or literally 'opening', is right, as in the Emmaus story: 'Did not our hearts burn within us . . ., while he opened to us the scriptures?' (Lk. 24:32; *cf.* Acts 17:3.)

131. This uses a different word for *open* from that of verse 130. It expresses the eagerness of a hungry or thirsty animal (*e.g.* Jb. 29:23).

133. 'By (or, in) thy word' is the meaning of the Hebrew, which makes very good sense. But *b*ᵉ ('by' or 'in') and *k*ᵉ ('according to') are easily confused, and some early evidence favours the latter, which is followed, perhaps unnecessarily, by most modern versions.

136. See the account of the psalmist and his contemporaries, in section IV.*a*, above.

119:137–144. Everlasting righteousness   *Tsade*

On the self-portrait glimpsed in verses 139 and 141, see again section IV.*a*.

142. A companion to this verse, though an inexact one, is Psalm 145:13, '. . . an everlasting kingdom'; to which could be added Jeremiah 31:3 (2, Heb.), '. . . an everlasting love'.

119:145–152. Hope deferred   *Qōph*

150, 151. Note the realism of the double statement, *They draw near . . . but thou art near*. The threat is not glossed over; it is put in perspective by a bigger fact.

119:153–160. Precious life   *Resh*

There is a mounting urgency, if repetition is any sign of it, in the plea for *life*, heard three times in this stanza in an identical exclamation (a single word in Hebrew) to end verses 154, 156, 159. On the meaning of it, see section III.*c*, above.

160. *The sum* is literally 'the head'; hence AV, 'from the beginning'. Coupled with 'from', this word can indeed mean the beginning (*e.g.* Is. 40:21; Pr. 8:23); but here it only says

---

[1] For the MT *'al-kēn* ('therefore'), one suggestion is *'al-kōl* ('above all'); another is to omit *'al*, leaving *kēn* by itself ('truly', NEB; 'yes', JB).

'the head of thy word'. In this kind of phrase it means, as in RSV, *the sum* (*cf.*, *e.g.*, 139:17); and its use as an equivalent to 'a census' in Exodus 30:12; Numbers 1:2, *etc.*, shows that 'the sum of' is not a way of saying 'by and large', but rather, 'every part of'.

119:161–168. The place of peace *Shin*

The picture of the psalmist that emerges here is filled out in the rest of the psalm; see section IV, above.

168. Note the reverence for God Himself, not for Scripture in isolation; *cf.* the remarks at the end of section I, above, and note the personal piety in the final stanza.

119:169–176. Teach me, help me, seek me *Taw*

171, 172. In the two expressions, *pour forth* and *sing*, there may be a hint of, respectively, the spontaneously personal and the corporate: the former word suggesting the bubbling up of a spring, and the latter (lit. 'my tongue will answer') the antiphonal praise of a choir (*cf.* the same word 'answer' for 'sing' in 147:7; and, using other terms, the calling of the seraphim one to another in Is. 6:3).

176. The note of urgent need on which the psalm ends (*lost* could be translated 'perishing') is proof enough that the love of Scripture, which has motivated the scribes of every age, need not harden into academic pride. This man would have taken his stance not with the self-congratulating Pharisee of the parable, but with the publican who stood afar off, but went home justified.

Psalm 120

The Outsider

This is the first of the fifteen Songs of Ascents (Pss. 120–134), a group whose name is briefly discussed in the Introduction, p. 43). They were evidently songs used by the pilgrims on their way up to the Temple at Jerusalem for the feasts. Not every psalm in the group was necessarily composed for this purpose. The present psalm, for example, seems sharply personal,[1]

[1] See, however, Additional note on verse 5.

although in a pilgrim context it voices very well the home-sickness of those who have settled among strangers and enemies. It appropriately begins the series in a distant land, so that we join the pilgrims as they set out on a journey which, in broad outline, will bring us to Jerusalem in Psalm 122, and, in the last psalms of the group, to the ark, the priests and the Temple servants who minister, by turns, day and night at the House of the Lord.

120:1-4. Deadly arrows

1, 2. The *distress*, or 'straits' into which human words can drive a man, contrasts cruelly with the liberty, or 'breadth', which Psalm 119 found in the words of God (*e.g.* 119:45, 96).

Instead of answering back, this man has looked in a better direction and received a more resounding answer, as he now recalls.[1]

3, 4. In short, the answer is that the liar, wounding though his weapons are, will be destroyed with far more potent shafts than lies: God's *arrows* of truth[2] and *coals*[3] of judgment.

120:5-7. Drawn swords

Now the singer's special situation as an alien comes to light, and with it the motivation of these slanders, which is simply the resentment of one way of life against its opposite. This little passage is a classic comment on the 'unequal yoke', the in-compatibility of light and darkness which no amount of goodwill, short of capitulation or conversion, can resolve. The New Testament counsels the Christian in this context against two opposite errors: on the one hand, compromise (2 Cor. 6:14ff.; 1 Jn. 2:15ff.), and on the other, animosity (Rom. 12:14-21).

Additional note on verse 5

Meshech and *Kedar* are so far apart (steppe-dwellers of the far north, Ezk. 39:1f., and Arab neighbours of Israel to the south-east) that they can only be coupled here as a general term for

---

[1] The most natural translation of verse 1 points to a past event, '. . . I cried . . . and he answered me', as in most versions. Verse 2 then recalls his prayer, and verses 3f. declare its outcome.

[2] *Cf.* Ps. 64:3f., 7f., where God's arrows turn the slanderers' verbal arrows against them.

[3] The roots of the *broom tree* apparently burn well and yield notable charcoal. On *coals* as a symbol of judgment *cf.*, *e.g.*, Ps. 140:10 (11, Heb.).

the heathen. If the 'I' of the psalm is Israel personified, these two names will summarize the Gentile world, far and near, in which Israel is dispersed. Otherwise, unless the text is emended,[1] they must be taken as the psalmist's figurative names for the alien company he is in: as foreign as the remotest peoples, and as implacable as his Arab kinsmen (*cf.* Gn. 16:12; 25:13).

Psalm 121

'I lift up my eyes'

The word 'keep', or 'keeper', comes often in this psalm. Protection is a burning issue for a pilgrim who is travelling arduously and through lonely country.

1. *The hills* are enigmatic: does the opening line show an impulse to take refuge in them, like the urge that came to David in Psalm 11:1, to 'flee like a bird to the mountains'? Or are the hills themselves a menace, the haunt of robbers?

2. Either way, he knows something better. The thought of this verse leaps beyond the hills to the universe; beyond the universe to its Maker. Here is living help: primary, personal, wise, immeasurable.

3, 4. The rest of the psalm leads into an ever expanding circle of promise, all in terms of 'he' and 'you' (the 'you' is singular). Another voice seems to answer the first speaker at this point in the pilgrims' singing, and yet another in verse 4; or else the whole song is an individual utterance, and the dialogue internal, as in, *e.g.*, Psalm 42:5.

In verse 3 the word for *not* is the one used normally for requests and commands. So this verse should be taken, not as a statement which verse 4 will virtually repeat, but as a wish or prayer (*cf.* TEV[2]), to be answered by the ringing confidence of 4 and of all that follows. *I.e.*, 'May he not let your foot be

---

[1] Two suggested emendations are: (a) to read Massa (Gn. 25:14) instead of Meshech, a difference of one Heb. consonant; (b) to see Meshech as an accidental abbreviation of *mōš⁼ḵê qešeṭ*, 'those that stretch the bow': *cf.* the reputation of Ishmael and his descendants through Kedar, Gn. 21:20; Is. 21:17. Both LXX and Vulg. read this verb 'stretch' instead of the name Meshech, which has the same consonants.

[2] But TEV alters the 'you', *etc.*, to 'me'.

moved, may he . . . not slumber!'—followed by the answer, 'Look, he who keeps Israel neither slumbers nor sleeps.'

5, 6. Now Israel's privilege is made sure to the single Israelite: a protection as individual as he himself. It starts where he is now, out on his journey, looking at the hills. The Lord is closer than they (5c), and His protection as refreshing as it is complete. It avails against the known and the unknown; perils of day and night; the most overpowering of forces and the most insidious.[1]

7, 8. The promise moves on from the pilgrim's immediate preoccupations to cover the whole of existence. In the light of other scriptures, to be kept *from all evil* does not imply a cushioned life, but a well-armed one. *Cf.* Psalm 23:4, which expects the dark valley but can face it. The two halves of verse 7 can be compared with Luke 21:18f., where God's minutest care ('not a hair of your head will perish') and His servants' deepest fulfilment ('you will win true life', NEB) are promised in the same breath as the prospect of hounding and martyrdom (Lk. 21:16f.). *Your life*, in the present passage (7), is as many-sided a word as in Luke; it means the whole living person. Our Lord enriched the concept of keeping or losing this by His teaching on self-giving and self-love (*e.g.* Jn. 12:24f.).

The psalm ends with a pledge which could hardly be stronger or more sweeping. *Your going out and your coming in* is not only a way of saying 'everything' (*cf.* the footnote to verse 6): in closer detail it draws attention to one's ventures and enterprises (*cf.* Ps. 126:6), and to the home which remains one's base; again, to pilgrimage and return; perhaps even (by another association of this pair of verbs) to the dawn and sunset of one's days. But the last line takes good care of this journey; and it would be hard to decide which half of it is the more encouraging: the fact that it starts 'from *now*', or that it runs on, not to the end of time but without end; like God Himself who is (*cf.* Ps. 73:26) 'my portion for ever'.

---

[1] The two lines of verse 6 are not only poetic parallels (*cf.* Introduction, pp. 2ff.) but use a favourite Heb. way of expressing totality: naming a pair of opposites to include everything between (*cf.* 8a). On the effects of *the moon* on certain people, little is understood; but some kinds of mental disturbance vary with its phases. Not all popular belief on the subject is unfounded.

Psalm 122

Beloved City

122:1, 2. Joy of arrival

At last Jerusalem and the House of the Lord come into sight, and we have arrived. The delight of verse 2 is captured by Gelineau: 'And now our feet are standing within your gates, O Jerusalem.' The trials of an expatriate (120) and the hazards of travel (121) are eclipsed now by the joy which had first drawn the pilgrim on his journey. There is a miniature of this gladness in any meeting for true worship (expressed particularly in the 'Song for the Sabbath', Ps. 92); but here the sight of the Lord's House is the climax of a longer and stiffer pilgrimage than a 'sabbath day's journey'. The Christian's equivalent to this progress and arrival is finely expressed in the doxology of Jude 24, offered to 'him who is able to keep you from falling' (*cf.* Ps. 121) 'and to present you without blemish before the presence of his glory with rejoicing' (*cf.* Ps. 122).

122:3-5. Bonds of unity

Nothing (except, at times, the church) could be further from this picture of 'a city that is at unity in itself' (PBV) than the Jerusalem which our Lord described: 'killing the prophets and stoning those who are sent to you' (Lk. 13:34). The expression '*bound firmly together*' uses (as Anderson points out) the same verb as is found in the instructions for making the tent of worship: 'couple the tent together that it may be one whole' (Ex. 26:11). Such was the blueprint; such will be the ultimate reality (Rev. 21:10ff.).

4. The unity was never meant to be uniform; Israel was a family of *tribes*, each with its well-marked character (*cf.* Gn. 49; Dt. 33). But the ties were more than those of blood or convenience: these were the tribes *of the Lord*, and Jerusalem was where they were to meet Him, not simply one another. King Jeroboam, with his breakaway kingdom, feared this rallying-point (1 Ki. 12:26ff.), forgetting that what was *decreed for Israel* (Dt. 12:13f.) could never be at odds with what was conditionally promised to him by the same God (*cf.* 1 Ki. 11:38).

Note that the object of these pilgrim feasts was *to give thanks*, not primarily to seek unity or prosperity. These were gifts over and above the occasion, not its *raison d'être*; whereas pagan worship was all too blatantly a means to securing what one wanted: *cf*. Hosea 2:5.

5. *Judgment* may seem an anticlimax among the glories of Jerusalem, but it means justice, which is a ruler's first duty and best gift: *cf*. Isaiah 2:4; 42:3f. See also on Psalm 72:1-4.

122:6-9. Vision of peace

The sound and sense of the name *Jerusalem*, whose final syllables suggest the word *peace* (*cf*. Heb. 7:2), set the tone of these verses, in which *šālôm* (peace) and *šalwâ* (security, prosperity[1]) make their pleasant influence felt. They are the proper fruits of justice, the subject of verse 5.

The inverted commas enclosing verses 6b, 7 in most modern versions rightly treat these words as the intercession that was called for in 6a. It is more than a prayer against external foes, although its mention of *walls* and *towers* takes due note of them (*cf*. Ps. 48:12ff.): it asks above all for concord: peace 'within . . . within . . . within . . .'.

Our Lord's lament for the Jerusalem of His day throws new light on such a prayer. To the authorities of the time, 'the things that make for peace' had looked at first sight divisive and dangerous (Jn. 11:48), and had eventually become unthinkable (Lk. 19:41ff.). In playing for safety Jerusalem had achieved disaster.

8, 9. What Jerusalem was to the Israelite, the church is to the Christian. Here are his closest ties, his *brethren and companions*, known and unknown, drawn with him to the one centre as fellow-pilgrims.

> 'Before Thy throne we daily meet
>   As joint-petitioners to Thee;
> In spirit we each other greet,
>   And shall again each other see.'[2]

And whatever the limitations of its citizens, Jerusalem was where God saw fit to build His House. The simple response to this, *I will seek your good*, was the least that such a fact demanded; and it had no upper limit. For the Christian it has, besides,

---

[1] *Prosper* (6) is the verb from which *security* (7) is derived. The root idea is of prosperous tranquillity.

[2] R. Baxter, 'He wants not friends that hath Thy love'.

no territorial boundary. For the inspiring implications of this, see Hebrews 12:22-24; for its immediate application, Hebrews 13:1-3.

Psalm 123

Our Longing Eyes

Like the Psalter itself, these pilgrim songs preserve many moods, reflecting something of the turbulent history of Zion, a history which continues in the story of the church. This cry from the heart can still speak for our contemporaries under persecution, and give us words to pray in unison with them.

1. If the traveller in Psalm 121 had to learn to look higher than the hills, this sufferer, even more hemmed in, has won the same victory. His words, soaring above his circumstances, set his troubles in a context large enough to contain them. God, *enthroned in the heavens*, 'does whatever he pleases' (115:3), and His faithful love and wisdom are equally beyond our calculating (36:5; Is. 55:9). The Lord's Prayer opens with an upward look like this; the psalm may correct the perfunctory glance to which familiarity often reduces it.

2. There was immense length of focus in verse 1; now the gaze is fixed intently on a single point near at hand, with the trained watchfulness of the servant who is ready for the smallest gesture. The comparison must not be pressed: these servants are watching for relief, not for orders; yet servants they are, still loyal and submissive. They have refused to ease the strain of waiting for God by renouncing Him, or to buy off 'the contempt of the proud' (4) by joining them. The hymn which links this psalm with our Lord's injunction to be servants watchful for His return is true to its spirit:

> 'Mark the first signal of His hand,
> And ready all appear.'[1]

3, 4. It is illuminating that *contempt* is singled out for mention. Other things can bruise, but this is cold steel. It goes deeper into the spirit than any other form of rejection; in the Sermon on the Mount it ranks as more murderous than anger

[1] P. Doddridge, 'Ye servants of the Lord'.

(Mt. 5:22). It is particularly wounding when it is casual or unconscious; but if it is deserved and irreversible it is one of the pains of hell (Dn. 12:2); *cf.* the quotation from C. S. Lewis in the comment on Ps. 14:4–6.[1]

Yet as part of the Christian's lot, in his capacity as Christian, its sting is drawn. It can be an honour (Acts 5:41), and it is something Christ Himself accepted and made redemptive.

Among the many repetitions which reinforce the urgency of the psalm is the expression '*had . . . enough*', or '*sated*' (the same Heb. verb). The psalm breaks off unanswered; but from the same kind of situation another sufferer replies, resolutely accepting this word (RSV 'filled'), in Lamentations 3:30f., 33:

> 'Let him give his cheek to the smiter,
>   and be *filled* with insults.
> For the Lord will not
>   cast off for ever . . .
> for he does not willingly afflict
>   or grieve the sons of men.'

Psalm 124

'When earthly armour faileth'

As a psalm of David, this gives us a rare insight into the early peril of his kingdom, particularly from the Philistines, who had thought to see the last of Israel when they shattered the kingdom of Saul. 2 Samuel 5:17ff. shows how serious the threat was, and how little confidence David placed in his own power to survive it. This was no mere raid to gain territory: it was meant to put an end to David and the hope of Israel.

1, 2. We overhear the cantor declaiming his opening line, then bringing the congregation in to thunder it out again in verse 2 (*cf.* JB, '—let Israel repeat it—'; see, likewise, 129:1).

3. The rest of the psalm, apart from the final verse, consists simply of three or four vivid figures to bring home to us the total disaster that had loomed so near. The first is of some monster large enough to need only one gulp at its prey (*alive* is, of course, the meaning of 'quick' in the familiar AV, PBV).

---

[1] See the top of p. 80, above.

4, 5. The raging torrent may be doubly apt, since in fact it was God who broke through the Philistines 'like a bursting flood' on what seems to have been this very occasion (2 Sa. 5:20; *cf.* the introductory comments, above). For another instance of such a picture of an all-conquering army see Isaiah 8:7f.

6. This is not quite the same figure as that of verse 3. In these jaws we feel the slower agonies of defeat, like the tearing and grinding of the prey.

7. Most vividly of all, the last metaphor presents the ordeal as one that had been already far advanced, with the enemy's grip a present fact, his army already in a dominating position (*cf.* 2 Sa. 5:18). It makes the psalm, incidentally, all the more accessible to the Christian as a vehicle of his own praise—that of a captive released, whose own struggles would merely have entangled him the more. But primarily the praise is corporate, blessing God for the survival of His people (in whom we may now see not only Israel but the church) under the most formidable attacks and most pitiless bondage.

8. David's example, in looking to the Maker, not to things made, seems to have inspired a later pilgrim (121:2); but the mention of *the name* may be an echo of his own Psalm 20:7, where this invisible aid is shown to be more real and more potent than the most advanced equipment of the day. It is the lesson of the whole psalm.

Psalm 125

Guardian of the Right

The hills and the holy city, much in view and much in mind to the pilgrims, make their presence felt again; and once more the thoughts they arouse are searching and fundamental, piercing to the realities behind these impressive sights.

1. Carnal religion will fasten on what seems sacrosanct, and will shelter behind Mount Zion from even God Himself (see the 'den of robbers' sermon in Je. 7). True religion starts at the centre, *the Lord* in whom all things—Mount Zion included—hold together. The phrase, *Those who trust in the Lord*, shows one of the several facets of our relationship named in the Old

Testament, along with the mention of those who 'fear', 'love' and 'know' Him; a personal bond too intimate to be a passing liaison. Its own logic makes it *for ever*.

2. As Zion prompted thoughts of its living counterpart the church, so the encircling hills draw the mind beyond themselves to God. But Psalm 121:1 shows that the mind is tempted to stop far short of this.

3. Now emerges the bleak situation in which these bold words have been spoken: one in which evil has apparently the upper hand and the righteous are wavering. This may or may not point to foreign domination: the heathen have no monopoly of sin. The conviction that this state of affairs cannot last is not based on the view that evil will be shamed into quitting, as 3a by itself might suggest. On the contrary, evil is always glad of something to corrupt; and 3b takes this seriously. *Cf.* the saying in Matthew 24:12 on wickedness and the cooling of love. It must be God who shortens its reign, and we are assured that He will.

4, 5. Assurance blossoms into prayer; verse 5, as well as 4, should be taken in that sense: *i.e.*, '. . . may the Lord lead away . . .'. The *crooked ways* bring back a reminder of Judges 5:6, when travellers had to take to devious routes; but these men are devious by choice. It is their way, no doubt, of pursuing peace, as they see it.

By contrast, the final words of the psalm have arrived at *peace*, not by compromise but by the only road that leads to it: the way of righteousness.

Psalm 126

'It was like a dream!'

Delirious happiness and relief—such is the mood recaptured in the first half of the song. But now it is only a memory, and the psalm turns into prayer for a comparable transformation of a barren and cheerless scene. What kind of deliverance God had given and would yet give, is the question raised in the comment on verses 1-3.

126:1–3. Joy re-lived

The old translations, and some of the new (*e.g.* JB, TEV), take this psalm to be about captivity and release. But the key phrases in verses 1 and 4 can embrace much more than this, and indeed verses 4–6 give a picture of toil crowned at last with blessing, rather than of the bare mercy of homecoming. So RSV (*cf.* NEB) is wise to use the general terms of restored fortunes[1] in both verses. Job's restoration is described in the same way (Jb. 42:10). Whether Zion's was from famine or siege, captivity or plague, it had been obviously miraculous and widely talked about.[2] It remained a vivid national memory (*cf.* the lively paraphrase in TEV: 'it was like a dream! How we laughed, how we sang for joy . . . how happy we were'), as inspiring as the outbreaks of revival in the Christian church.

Verse 3 is still looking back to it, as the Hebrew suggests and as verse 4 demands. RSV should run, 'The Lord did great things for us; we were overjoyed.'

126:4–6. Joy re-claimed

Memory, so far from slipping into nostalgia, now gives the impetus to hope. Verse 1 could have been echoed as a sigh; instead, it sets the tone and scope of confident intercession.

The two images of renewal (4b, 5–6) are not only striking: they are complementary. The first of them is all suddenness, a sheer gift from heaven; the second is slow and arduous, with man allotted a crucial part to play in it.

Sudden bounty has its perfect illustration here, since few places are more arid that *the Negeb*,[3] and few transformations more dramatic than that of a dry gully into a torrent. Such can

---

[1] See the comment and footnote on Ps. 14:7. The existing text of 126:1 possibly gives slight further support to RSV, in that *šîḇaṯ* can hardly mean captivity. But it is generally accepted to be a scribal error for *šᵉḇûṯ/šᵉḇîṯ* as in verse 4 and elsewhere.

[2] This tells against the view that the psalm is a product of the cultus, a liturgical thanksgiving and prayer for harvest and the seasonal rains. Even if 'dream' (1) is replaced by the prosaic alternative, 'are healthy' (*cf.* NEB and the occurrences of this second root in Jb. 39:4 Is. 38:16), there remains the surprise of the nations (2), which would seem a little excessive if it related to the due sequence of the seasons.

[3] This name, meaning 'dry' or 'parched', is given to the southernmost part of Judah, extending down towards the Sinai peninsula. In AV, RV it is called 'the South'.

be the effect of a downpour, which can also turn the surrounding desert into a place of grass and flowers overnight.[1]

Matching this is the other picture of revival, in terms of farming at its most heart-breaking; all its joys hard-won (*cf.* 2 Cor. 9:6) and long-awaited (Gal. 6:7–10; Jas. 5:7f.). But whatever the uncertainties of literal farming, the psalmist is as sure of this harvest—God's blessing of seed sown,[2] and His visiting of His people—as are the apostles. The modern translations tend to omit the extra words of emphasis in the final verse, which are partly preserved in AV, PBV. Both the going forth and the coming home are stressed by a doubling of the verb, and might be translated, 'He that surely goes forth weeping . . . will surely come home with shouts of joy.'

So the psalm, speaking first to its own times, speaks still. Miracles of the past it bids us treat as measures of the future; dry places as potential rivers; hard toil and good seed as the certain prelude to harvest.

Psalm 127

In Vain?

One of the most telling features of this short poem is that it singles out three of our most universal preoccupations—building, security, raising a family—and makes us ask what they all amount to, and to whom we owe them. The psalm is ascribed to *Solomon*, and has perhaps a concealed signature in the expression *his beloved* (2), which is the word from which Jedidiah, his personal name from God, was formed (2 Sa. 12:25). Yet, like much of Solomon's wisdom, the lessons of this psalm, relevant as they were to his situation, were mostly lost on him. His building, both literal and figurative, became reckless (1 Ki. 9:10ff., 19), his kingdom a ruin (1 Ki. 11:11ff.) and his marriages a disastrous denial of God (1 Ki. 11:1ff.).

The two parts of the psalm are so well marked that some

---

[1] See, *e.g.*, N. Glueck, *Rivers in the Desert* (Norton, New York, ²1968), pp. 92f.

[2] AV's beautiful expression, 'precious seed', cannot be sustained. For NEB's 'bag of seed' see K-B. The most likely meaning, in view of Am. 9:13, is 'a trail of seed' (lit. 'a drawing-out of seed'); hence RSV, *seed for sowing*.

have thought them to be separate poems. But both parts proclaim that only what is from God is truly strong; and further, the two senses of the word 'house' (a dwelling or a family) make a well-known word-play in the Old Testament,[1] all the more ready to hand for the similarity of the Hebrew words *bōnîm*, 'builders' (1), and *bānîm*, 'sons' (3).

127:1, 2. Fruitless efforts?

The two human activities of verse 1 are samples of a great area of life: its enterprises and its conflicts, the work of creating and of conserving. For each of them this verse sees only two possibilities: either it will be the Lord's doing or it will be pointless; there is no third option.

In vain is not the same word as the 'vanity' which dominates Ecclesiastes to take the relish out of worldly success; but it is no less sweeping. Verse 2 underlines the fact that to work still harder is no answer to it: it can be a fresh enslavement.[2] It is not simply that our projects will fail—there is at least 'bread' to show for them—but that they lead nowhere. In terms of verse 1, the house and city may survive, but were they worth building?

For he gives to his beloved sleep: from this point on, the psalm presents the alternative (already hinted at in the phrase 'Unless the Lord . . .') to our elaborate failures. (On the translation of this line, see the Additional note on p. 442.)

127:3-5. Living assets

God's gifts are as unpretentious as they are miraculous. The two halves of the psalm are neatly illustrated by the first and last paragraphs of Genesis 11, where man builds for glory and security, to achieve only a fiasco, whereas God quietly gives to the obscure Terah a son whose blessings have proliferated ever since.

The picture in these verses is not to the scale of the Genesis events, but the values are similar. Nothing is said of monetary wealth or of position: an upstanding family is wealth enough and honour enough.

---

[1] *Cf.* especially 2 Sa. 7:5, 11ff.

[2] *Anxious toil* is a Heb. word which, with a synonym from the same root, was prominent in the sentence of 'pain' and 'toil' on Adam and Eve (Gn. 3:16f.).

And it is not untypical of God's gifts that first they are liabilities, or at least responsibilities, before they become obvious assets. The greater their promise, the more likely that these sons will be a handful before they are a quiverful.

Additional note on verse 2[1]

The last half-line of verse 2 contains two problems for the translator. First, the word 'for '($k\hat{\imath}$), which makes good sense, is not the only reading: the standard text has $k\bar{e}n$, which AV, RV translate as 'so'; but it can also mean 'truly', which again makes good sense.[2]

The second crux is the word translated *sleep*. This could signify the blessing God gives (*cf.* RSV), or (taken adverbially) the time or way in which He gives it (*cf.* Weiser, in the footnote just referred to). But while a contrast between fruitless toil and effortless enrichment is attractive, the opening verses are in fact contrasting two attitudes to God (dependence and independence) rather than two attitudes to work or, still less, the rival merits of toil and sleep. So this line must be implying much that it leaves unsaid if it is to arrive at a contrast between the fruitless strain of self-effort and the relaxed but not slothful fruitfulness of the godly.

While this looseness of expression would be far from unique, it would be fairly considerable; therefore other meanings have been sought for the word translated 'sleep'. Among various suggestions surveyed in J. A. Emerton's article referred to above, we may note 'prosperity' (Dahood) and 'high estate' or 'honour' (Emerton), each of which can claim some linguistic support and would ease the difficulty of this enigmatic line.

To me, however, it seems probable that the psalmist did speak of *sleep*, content merely to sketch the contrast to the picture of frantic activity, in the simplest and most graceful terms, whatever logical objections a minute scrutiny might uncover. Is there a parallel to this *seemingly* escapist outlook, in the incident of the sleeping Christ in the storm?

---

[1] This note is much indebted to J. A. Emerton, 'The meaning of *šēnā*' in Psalm CXXVII 2', *VT* 24 (1974), pp. 15–31.

[2] Taken as a noun, it can mean 'what is right'; hence Weiser renders the line, 'for he gives to his own in sleep what is proper'. This seems possible rather than probable.

Psalm 128

Peace

The quiet blessings of an ordered life are traced from the centre outwards in this psalm, as the eye travels from the godly man to his family and finally to Israel. Here is simple piety with its proper fruit of stability and peace.

128:1, 2. A man before God

The ingredients of true happiness (for the psalm should open with the word 'Happy', the same word as in 2b) are not far to seek. Here they are summed up as reverence (the right relationship to God, 1a) and obedience (the habits learnt from Him, 1b). Hard work (2a) is taken for granted, but this psalm makes it as clear as Psalm 127 that enjoyment of its fruits is a gift from God (*cf.* Is. 62:8f.).

If these promises seem modest, and the programme of verse 1 unadventurous, they can be compared with their high-sounding alternatives: '*You shall be happy*' with 'ye shall be as gods' (Gn. 3:5, AV); and walking '*in his ways*' with 'every one to his own way' (Is. 53:6). Psalm 14 shows what comes of these ambitions.

128:3, 4. The family circle

The *vine* was a symbol not only of fruitfulness (here explicitly so) but of sexual charm (Ct. 7:8ff.) and of festivity (Jdg. 9:13). The strong word for *within* (*cf.* NEB, 'in the heart of your house'), which refers to the wife directly, not to the vine, is in marked contrast to what is said of the promiscuous wife in Proverbs 7:11, as Keet points out: 'She is loud and wayward, her feet do not stay at home.' In the psalm the attractiveness of this wife is wholly matched by her faithfulness.

The *children ... around your table* are the hope and promise of the future. The simile of *olive shoots* is no more photographic than are the 'arrows' of 127:4. In the two psalms these two aspects or stages of youth, as tender growth to be nurtured and as the embodiment of fiery zeal, make a complementary pair. *Cf.*, further, 144:12.

128:5, 6. The wider horizon

If piety can be too individualistic, and a family too selfcontained, the final strophe takes care of both these dangers. *Zion*, where the faithful gather, is where 'you' (singular) can expect to find blessing (*cf.* Heb. 12:22ff.); and your family's future is bound up in Zion's welfare and that of *Israel*.

There is perhaps a New Testament echo of the last exclamation, *Peace be upon Israel!* in Galatians 6:16. It is no empty phrase there: it sums up the urgent concern of Paul that God's people should not put up barriers against each other, but show themselves true citizens of 'the Jerusalem above' (Gal. 4:26), our common metropolis. It is still a prayer to echo.

Psalm 129

Persecuted Zion

Whereas most nations tend to look back on what they have achieved, Israel reflects here on what she has survived. It could be a disheartening exercise, for Zion still has its ill-wishers. But the singers take courage from the past, facing God with gratitude and their enemies with defiance.

129:1–4. The scarred survivor

We hear the cantor in verse 1 (as in 124:1) declaiming the words which the rest of the company will take up. The mention of Israel's *youth* leads the mind back to the Exodus, the event which two of the three pilgrim feasts commemorated. 'When Israel was a youth,[1] I loved him, and out of Egypt I called my son' (Ho. 11:1). This was the best starting-point for reflections on suffering, as the cross and resurrection are for the Christian. Many of the later ordeals of Israel, unlike the Egyptian bondage, were punishments; but God's character as *righteous* (4; *cf.* on 23:3b) and as rescuer (4b) shines through them all.

The two-stage metaphor showing Israel as a scourged man, and the weals on his back as *furrows* of a ploughed field (3), could hardly be stronger or more horribly apt. The survival

---

[1] RSV has 'child', but the word in Ho. 11:1 is basically the same as in the psalm.

of this people, so hated but so resilient, bore silent witness to their Preserver (as, one may feel, it has continued to do). Such involuntary evidence is strong, as far as it goes. But the Servant Songs visualize this witness lifted to a higher plane altogether: that of a willingly accepted suffering, first as the cost of speaking out for God (which is the context of the words, 'I gave my back to the smiters', Is. 50:6), and finally as vicarious sacrifice—a task beyond the capacity of Israel itself ('with his stripes we are healed', Is. 53:5). The New Testament, while showing its fulfilment in Christ (and in Him alone, as to its atoning aspect), calls the church to follow in His steps, and shows the apostles rejoicing to do so.

On verse 4, see the end of the first paragraph on verses 1-4.

129:5-8. The price of hatred

If *Zion* were no more than a capital city, this imprecation on its enemies would be mere petulance and bluster. But in the Psalter Zion is 'the city of our God' (48:1), 'the mount . . . for his abode' (68:16) and the destined mother-city of the world (87). In the Psalm just referred to, the Gentile converts say to her, 'All my springs are in you' (87:7). It is only appropriate, speaking in those terms, that those who reject her should wither (6f.); leaving metaphors aside, they are not only choosing the way of hate, which is soul-destroying, but setting themselves against God, which is suicide.

The simile of fading grass (6f.) is not reserved for enemies alone, but applied to man in general in 90:5f.; Isaiah 40:6-8, over against the Word of God, whose eternity we can share (1 Pet. 1:23ff.; 1 Jn. 2:17). Here the contrast between these futile wisps and the sheaves of corn which the reapers bring in, calls to mind the cheerful exchange of *blessing* (8) which we overhear in another harvest scene (Ru. 2:4). For what is ephemeral and finally irrelevant there is only silence.

Psalm 130

'Out of the depths'

The opening words of this psalm make a fitting title to it, since they suit the progress as well as the starting-point of the prayer. There is a steady climb towards assurance, and at the end there is encouragement for the many from the experience of the one.

This is traditionally the sixth of the seven 'penitential psalms', which are listed in the first comment on Psalm 6.

1, 2. *The depths* are eloquent enough in themselves as a figure of near despair, but Psalm 69:1f., 14f. fills out such a picture with the victim's sense of floundering and terror. What is clear in all such passages is that self-help is no answer to the depths of distress, however useful it may be in the shallows of self-pity.

3, 4. Now the nature of the trouble comes out, as something different from the depression of illness, homesickness or persecution seen in some other psalms (*e.g.* Pss. 6, 42, 69). Here it is guilt. The confession of verse 3 throws light on the professions of righteousness found elsewhere in the Psalter, for it implies that such claims could never be absolute (see on Ps. 5:4–6); but it also reveals how slight, on the whole, was the assurance of atonement at this stage. A Christian could have looked to the fullness of the ransom rather than the mildness of the reckoning. By the end of the psalm, the writer is doing just this, in relation to Israel; but the basis of redemption (Rom. 3:25) is still unrevealed to him.

For all that, the *fact* of forgiveness (4) is not in doubt. Paul, had he wished, could have added this verse to Psalm 32:1 in his proof that the Old Testament already knew about un-merited pardon (Rom. 4:7). But verse 4 is notable, too, for its second line, *that thou mayest be feared,*[1] which may sound a strange outcome of forgiveness. In reality it confirms the true sense of the 'fear of the Lord' in the Old Testament, dispelling any doubt that it means reverence and implies relationship. Servile fear would have been diminished, not increased, by forgiveness.

5, 6. The above understanding of 'fear' is clinched by these verses. It is the Lord Himself, not simply escape from punish-ment, that the writer longs for. Notice that this is more than wistfulness or optimism. In plain terms, he speaks of a promise (*his word*) to cling to, and in picturing the *watchmen* he chooses

---

[1] Symmachus and Theodotion took the consonants of this verb (*twr'*) to be those of *tôrâ* (law), spelt with a different final letter (*twr'* for *twrh*). LXX has 'on account of thy name'. These variants seem, however, to be ways of escaping the paradox of 'feared'.

as his simile a hope that will not fail. Night may seem endless, but morning is certain and its time determined.

7, 8. Nothing could be further from the shut-in gloom and uncertainty of 'the depths' than this. The singer is now liberated from himself to turn to his people and to hold out hopes that are far from tentative. Coverdale's beautiful expression, *plenteous redemption*, adopted by AV, RV, has been happily retained in RSV; it shines very brightly against the darkness of the psalm's beginning. But the less spectacular final verse, confirming it and spelling it out, is perhaps even more heartening. It is already a far cry from the 'trembling hope' of verses 3f. There is no arguing with the bold inclusiveness (answering the rueful inclusiveness of 3) of the last words: *from all his iniquities.* 'Where sin abounded, grace did much more abound.'

Psalm 131

The Childlike Spirit

The name of David at the head of this psalm exposes his character to comparison with the profession he makes. This has its ironies in the light of his middle and later years, but it also wakens memories of his early modesty, simplicity and lack of rancour, among the qualities which helped to make him great. The demure little psalm anticipates the object lesson of Matthew 18:1–4, where Jesus called a child to Him in answer to the question, 'Who is the greatest in the kingdom of heaven?'

1. It would be easy to make this verse an excuse to avoid the challenges of life. But the sin rejected in 1a is pride (*cf.* the little portrait of the supercilious in Pr. 30:13), while the sin of 1b is presumption. By the first of these, one undervalues other people (unless they seem worth cultivating); by the second, one overestimates and overreaches oneself, forgetting, *e.g.*, Deuteronomy 29:29. In Philippians 2 we are shown the constructive answer to the first of these temptations, in the honour of being a servant; and in Philippians 3, 1 Corinthians 2, the answer to the second, not by stifling adventurousness but by rightly directing it.

2. The point of this verse is blunted by RSV, which pictures a baby pacified at its mother's breast; whereas the psalm emphasizes the word 'weaned', thereby drawing an analogy between the child which no longer frets for what it used to find indispensable, and the soul which has learnt a comparable lesson. The RV translates it most faithfully: 'Like a weaned child with[1] his mother, My soul is with me like a weaned child.' It is freedom (in the light of verse 1) from the nagging of self-seeking, and, as verse 3 would add, from the bondage of delusive frets and fears. In terms of the New Testament again, it embodies the lessons of both Philippians 2:3ff. ('Do nothing from selfishness or conceit') and 4:11ff. ('I have learned . . . to be content').

3. The last verse rouses us from contemplating David to following his example and that of his greater Son: not through introspection but through being weaned from insubstantial ambitions to the only solid fare that can be ours. 'My food is to do the will of him who sent me, and to accomplish his work' (Jn. 4:34).

Psalm 132

The Ark Ascends to Zion

When the ark covered the short distance from Kiriath-jearim to the newly captured Jerusalem, it was the climax of a journey of centuries, begun at far-off Sinai. At least two other psalms bring this event vividly to mind: Psalm 24, awestruck at the holiness of the King of glory, and Psalm 68, exultant at the great march of God and at His choice of little Zion as His royal seat. In the present psalm another strand of the pattern comes into view: the place of David in this enterprise. The first half reveals his sworn resolve to see the matter through, and re-lives the great occasion; the second half matches it with God's resolve and oath to stand by David's dynasty and by His own choosing of Zion.

Verse 10, in which a new 'anointed one' looks back to David, makes the psalm subsequent to David's time. But 2 Chronicles 6:41f., quoting verses 8–10, shows that it existed

---

[1] More literally 'upon', in both lines. The child is pictured in its mother's arms, but not intent on being fed.

early enough in the reign of Solomon to be ready for the dedication of his Temple, when the ark completed the journey to which David had committed it.

132:1–5. David's oath to God

This is a unique glimpse of David's motive in bringing the ark to Jerusalem (2 Sa. 6; 1 Ch. 13–16). Without it we might have mistaken the operation (as some have done) for a political stroke: a crowning touch to his prestige and that of his new capital. Instead, he is shown to be zealous for God's honour, conscious of his people's heritage (*the Mighty One of Jacob* is a title last heard on Jacob's lips as he prophesied the destinies of the twelve tribes, Gn. 49:24), and pledged (2) to see this matter through at all costs (1) and with all speed (3–5).

The *hardships*, here, are unlikely to mean the youthful trials of David; rather, the heart-searchings[1] which he brought to his task; perhaps also his shock and distress at the death of Uzzah (2 Sa. 6:6ff.). His dancing before the Lord may have owed some of its exuberance to his relief at finding himself accepted again.

3, 4. *My house* and *my bed* are literally 'the tent of my house' and 'the couch of my bed'—the extra words being probably no more than poetic embellishments. Likewise the refusal of *sleep* is a common figure of speech (*cf.* Pr. 6:4), not necessarily to be taken literally. In the event, the enterprise was to hang fire for three months.

132:6–10. The procession to Zion

Scattered allusions (the ark is merely 'it') and snatches of song create an impression of the excited cavalcade which set out to bring the ark to Zion, and these could well be the phrases used for a ritual re-enaction of the scene. The search for the ark in verse 6, as for something almost totally forgotten, brings out the fact that, as David put it, 'we neglected it in the days of Saul' (1 Ch. 13:3). The ark had stayed in the obscurity of Kiriath-jearim (1 Sa. 7:1f.),[2] which is the place alluded to in

---

[1] The phrase, *the hardships he endured*, is lit. 'his being afflicted', which is close to the Heb. for 'whoever is not afflicted . . .' in the directions for observing the Day of Atonement (Lv. 23:29).

[2] In 2 Sa. 6:2 this is called Baale-Judah, which 1 Ch. 13:6 shows to be an alternative name for 'Kiriath-jearim which belongs to Judah'. There it is spelt Baalah.

the names Ephrathah and Jaar (6)[1]—the latter (meaning 'wood' or 'thicket') drawing pointed attention to this incongruously rustic abode: *cf.* PBV, '. . . and found it in the wood'.

7. So, after the ritual search, the worshippers set their faces to Jerusalem, summoned with a call like the biddings of 99:5, 9, and 122:1; words which put all shallowness and apathy in worship to shame.

8. *Arise, O Lord*, was the invocation 'whenever the ark set out' in the days of Moses (Nu. 10:35); another echo of it introduces the great processional Psalm 68. In the wilderness the ark had led the people, stage by stage, 'to seek out a resting place for them' (Nu. 10:33), but now the pilgrimage is almost over, as verse 14 will emphasize. In Psalm 23 there is a similar progress, in the individual's experience, by daily 'waters of rest' (or of resting places) to the settled home at the end.

9. David's first encounter with the ark had begun in carelessness and ended in tragedy (1 Ch. 13:11f.). Such is the dismal background to the ideal sequence here, which begins with righteousness and ends with joy—reminiscent of David's second attempt, which started with the bidding, 'sanctify yourselves' (1 Ch. 15:12), and ended in festivity. Our verse, which captures this, has been adapted in the Anglican Prayer Book as a Christian petition for ministers and people. There is an answering assurance in verse 16. Compare Isaiah 61:10 for the promise of 'garments of salvation' and 'the robe of righteousness'.

10. From this verse we gather that the reigning king (*thy anointed one*) is singing the psalm in procession. He seeks admission on David's account rather than his own, to the city which is God's rather than his. Like the Christian, he can come boldly: *cf.* what God granted 'for David's sake' in, *e.g.*,

---

[1] *Jaar* is the singular of *jearim*; the name Kiriath-jearim means 'city of woodlands'. *Ephrathah* is usually a term for Bethlehem or its environs, and has been explained here by some expositors to mean that the search (or the summons to it) started at Bethlehem, but finished at Kiriath-jearim. Delitzsch, however (*Psalms*, III, p. 310), pointed out that Caleb's wife Ephrathah bore a son (Hur) who is called 'the father of Bethlehem' (1 Ch. 4:4), and whose son Shobal in his turn is called 'the father of Kiriath-jearim' (1 Ch. 2:50); hence the district round Bethlehem seems to have been known as Ephrathah (Mi. 5:2), and that of Kiriath-jearim as Caleb-Ephrathah (1 Ch. 2:24, RV, RSV mg.).

1 Kings 15:4. Solomon may have used these words before the time which 2 Chronicles 6:41f. records; and other kings may have used them after him. But this periodic re-enaction remains a conjecture, though a likely one.

132:11, 12. God's oath to David

The second half of the psalm is the bright counterpart of the first, with God's oath now matching David's, and His promise crowning the people's prayers. This pledge to perpetuate the house of David (2 Sa. 7:11b-16) included further promises which were to flower into the Messianic hope: see on Psalm 89:19-37. It was a typically divine response to a well-meaning gesture, to refuse a perishable house and bestow an imperishable one.

132:13-18. His presence in Zion

The warmth and wealth of these promises spring from love, and require an answering love for their fulfilment. Instead, the human response was all too often cynical, treating God's choice as something to be exploited: a shelter against His judgment (Je. 7, especially verses 8-15) or an asset to be commercialized (Mt. 21:12f.). How total was this misconception of God's commitment to Zion, many events have shown and many scriptures expounded. See on Psalms 46:4; 48:1-3; 87; 122:8, 9; *cf.* the New Testament passages referred to in those comments.

16. Within the general answer of verses 11-18 to verses 1-10, this promise grants the request of verse 9, where see comment.

17, 18. Here, too, is the abundant answer to the prayer of verse 10. The three terms, *horn*, *lamp* and *crown*, scarcely need comment, with their evident implications of strength, clarity[1] and royal dignity. But note that the word used for *crown* (the same as for the high priest's mitre) draws attention to the fact that it symbolized the king's hallowing. Not power alone, but holiness is this king's—our King's—glory.

And the expression, *will shed its lustre*, is literally 'will blossom': perhaps a reminder (like the unexpected verb, 'to sprout', 17) of the vitality and freshness of what God creates, unlike the glitter of the man-made; perhaps a reminder, too,

---

[1] But 2 Sa. 21:17, where David is called 'the lamp of Israel', may imply that the promise in the psalm is of a worthy successor to the throne.

of the rod whose blossom was God's accrediting of His high priest, Aaron (Nu. 17:8 [23, Heb.]).

So the psalm, which began with hardships and grim determination, ends with the glory which is their proper aim and outcome: the victory and radiance of the promised King.

Psalm 133

Rich Concord

This vivid little psalm is ascribed to David (a fact overlooked by RSV, at least in its early editions). Whether it marked the moment he had waited for, when at last all Israel had rallied to him, and God had now given him Jerusalem (2 Sa. 5:1–10), or whether it was an isolated meditation, we have no means of knowing. David's later life lent tragic emphasis to his words, but here there is no trace of irony or regret. He has not yet exchanged this peace for the sword which would 'never depart' from his house (2 Sa. 12:10).

1. The clause, *when brothers dwell in unity* (lit. 'when brothers dwell also together'), has a fairly close parallel in Deuteronomy 25:5, where it merely refers to an extended family living at close quarters. Some have therefore seen the psalm as a plea to restore or preserve this social pattern, or as praise for the family reunions which the pilgrim feasts made possible (note the emphasis on Zion, 3).

But this is unduly narrow. All Israelites, including even debtors, slaves and offenders (*cf.*, *e.g.*, Dt. 15:3, 12; 25:3), were brothers in God's sight. The psalm is surely singing, as most versions have taken it to be, of living up to this ideal, giving depth and reality to the emphasized word, 'together'.

2. The older translations, AV, PBV, RV, made too much of this picture by taking the 'mouth' or 'opening' of Aaron's robes to be not *the collar* (*cf.* Ex. 28:32) but the skirts, an interpretation which would imply not so much an anointing as a deluge. The psalm needs no such exaggeration to portray, by this figure, a people as differentiated, but also as integrated, as a priest and his robes; a people among whom God's blessings are not the preserve of a few but are free to spread and be shared, unifying the recipients all the more, just as the anointing oil intended for the head (Ex. 29:7) was not confined to it, nor could its fragrance be contained. Exodus 29:21 provided explicitly that after the pouring of the oil on the head, some was to be sprinkled on the robes: 'and he and his garments shall be holy'.

Although fragrance is not directly mentioned here, it is implied in the expression '*the precious oil*' (lit. 'the good oil'), whose spices, 'blended as by the perfumer', are specified in Exodus 30:23ff.

3. *Hermon*, the highest mountain in Israel, was evidently proverbial for its heavy dew; yet the little Mount Zion enjoyed the same gift. 'High and low drink in the same sweet refreshment' (Perowne); it is essentially the thought already presented in verse 2.

The second half of verse 3, with its strong accent on God's initiative (*commanded*) and on what is only His to give (*life for evermore*), clinches another emphasis of the psalm, which is made by a threefold repetition, partly lost in translation: literally, 'descending (2a) . . . descending (2b) . . . descending' (3a). In short, true unity, like all good gifts, is from above; bestowed rather than contrived, a blessing far more than an achievement.

Coming from David's lips, however, there is unconscious irony in the emphatic '*there*' of 3b, which gives a parting thrust to the message of the psalm. 'There', *i.e.* Jerusalem, where Israel met in God's courts, was where heaven's concord could be found. Yet 'there' instead (2 Sa. 11:1), King David was to bring down on his people the discord which would spill and spread from his own house to every corner of his kingdom.

Psalm 134

Unceasing Praise

The Songs of Ascents, which began in the alien surroundings of Meshech and Kedar (Ps. 120), end fittingly on the note of serving God 'day and night within his temple'. It is possible that there is greeting and response here: the pilgrims addressing the priests and Levites in verses 1 and 2, and receiving in reply the blessing which closes the psalm.

1. We learn from 1 Chronicles 9:33 that Levitical singers (whose turns of duty are outlined in 1 Ch. 25) 'were on duty day and night'. The law of Moses had summed up the role of this tribe in the words 'to carry the ark ... , to stand before the Lord to minister ... , and to bless in his name' (Dt. 10:8). When the ark found its resting-place, David gave them new responsibilities, but worship remained paramount: 'they shall stand every morning, thanking and praising the Lord, and likewise at evening' (1 Ch. 23:30; *cf.* verse 26). These, rather than the congregation at large, are the particular *servants of the Lord* addressed here.

2. The phrase, *to the holy place*, translates a single word, 'holiness', which in Hebrew usage can mean either 'sanctity' or 'sanctuary', and is here used adverbially. So it may speak of worshipping 'in holiness' (RV mg.), and be the passage underlying 1 Timothy 2:8, 'lifting up holy hands'; or, as most versions prefer, it may mean 'to (or, in) the holy place'.[1]

3. The word *bless* is perhaps the key-note of the psalm, sounded as it is in each verse. So far, it has been directed Godward; now it returns from God to man. But the exchange is quite unequal: to bless God is to acknowledge gratefully what He is; but to bless man, God must make of him what he is not, and give him what he has not.

Note, finally, the place God has for both 'the mighty small' and 'the mighty great' (to borrow a phrase from a hymn).[2] As the one *who made heaven and earth*, He gives without measure; and His ways are past finding out. Yet His blessing is *from Zion*, a particular and discoverable place to which the Israelite could get up and go. Like His commandment, His blessing is not 'far off'; not 'in heaven' nor 'beyond the sea', but 'very near you' (Dt. 30:11–14; *cf.* Rom. 10:6ff.). His true Mount Zion is, as Hebrews 12:22–24 shows, where 'Jesus, the mediator of a new covenant', reigns in the midst of His people. In the words of the previous psalm, 'There the Lord has commanded the blessing, life for evermore'.

---

[1] The holy place, in turn, could stand for the whole temple complex, with its courts, or for the building which only the priests could enter.
[2] Sir Ronald Ross, 'Before thy feet I fall'.

Psalm 135
An Anthology of Praise

Every verse of this psalm either echoes, quotes or is quoted by some other part of Scripture. Alongside these familiar and great passages it builds up its own coherent structure of praise, beginning and ending with a worship-call to Israel, which the main body of the psalm substantiates by contrasting the true Sovereign and Redeemer with the helpless idols of the heathen.

135:1-4. Acclamation from His chosen

The first verse rearranges the phrases of Psalm 113:1 so as to lead into the summons to God's *servants* gathered in the temple courts (1b, 2, echoing 134:1). While the previous psalm greeted chiefly the Levites on night watch, this one has a great and varied throng in view, priestly and lay (see 19f.).

3. This is one of three related verses in the Psalter in which we are reminded that the Lord's name (the reputation He deserves) is good (52:9 [11, Heb.]), that He Himself is good (135:3) and that praising Him is good (147:1); further, that both His name (here) and the act of worship (147:1) are delightful.[1] See also 33:1; 92:1.

4. If the first ground of praise is the Lord's character (3), the next is His love for us. The word *Jacob* (and consequently *Israel* too) is emphatic: 'For it was Jacob that the Lord chose . . .'. In this, and in the strong word *s^eḡullâ*, 'treasure' or *own possession*, the psalm looks back to Deuteronomy 7:6 (lit.): '. . . it was you that the Lord your God chose . . . for his own possession'; and the next two verses of that passage make the sheer grace of such a choice very clear.

135:5-7. The Lord omnipotent

These three verses can be paralleled from Exodus 18:11; Psalm 115:3; Jeremiah 10:13.[2] But they are more than quotations: they are given the force of personal conviction by the opening clause, *For I know . . .* ; and the 'I' is emphatic,

---

[1] While RSV, 'for he is gracious', is possible in both places, the more straightforward translation appears to be 'for it is pleasant' or 'lovely'.
[2] See the whole of Je. 10 for the implications of this verse, for faith and conduct, powerfully expounded.

making Jethro's testimony (Ex. 18:11) one's own. This is truth to live by. Its reference to the physical world about us forbids us to relegate God's miracles to the past (8–12) or to the future (14), important as these dimensions are.

135:8–14. The Lord our Saviour

Most of the phrases of verses 8–12 reappear in the next psalm, word for word (136:10, 18–22). Whether that psalm has taken them from here, interspersing its refrains, or whether the present psalm has done the borrowing (possibly through the memory of words constantly sung), is of little consequence. But their double occurrence, and the presence of similar reviews of history (*e.g.* Pss. 78, 105, 106), draws attention to the role of grateful, factual remembrance in worship. God has begun a good work; it follows that He will complete it, as indeed verse 14 concludes. The Christian creeds have a similar pattern, progressing from the creation to the acts of our redemption, and thence to the certain prospect of Christ's second coming and the consummation.

11. The victories over *Sihon* and *Og* are recounted in Numbers 21:21ff., 33ff.; *cf.* Deuteronomy 3:11.

13, 14. These verses allude to Exodus 3:15 and Deuteronomy 32:36. The latter (from the Song of Moses) makes it very clear that the rescue of God's people will be wholly undeserved: the saving of fools and apostates from the predicament they deserved to find themselves in.

135:15–18. The absurdity of idols

This stanza reproduces 115:4–6, 8 almost exactly,[1] in spite of RSV's terser style here, which corresponds to no change in the Hebrew text. Verse 18 is translated better here than is its equivalent, Psalm 115:8 (where see comment), where again the Hebrew is identical.

135:19–21. Antiphons from His chosen

On these verses see the comments on 115:9–11, where three of these four groups of names are bidden in turn to glorify God. There, the call was to honour Him at the centre of one's being, by trust; here, by the outward display of gratitude and praise.

---

[1] Ps. 115:7 is omitted, and 115:6b is given a new twist after our psalm has taken its opening word, $'a\bar{p}$, not in the sense of 'nose' but as the emphatic conjunction rendered here 'nor'.

The responsive blessing that ascends to Him *from Zion* (21) bears no comparison with the creative blessing He imparts from there (134:3, where see note); but, as Matthew 21:16 reminds us, He is not too proud to be delighted to be offered it.

Psalm 136

His love has no end

Our versions of this psalm are mostly cumbersome: they lack the swiftness which should rid its repetitions of their tedium. The six Hebrew syllables of the response have their happiest equivalent in the Gelineau version of Psalm 118:1 (117:1 in Gelineau's numbering):[1] '*for his love has no end*'. Unaccountably, Gelineau substitutes here a laboured alternative, although the Hebrew is unchanged. See also on verses 1–3, below.

In Jewish tradition this psalm is often known as the Great Hallel ('the Great Psalm of Praise'). It follows much the same pattern as the previous psalm, with which it shares a series of identical phrases. The interspersed responses give us a glimpse of the congregation's part in psalm-singing; a comparison of verses 18–22 with 135:10b–12 suggests that other psalms, or parts of them, may have been intended to be sung in this way.

136:1–3. God of gods

Give thanks is not the whole meaning of this word (which introduces not only each of the first three verses and the final one, but also, unheard, every verse or sequence in the psalm): it basically means 'confess' or 'acknowledge' (*cf.*, *e.g.*, Lv. 5:5; Pr. 28:13, in a less happy context), and therefore calls us to thoughtful, grateful worship, spelling out what we know or have found of God's glory and His deeds. The psalm proceeds to do this, speaking here of His character (1) and sovereignty (2, 3); then of what He has made and done (4ff.), and what He continues to do (25).

Steadfast love is the word *ḥeseḏ*, discussed at 17:7. Provided that this background of covenant-fidelity is understood, the

[1] Gelineau follows the numeration of the LXX and Vulg., which diverges from that of the Heb. text from Pss. 9 to 147 inclusive. On these differences see the opening comments on Pss. 9, 115, 116, 147.

response 'For his love has no end' will be preferable to RSV's ponderous refrain. The word *endures* is a translators' addition.

136:4-9. Creator

These biddings bring together two Old Testament treatments of the creation theme: that of Proverbs, which enlarges on the wisdom and *understanding* (5) which creation presupposes (*cf.* Pr. 3:19f.; 8:1, 22-31), and that of Genesis which tells the story of it (*cf.* verses 6-9 with Gn. 1:9f., 16-18).

This theme, wherever it comes in the Psalter (*cf.* such varied treatments as Pss. 8, 19, 33, 104, 147, 148), invites the Christian, not to wrangle over cosmological theories but to delight in his environment, known to him as no mere mechanism but a work of 'steadfast love'. No unbeliever has grounds for any such quality of joy.

136:10-16. Rescuer

What 'the judgment of this world' and of its 'ruler'[1] means to the Christian since the cross and resurrection, the overthrow of Pharaoh and his host meant in some degree to Israel. It is also part of our own history, illuminating our own redemption and the meaning of our baptism and pilgrimage (1 Cor. 5:7; 10:1-13).

136:17-22. Victor

This passage runs parallel, almost exactly, to 135:10-12, where see comments.

136:23-25. Friend in need

Verses 23f. may be summarizing the story already told, but more probably bringing it down to the present. After all, 'his steadfast love endures for ever', and the refrain is designed to show the relevance of every act of God to every singer of the psalm. Then verse 25 proceeds to enlarge the horizon in terms of space, not only of time.

136:26. God of heaven

This final verse takes up the style of verses 1-3, to return the psalm effectively to the key-note from which it started.

[1] Jn. 12:31; 16:11.

Psalm 137

By the Waters of Babylon

This psalm needs no title to announce that its provenance was the Babylonian exile. Every line of it is alive with pain, whose intensity grows with each strophe to the appalling climax. The relation of this outcry to other parts of the Old Testament and to the teaching of the New is discussed in the Introduction, pp. 25–32.

137:1–3. Pathos

The scene has the vividness of first-hand experience. *The waters of Babylon* included a system of canals across the huge plain, a landscape alien enough in any circumstances to natives of the hills and valleys of Judah. As for *lyres* and the demand for *songs*, it happens that a relief from Sennacherib's palace at Nineveh, in the neighbouring land of Assyria, portrays a situation not unlike this, with three prisoners of war playing lyres as they are marched along by an armed soldier.[1]

Our tormentors (3) is as likely a meaning as most that have been proposed or substituted for this word, which occurs only here.

137:4–6. Defiance

A fine stubbornness has already been implicit in the gesture of verse 2, refusing to expose the songs and high claims of Zion to ridicule. The question of verse 4, *How shall we sing the Lord's song . . . ?* might well have been the prelude to a defeatist answer, repudiating the hope of Israel. Instead, as verses 5 and 6 reveal, it springs from a burning loyalty which the disaster has only raised to a new pitch of intensity.

137:7–9. Imprecation

The first thing to notice about this strophe is its juridical background, indicated by the expression *Remember . . . against*, which 'has its roots in the legal life of Ancient Israel'.[2] The divine Judge is being presented in verse 7 with evidence

---

[1] See M. A. Beek, *Atlas of Mesopotamia* (Nelson, 1962), plate 219.
[2] B. S. Childs, *Memory and Tradition in Israel* (SCM Press, 1962), p. 32.

against Edom (the facts, which are damning, emerge more
fully in Ob. 10–14). Then the plaintiff rounds on Babylon, the
chief offender (8, 9). Although this is an outburst, not a direct
plea to the Judge, and reveals only obliquely what Babylon
has done, the words are by implication spoken in the Lord's
hearing, continuing from verse 7. This inference is confirmed
by the appeal of verse 8b to the *lex talionis*, or principle of
retribution, which applied to legal but not personal decisions
(*cf.*, *e.g.*, Dt. 19:19ff. with Pr. 24:29). The wording of verse 8
agrees with God's general pledge, 'I will repay',[1] and, we may
add, with His specific sentence on Babylon in Jeremiah 51:56.
The latter seems in fact to be the ground of the present
verse (8), for it can hardly be coincidence that three of
Jeremiah's principal words are related to the three verbs of
137:8.[2] The psalm is therefore a response to Scripture as well
as to events.

What those events had been is disclosed in verse 9, which is
the mirror of *what you have done to us* (8c). There is ample
evidence that 'to dash in pieces their little ones' was a common
enough sequel to a heathen victory,[3] and that Babylon had
been in no mood for restraint at the fall of Jerusalem (2 Ki.
25:7; La. 5:11f.). To the question, What do the perpetrators
of such acts *deserve*? the dispassionate answer would presumably
be 'the degree of suffering they imposed on others', leaving
aside the further question of what should in fact be done to
them, and by whom. To that further question the New
Testament replies that ultimately God 'will render to every
man according to his works', but also makes it clear that
wrath is only for the 'hard and impenitent heart' (Rom.
2:5f.).

This, we may feel, is what the psalmist might have said in a
cooler moment. But we are not given it in that form: it comes

---

[1] *Cf.* '*requite*' here with the Heb. of Dt. 7:10; 32:35; Is. 65:6.

[2] In RSV the related words are rendered, here and in Je. 51:56 respectively:
devastator/destroyer ($\sqrt{sdd}$); requites/requite ($\sqrt{slm}$); done/recompense
($\sqrt{gml}$). But it should be added that 'devastator' should be read as a passive
here: *cf.* RV, 'that art to be destroyed'.

[3] See 2 Ki. 8:12; Is. 13:16; Ho. 10:14; 13:16 (14:1, Heb.); Na. 3:10.
For a modern example, *cf.* the account by S. S. Stubaf. Haller of the method
used in the Second World War at Bromberg: viz., 'to take the Jewish
children by their feet and to break their heads by striking against the
wall . . .' (transcript translated in P. Joffroy, *A Spy for God* (Collins, 1971),
p. 292. *Cf. ibid.*, p. 163).

to us white-hot. Our response to such a scripture should, we suggest, be threefold. First, to distil the essence of it, as God Himself did with the cries of Job and Jeremiah.[1] Secondly, to receive the impact of it. This raw wound, thrust before us, forbids us to give smooth answers to the fact of cruelty. To cut this witness out of the Old Testament would be to impair its value as revelation, both of what is in man and of what the cross was required to achieve for our salvation. Thirdly, our response should be to recognize that our calling, since the cross, is to pray down reconciliation, not judgment. This is discussed more fully in the Introduction, pp. 31f.

So this psalm takes its place in Scripture as an impassioned protest, beyond all ignoring or toning down, not only against a particular act of cruelty but against all comfortable views of human wickedness, either with regard to the judgment it deserves or to the legacy it leaves; and not least, in relation to the cost, to God and man, of laying its enmity and bitterness to rest.

Psalm 138

Goodness Beyond Measure

A group of eight psalms of David begins here, bringing to its conclusion his share in the Psalter, altogether nearly half the collection. We are again aware of the presence of enemies, and of the special gratitude of one who has been much threatened but much protected. On *David* as author, see Introduction, p. 33.

138:1-3. Help for one man
The repeated word *thanks* in verses 1, 2 and 4 (translated 'praise' in the last of these) points to the moment the psalmist has in mind for his song to be heard, when he will publicly sacrifice his thank-offering and tell 'the glad news of deliverance' to 'the great congregation' (*cf.* Ps. 40:10). There is a fine blend of boldness and humility from the outset: boldness to confess the Lord *before the gods*, humility to *bow down* before Him.

[1] See Introduction, pp. 27f.

David had once felt, but rejected, the pressure of 'other gods' (1 Sa. 26:19) within their territories—somewhat as we may feel the force of other ideologies, or of demonic powers, where they are cultivated. So verse 1b is no empty gesture, any more than 2a.[1]

2b. The Hebrew text, as we have it, runs as in AV, RV: '. . . hast magnified thy word above all thy name' (*cf.* RSV mg.). This is a strange expression (one would expect 'even' rather than 'all'), and a strange statement if 'thy name' has its usual meaning of 'thyself revealed', as it has in the first half of the verse. For all its high claims, Scripture does not encourage bibliolatry; so the meaning of such a sentence could only be that God has fulfilled His promise[2] in a way that surpasses all that He has hitherto revealed of Himself. But this would be an obscure way of putting it, and RSV seems justified in assuming a copyist's omission of the letter *w*, meaning 'and',[3] from a text which will have read '. . . hast exalted above everything[4] thy name and thy word'.[5]

3. There is an attacking spirit in the second line of this verse, which RSV fails to catch (but see RSV mg.). It comes out in NEB: 'thou didst answer me and make me bold and valiant-hearted'. We are reminded of Paul, boasting in the Lord and even in his own infirmities; for it is possible that the answer here was first and foremost the boldness itself, which made David (like Paul in 2 Cor. 12:8–10) equal to the occasion. It is not always the situation which most needs changing; it is, as often as not, the man involved in it.

138:4–6. Light for the world
Rather as in Psalm 22:27ff., David is shown the implications of what he has found in his own dark hour. The true God, and so wonderful a God, cannot be for ever hidden, known only to a few. Every tongue must confess Him,[6] and His words must

---

[1] On the word *temple* (2a) in the psalms of David, see on 5:7, p. 59.

[2] This is a frequent meaning of '*imrâ*; *cf.* 119:38, 41, 50, *etc.*

[3] An alternative to postulating an omitted *w* ('and') is to assume that 'thy name' in 2b has crept in by dittography from 2a.

[4] A trace of the meaning 'everything' may be preserved in the long vowel of *kōl*, which is well attested though not undisputed (*BH* has the short vowel).

[5] LXX, omitting 'thy word', has 'thy holy name'.

[6] *Praise* (4) has this primary sense, and then often the secondary sense of 'give thanks' as in verses 1 and 2. See on 136:1.

spread through the earth. The perfect tense of verse 4b, *they have heard*, expresses the certainty of what is yet to come; see on Psalm 9:5f. But 4a and 5a may well be jussive tenses: 'Let all ... praise thee ..., and let them sing', as in NEB.

5, 6. David's experience of grace clarifies his vision of *glory*, which he sees in terms not simply of power but of magnanimity. God's caring, no less than His sovereign might, is His glory. And this in turn reveals men in their true colours: the pretentiousness of *the haughty* belongs to quite another world than His. The two concepts of greatness have no meeting-point.

138:7, 8. Help to the end

Meanwhile the vision of verses 4–6 waits to be realized, and times are hard. If the inner resilience of verse 3 was the first part of God's help, it is not the last. Verse 7 shows His control over the battle, both as 'the Lord and giver of *life*'[1] and as stronger than the enemy; and verse 8 looks beyond the immediate scene to the finished product that God must have in mind in relation to His servant (8a), a work to which He has set His hand (8b). The old translation of 8a is perhaps as memorable as any: 'The Lord will perfect that which concerneth me' (AV, RV). So the first and last lines of this verse make personal, confident and urgent use of the familiar truth which they embrace in the middle line. To David, hard-pressed and threatened, the words come new-minted: God's *steadfast love ... endures for ever*.

Psalm 139

'Too wonderful for me'

Any small thoughts that we may have of God are magnificently transcended by this psalm; yet for all its height and depth it remains intensely personal from first to last.

One manuscript of the Septuagint ascribes the psalm to Zechariah, adding the note 'in the dispersion' (which looks

---

[1] As in Ps. 119:25, 37, *etc.*, the single word translated *preserve my life* can also mean 'revive me' (*cf.* AV, RV here). See the introductory comments to Ps. 119, section III. *c*, pp. 421f.

like a gratuitous inference from verses 7–12). Some resemblances to Job (*e.g.* the term Eloah for God, verse 19), and some affinities to Aramaic, have raised doubts over David's authorship; but Aramaic influence is no proof of late dating. For some tentative observations on this feature, see Introduction, p. 34, footnote 2. On the note, *To the choirmaster*, see p. 40.

The Gelineau version gives the psalm the heading 'The Hound of Heaven', a reminder that Francis Thompson's fine poem of that name owed its theme of flight and pursuit largely to the second stanza here (verses 7–12), which is one of the summits of Old Testament poetry.

139:1–6. The All-Seeing

This statement of omniscience is characteristically vivid and concrete: not formulated as a doctrine but, as befits a psalm, confessed in adoration. This divine knowledge is not merely comprehensive, like that of some receptor that misses nothing, capturing everything alike. It is personal and active: discerning us (2b); sifting us (3a, where *searchest out* is based on a term for winnowing); knowing our minds more closely (*altogether*) than we know them ourselves (2b, 4; *cf.* Am. 4:13); surrounding us (*beset*), handling us (5).

If one's first reaction to this is the wonder of verse 6, one's second may be the urge to escape, which appears to animate the next stanza.

139:7–12. The All-Present

The impulse to flee from God's face (the literal meaning of *thy presence*) is as old as the Fall. Admittedly the talk of flight may be a purely literary device to dramatize the fact of God's ubiquity; but there seems to be at least an ambivalent attitude to Him here, like that of a child running from its parent. Verse 10 appreciates that God's long arm is moved by love alone, yet the language of verses 11f. suggests a last and unavailing bid to hide. Amos 9:2ff. uses imagery that recalls this very passage to describe the hunting down of those who are fugitives from justice. If no thought of escape had come to mind here, David could have cried 'What shall separate me from thy Spirit, or drive me from thy presence?', somewhat as Paul did in Romans 8:38f. But the end of the psalm will see no doubts or hesitations.

8. On *Sheol*, see the review of its Old Testament aspects at Psalm 6:5. The gospel has given the second line of the present verse a wholly new flavour, first in that Christ descended into Sheol on our behalf, and could not 'be held by it' (Acts 2:24, 31), and secondly that for us Sheol has become Paradise. David's exclamation, '*thou art there!*', loses all its ambiguity with Paul's eager phrase, 'With Christ, which is far better'.

9. On the superb expression, *the wings of the morning*, see on 57:8. There may well be the thought of the great span of the heavens from one horizon to the other, since in Israel *the sea* was a natural synonym for the west.

10–12. On the implications of these verses see the opening comments on this stanza, above. RSV translates the Hebrew of verse 10 faithfully; TEV is perhaps unduly free. But in verse 11 the Hebrew text has 'the darkness will bruise me', which seems to be a scribal error for 'cover me',[1] unless (improbably) darkness is a metaphor here for distress (*cf.* Anderson), which would yield sense of a sort, only obscurely expressed.[2]

139:13–18. The All-Creative

The third stanza brings together and carries forward the thought of the first two: God not only sees the invisible and penetrates the inaccessible, but is operative there, the author of every detail of my being. And the dimension of time is now added to those of space, from before my existence to whatever is implied in the phrase 'when I awake' (18).

13. *Form* (or 'create') and *knit . . . together* make better sense here than 'possessed' and 'covered' (AV, RV), and are well established alternative meanings of the Hebrew words in question.

14. Here, however, RSV follows LXX *et al.*, and is a little unfair in its marginal note, since the Hebrew can be legitimately translated 'I praise thee, for I am awesomely[3] wonderful'; hence AV, RV, '. . . I am fearfully and wonderfully

---

[1] *I.e.*, *yᵉšûp̄ēnî* in error for *yᵉśukkēnî*?

[2] In the next line, NEB's 'night will close around me' is derived from a Qumran MS which has the consonants *'zr* (gird) instead of *'wr* (light). But LXX agrees with MT.

[3] The same plural noun is used adverbially in Jb. 37:5 ('wondrously', RSV).

made'. *Cf.* JB, freely: 'For all these mysteries I thank you: for the wonder of myself, for the wonder of your works.'

The last line of this verse, as it stands, reads 'And my soul knows (it) very well' (*cf.* LXX, AV, RV). Most modern versions put this the other way round, with RSV (*Thou knowest me . . .*); but this requires a change in the traditional vowels, which is hardly called for.

15. *The depths of the earth* are a metaphor here for deepest concealment, *i.e.*, the hiddenness of the womb. This line (15b) is close in thought to 13b, whose term, 'knit together', is taken a step further in the expression *intricately wrought*, suggesting the complex patterns and colours of the weaver or embroiderer.

16. The rather cryptic Hebrew may mean either that *the days* of my life were mapped out in advance (RSV, JB, TEV), or that my embryonic members were likewise planned and known before the many stages ('day by day')[1] of their development (AV, RV, NEB). The former option gives perhaps a slightly more straightforward sentence than the latter; but in either case the stanza so far has laid its main emphasis on our pre-natal fashioning by God (13–16a at the least)—a powerful reminder of the value He sets on us, even as embryos, and of His planning our end from the beginning.[2]

17, 18. David has moved on from contemplating his own thoughts and their nakedness before God (2), to considering God's innumerable thoughts towards him (*cf.* Ps. 40:5, and the comment there). He is not exaggerating. Even in his own body (13ff.) there is an unimaginable wealth of detail, every point of it from the mind of God. Such divine knowledge is not only 'wonderful' (*cf.* verse 6) but *precious*, since it carries its own proof of infinite commitment: God will not leave the work of His own hands (138:8c), either to chance or to ultimate extinction. Already the metaphor of *thy book* (16; *cf.* 56:8) has ruled out so casual a divine attitude; and the words *I am still with thee* (18b), taken with the vast background of verses 7–12,

---

[1] The plural noun, 'days', can be used adverbially ('daily'); *cf.* the previous footnote. But then 'my members' or 'my limbs' have to be inferred from the singular noun 'my embryo' ('my unformed substance') as the unexpressed subject of the verbs.

[2] This appears to raise important ethical questions concerning the resort to abortion in the interests of, *e.g.*, social convenience or an 'acceptable' level of health.

can be given no limit, even by death. *When I awake*[1] may therefore have its strongest sense, a glimpse of resurrection. On this theme see also on 17:15.

139:19–24. The All-Holy

The very clarity of the vision makes the anomaly of evil, boasting in full view of God, intolerable; so David's re-entry to the atmosphere of earth creates, as we might say, a sudden incandescence. The abrupt change in the psalm from reverie to resolve is disturbing, but wholly biblical in its realism; and the last two verses emphasize the continuity of this stanza with what has gone before, transposing the truths of the opening verses into the key of willing acceptance and surrender.

19–22. For all its vehemence, the hatred in this passage is not spite, but zeal for God. In 'the day of salvation' the New Testament will re-direct this fighting spirit, but it will endorse its single-mindedness ('What fellowship has light with darkness? What accord has Christ with Belial?'[2]). It is worth noting that David's resolve was not necessarily easy, since the unscrupulous can be convenient allies, and the scoffers can be daunting opponents. For a fuller statement of it, see the kingly vow of Psalm 101, with the prefatory comment there. See also the Introduction, p. 32.

23, 24. David does not confine his attack to the evil around him: he faces what may be within him. If there was any dismay in the confession of verse 1, 'Thou hast searched me and known me', it has changed to gratitude and eager welcome. Two expressions in particular, as translated by NEB, reveal his sensitive awareness of his need: first, 'my misgivings' (23b); not merely 'thoughts' as in verse 2, but the restless, ramifying cogitations translated 'cares' in 94:19 (*cf.* perhaps the inner conflict confessed in Mk. 9:24). Secondly 'lest I follow any path that grieves thee' (24a)—or simply ' . . that is hurtful', whether to God or man—recognizing that sin is never an isolated incident.

---

[1] The tense is perfect, hence Delitzsch takes it that David had fallen asleep as he mused, and has now woken again (*cf.* Je. 31:26). But a prophetic perfect, *i.e.*, a perfect of anticipation, is equally possible, as in RSV, *etc.* The alternative suggestion, 'Were I to come to the end' (RSV mg.; *cf.* RP, NEB), is based on another verb (properly 'to cut off') assumed from a variant spelling found in three MSS. But LXX supports 'awake'.

[2] 2 Cor. 6:14f.

The final words could be translated 'the ancient way' as in Jeremiah 6:16 (*cf.* RSV mg., NEB); but the majority of translators would appear to be right in rendering them *the way everlasting*, in contrast to the way of the wicked which will perish (Ps. 1:6), and in harmony with what is said of the path of the just, which shines 'more and more unto the perfect day' (Pr. 4:18, AV).

Psalm 140

Poison

The single theme of malicious intrigue dominates this psalm, as it has dominated many others, especially those of David. The New Testament treats the Psalter as a major witness to human depravity (most of Rom. 3:10–18 is from the Psalms), largely because it exposes this element in us of sheer malice, a poison which can be secreted and employed not only without provocation (69:4) but even in face of generosity and love (*cf.* especially 35:12–16; 55:12–14).

The prayers of verses 1–5 are coloured chiefly by thoughts of the plotters and their ways; those of 6–11 by the interventions sought from God: finally verses 12 and 13 crown the prayer with affirmation.

Title
On *the choirmaster* and *David*, see Introduction, pp. 40, 33.

140:1–5. The conspirators
What emerges clearly from this passage is the evil that can arise, not from any pressure of circumstances but from a love of violence, cruelty and intrigue for their own sake. David has no illusions and makes no excuses for these men, as our Lord made none for those who opposed Him in, *e.g.*, John 8:34–47. They have chosen the alternative way to God's way, and it is that of the 'murderer from the beginning' and 'the father of lies'. The reader of the psalm can reflect that this pattern of hurting, slandering and deceiving has its gentler manifestations, and is no rarity.

140:6–11. The counterblast
The first ground of David's appeal is personal (6–8). Not only is there already a bond between him and God, which he states with some emphasis in 6a (and elaborates in the further possessives of 7a, *my Lord, my strong deliverer*), but God has helped him before, in even greater perils. What availed him in *the day of battle* will suffice against the *evil plot. Cf.* Paul in 2 Corinthians 1:10: 'he delivered us from so deadly a peril, and he will deliver us'. Or John Newton, with salty simplicity:

> 'His love in time past
> Forbids me to think
> He'll leave me at last
> In trouble to sink.'[1]

The second ground is punitive (9–11). These men must have their deserts, and taste their own medicine. The *burning coals* and *pits* are probably metaphorical, the former for the searing words which they have loved to use (but those that come back to them will be more deadly, because unanswerable; *cf.* on 120:3f.), the latter for the traps and pitfalls they have made for others (*cf., e.g.*, 141:10). The appropriateness of judgment is brought out again in 11b, where evil appears as a kind of nemesis. *Cf.* 109:17ff.

140:12, 13. The certainty
The word used for *cause* (12) is a legal one, and is reinforced by *justice* in the second line. The king's duty to his people in this sphere was a constant reminder that God as King will take this matter no less seriously. There can be ultimately no loose ends in His administration.

But even better than this note of certainty is David's release from obsession, for he finally lets the subject rest. The last line is wholly positive. His heart is free to find its true home, and his last words match the climax to which the whole of Scripture moves: 'His servants shall serve him: and they shall see his face' (Rev. 22:3f., AV).

---

[1] J. Newton, 'Begone, unbelief'.

Psalm 141

No Compromise

There is a Puritan vigour and single-mindedness about this psalm to put one in mind of Christian and Faithful at Vanity Fair, whose prayer was 'Turn away mine eyes from beholding vanity', and whose reply to the challenge 'What will you buy?' was 'We buy the truth'. The colourful Hebrew of the middle verses is difficult, but the thrust of the psalm is plain: a prayer against insincerity and compromise, and a plea for survival under the savage attacks which such an attitude has invited.

Title
On *David*, see Introduction, p. 33.

141:1, 2. Pure prayer
This evening psalm, matching the morning prayer referred to in Psalm 5:3, was prompted like its companion by the example of the daily sacrifices (2; Ex. 29:38ff.). David has caught the meaning of this disciplined[1] devotion, and applied it to his own praying. *Cf.* Revelation 5:8, with its 'golden bowls full of incense, which are the prayers of the saints', and Hebrews 13:15, with its verbal 'sacrifice of praise'.

But verse 1 shows how sharply this piety is under trial, and the rest of the psalm will enlarge on it. This is no cloistered situation, any more than that of Psalm 5.

141:3-6. Plain loyalty
The request of these verses grows naturally out of verse 2 with its concern for a pure offering of prayer. Out of the same mouth there must not flow both blessing and cursing (*cf.* verse 3 with Jas. 3:9f.); and if the house of God needed its guards and doorkeepers, how much more the man of God!

4. Now the prayer deepens and widens, going behind the lips to the mind and will (*my heart*), and thence to the actions and, above all, the attitudes and alliances which flow from the centre of one's being.

[1] See on Ps. 5:3; and *cf.* NEB in the present verse, where RSV's expression *'counted* as incense before thee' is well rendered 'like incense *duly set* before thee'.

Incline not my heart to evil is a petition framed in the same striking way as 'Lead us not into temptation'. This way of putting it, although it may invite a quibble about God's attitude to evil (answered by Jas. 1:13), entrusts to Him 'the first springs of thought and will', with the humility of a plea and the clarity of a renunciation—for one cannot pray it with either complacency or reservations.

To *eat of their dainties* implied a much closer bond of friendship than it necessarily would in our society. The New Testament recounts some of the problems this created for traditionalists and externalists, and shows how the gospel brought a new approach to the matter (*e.g.* Mk. 2:16f.). But David's fears were for his loyalty; and the threat to this was real enough. C. S. Lewis describes its equivalent with his usual penetration: 'There is a subtle play of looks and tones and laughs by which a mortal can imply that he is of the same party as those to whom he is speaking. . . . He will assume, at first only by his manner, but presently by his words, all sorts of cynical and sceptical attitudes which are not really his. But . . they may become his. All mortals tend to turn into the thing they are pretending to be.'[1]

5.[2] RSV and other modern versions have reasonably followed the Septuagint in the second line,[3] bringing clarity to the verse in harmony with the proverb 'Faithful are the wounds of a friend' (Pr. 27:6) and in line with the prayer of verse 4, which it carries a stage further.

6. RSV, surprisingly, has rewritten 6a, parting company with the text and with other versions. To a lesser extent it has also emended 6b and 7.

Literally, the Hebrew runs as in RV: 'Their judges are thrown down by the sides of the rock; and they shall hear my words; for they are sweet.' Hebrew idiom would allow this to be a temporal construction; and in the last clause the word 'for' could equally mean 'that'; so the sentence could be rendered, 'When their judges are thrown down . . . they will

---

[1] C. S. Lewis, *The Screwtape Letters* (Bles, 1942), No. 10.

[2] The obscurity of the Heb. of verses 5–7 suggests a damaged text. The variations between different translations at this point arise largely out of attempts to clarify or restore it.

[3] This involves a small variant (*rāšā'*, 'wicked', for MT *rō'š*, 'head', which looks like a partial dittography of *rō'šî*, 'my head', later in the line), and a seemingly better translation of a verb ('anoint', *cf. TRP, ad loc.*, rather than RV 'refuse', or AV 'break').

hear my words, that they are sweet.' In short, David affirms that judgment will overtake the leaders ('judges') of his opponents, and then at last their followers will listen to him gladly.

Obscure as the language of this verse is, it carries the previous thought forward to its climax, reinforcing the resolve to strike no bargains with evil, by looking ahead to the time when such a stand will prove its point and win its following.

141:7–10. Sheer faith

To include verse 7 in this section one must take it unaltered, when it is found to describe '*our*' plight, not that of the enemy.[1] With NEB's free translation accordingly adapted, it can be rendered: 'Our bones are scattered at the mouth of Sheol, like splinters of wood or stone on the ground.' Psalm 79 was to describe such a scene in actuality (79:1–3); and Ezekiel would see both the parable it offered and a vision of what God could make of it (Ezk. 37:1–14). Here there is no vision, but there is the prayer of faith, beginning with the emphatic phrases of verse 8, whose order gives due precedence to God: 'But *toward thee* . . . are my eyes; *in thee* I seek refuge.'

So the psalm ends on the urgent, personal note on which it had started. The enemies' blandishments have failed; there remains their malice, and David knows its subtlety. But the last line ('while, as for me—I pass right on!')[2] has a buoyancy worthy of the man who has slipped through many a net with the help of God, and is sure that his journey is by no means over.

Psalm 142

Hemmed In

The title in the text makes this a companion piece to Psalm 57 by the note, 'when he was in the cave'; and together the two psalms give us some idea of the fluctuating state of David's

---

[1] RSV, NEB, TEV follow some MSS of the LXX in reading *their bones*, but the standard Heb. text has 'our bones'. RSV adds a complication by gratuitously transferring the *rock* from 6a to 7a.

[2] The Heb. is lit. 'while together *I* pass on'. 'Together' (*yaḥad*), unless it is taken with the preceding line (RSV, repunctuating MT), may mean 'at the same time', or possibly 'all in one piece' (Anderson; *cf.* TEV 'unharmed'). LXX read it as *yāḥîd*, 'all alone' (*cf.* NEB).

emotions in the ordeal. Psalm 57 is bold and animated, almost enjoying the situation for the certainty of its triumphant outcome. In the present psalm the strain of being hated and hunted is almost too much, and faith is at full stretch. But this faith is undefeated, and in the final words it is at last joined by hope.

On the authenticity of the biographical notes in the psalm-headings, see Introduction, VII, pp. 43-46. On the terms *Maskil* and *A Prayer*, see p. 38.

142:1-3a. My plea

The urgency of the prayer comes through at once in the repetition 'aloud . . . aloud' (RSV *with my voice . . . with my voice*). David, like Bartimaeus in the Gospels, knows the value of refusing to relapse into silence. That way lies despair.

Some facets of his praying can be seen in these opening terms. To *make supplication* is to appeal to kindness (so the Hebrew word suggests); *my complaint* is not as petulant a word as in English, but might be rendered 'my troubled thoughts'; and we should not miss the note of frankness in the words *pour out* and *tell*, or the sense of access in the reiteration of *before him* (2).

But 3a is the first of three modest summits of the psalm, standing out all the more for the depth from which it rises (TEV, freely, 'When I am ready to give up') and for its emphasis on the word 'Thou'. This should be italicized: '*thou* knowest my way!'

142:3b, 4. My plight

Just how timely was the conviction that God knew David's way (3a) is now doubly clear. First, verse 3b shows the perils of the path ahead; he can be thankful that it holds no problem for God. Then verse 4 reveals the friendless state of David, whom no-one cares to know—or so he feels. Mercifully again, God knows and cares. In the event, it seems that God answered abundantly, soon sending David's 'brothers and all his father's house' to join him in his cave, and then by degrees a company that would become the nucleus of his kingdom (1 Sa. 22:1f.). This low ebb in his fortunes proved in fact to be a turning-point.

142:5, 6a. My portion

This is the second summit of faith in the psalm (*cf.* 3a): a second affirmation in the face of all appearances and feelings.

As to the latter, verse 6a is eloquently simple; its pathos anticipates our Lord's own confession, 'My soul is very sorrowful, even to death' (Mt. 26:38).

My refuge (5; not the same word as in 4b) is understandably a favourite word with David; see on 57:1. To say '*my portion*' goes as far beyond this as love goes beyond fear. TEV brings out the great force of this word by the phrase 'you are all I want' (*cf.* 73:26; 119:57; and in telling contrast, 17:14).

142:6b, 7. My prospect

Persecutors (6b) is perhaps too figurative here, for David is being hunted literally. 'Pursuers' (NEB) is a better word. *Prison*, on the other hand, is a metaphor for his frustrating situation, forced into hiding and cut off from normal life. (The old translation, 'Bring my soul out of prison', is probably too literal, since 'my soul' is frequently a longer way of saying 'me'.)

Verse 7b ends the psalm on a new summit (*cf.* 3a, 5), where faith, joined now by hope, looks into the future. Those who disallow David's authorship of the psalm, seeing it as a set piece for any individual worshipper to use in times of trouble, take 7b to be looking forward to the day when such a sufferer, his prayer now answered, will make his thank-offering in the presence of the congregation (*cf., e.g.,* Ps. 116:12–19). This is a useful reminder that the Psalms were (and are) for all to use and make their own. But in the first instance it is David who dares to visualize the day when he is no longer shunned or hunted, but thronged, or even crowned.[1]

Perhaps he looked forward simply to bringing a thank-offering, at a time of public worship, when he was a free man again. Yet he already knew himself to be the future king. Even in this dark hour, was his first vision renewed as he prayed?

---

[1] From 'surround', which is the root meaning of the verb in 7b (*The righteous will surround me*), there arises a word for a royal crown (Est. 1:11; 2:17; 6:8) and a further sense of the verb as 'to crown' (Pr. 14:18). NEB sees this sense here (but not in terms of royalty), translating 7b 'The righteous shall crown me with garlands', with a marginal alternative, 'crowd round me'.

Psalm 143
My Spirit Fails

By tradition this is known as the last of the seven penitential psalms (which are listed in the commentary on Psalm 6). But this is probably because of verse 2, with its admission of universal guilt: an important truth, but the only reference to sin and forgiveness in the psalm. The main concern of David is with the straits to which his enemies have brought him. If his preoccupation at first is mainly with his troubles, towards the end it is largely with finding and following God's way ahead.

Title
On *David*, see Introduction, p. 33.

143:1-6. Chastened thoughts

1, 2. God's *faithfulness* and *righteousness* are often appealed to in the Old Testament as being on the side of those who pray, just as the integrity of a judge would be welcomed by those who brought a case to court. But David is pulled up short by the word he has used (2; *cf.* 130:3). The paradox of a righteous judge who nevertheless 'justifies the wicked' (an act which Pr. 17:15 calls an abomination to the Lord) would not be resolved until the cross had settled it.[1]

3, 4. Every phrase here is so heavy with distress, that no sufferer need feel unique in what he experiences. And the similarity of these terms to those that describe our Lord's emotions (*cf.* Mt. 26:37f.; Heb. 4:15ff.) remind us that none need feel himself alone, or less than fully understood.

David's words in 3b were to be borrowed in Lamentations 3:6; but there it is emphasized that God's hand was behind the enemy's in judgment, which is not said here.

The strong word for *faints* (4) is found nearby in 142:3, where see comment and notice the telling phrase for it in TEV.

5, 6. The mood is not nostalgia, that fruitless yearning for other times and places, but recollection of what God can do. It may have included David's own experience, but the second

---

[1] *Cf.* Rom. 3:21-26; 1 Jn. 1:9.

and third lines of verse 5 take in a bigger scene, the acts of God in history and creation (*cf.* NEB, somewhat freely). Still more to the point, he reaches out towards God Himself, not only to the things He can be asked to do. It is this personal devotion that was David's greatness (*cf.* 63:1 for the metaphor of thirst) and is the continuing greatness of his psalms.

He is already escaping from the prison of his circumstances and his self-preoccupation; but there will be no dramatic change.

143:7-12. Stirrings of the will

7-10. The pressure is still extreme (7),[1] and the only promising sign is one that would escape the singer's notice: the fact that he is beginning to look ahead and seek direction. The phrase, *in the morning* (8), is already a token of this by its admission that the night is not endless; *cf.* Psalm 30:5.

Three times in verses 8-10 David prays for guidance; and each request has its own nuance. *The way I should go* (8b) gives slight prominence to the fact of individual destiny, *i.e.*, that each of us is uniquely placed and called (*cf.* Jn. 21:21f.). *Teach me to do thy will* (10a) settles the priorities, making the goal not self-fulfilment but pleasing God and finishing His work. The words *lead me* (10b) speak with the humility of one who knows his need of shepherding, not merely of having the right way pointed out to him. David, no less than Paul (Rom. 8:14; Gal. 5:18), teaches us to look to God's *good spirit* for this leading; in other words, for an inward work of inclining the will and awakening the mind. The plea for a *level path*, or more accurately 'level land'[2] (the term used for the broad plateau allotted to Reuben, Dt. 4:43), implies the admission that one is prone to stumble, not only to stray. It can also be translated, in less pictorial terms, 'the land of uprightness', which reinforces the prayer 'to do thy will' (10a).

11, 12. Meanwhile life itself is at risk; but David can look to God's firm commitment. This is the force of his appeal to God's *name* (*cf.* 106:8), *righteousness* and *steadfast love* (see on 17:7), for God is pledged to His servant (12c) as surely as His servant is pledged to Him. If God cared nothing for His name,

---

[1] The last line of verse 7 quotes Ps. 28:1. See the comment on that verse, and on 28:3-5 where this fear is enlarged on.

[2] RSV ('path') follows certain MSS which diverge from MT ('land').

for the cause of right or for His covenant, we might have doubts of His salvation. Not otherwise.

Psalm 144

A King's Song

There is a warrior's energy in this psalm, worthy of David at the height of his powers, the David of Psalm 18. Yet that psalm of triumph is quoted now more as a stimulus to prayer than as plain thanksgiving, for the enemies and agitators are pressing hard, and the idyllic scene of the closing stanza is still a vision, perhaps prayed for with all the greater fervour for its contrast to the present.

The psalm is a mosaic, not a monolith; most of its material, short of the final verses, is drawn from other psalms of David, most substantially Psalm 18. But occasionally other parts of the Psalter can be glimpsed here, which has led the majority of recent exegetes to infer that a later author has compiled the psalm for David's heirs, whereby on state occasions they might wear, so to speak, his mantle and invoke a renewal of the blessings and victories he enjoyed.

Only three or four phrases of this poem, however, are at all closely paralleled in other psalms, all of which happen to be anonymous;[1] and it would be hard to prove that these must be post-Davidic, or that none of these expressions was common religious parlance. Also it seems to me as likely that David himself might have drawn freely on his former work to meet a new situation, as that another author did so. In either case it is David's life and faith, and David's poetry, that stimulate us here to praise and intercession.

144:1-4. The strong and the fragile

It is a telling stroke to bring together in these four verses the triumphant mood of Psalm 18 and the searching reflections of the more pensive psalms, thereby not only magnifying the Lord but cutting down friend and enemy alike to size.

---

[1] *Cf.* verse 5b with 104:32b; verse 9 with 33:2f.; verse 15b with 33:12a. Verse 4b has some resemblance to 102:11, but equally to the Davidic 109:23 and to Jb. 8:9; Ec. 6:12, *etc.*, since it uses a standard simile.

477

1. David's thought leaps from a word he had used in Psalm 18:2 (*my rock*) to a phrase from 18:34, to which he adds a companion line, *and my fingers for battle* ('fingers' being used not in contrast to hands but as a poetic synonym; *cf.* Introduction, p. 3).

2. Here, too, he spans the earlier psalm, returning to its second verse and sweeping on to its forty-seventh, both of which he modifies. In quoting the former, instead of repeating *my rock*, as RSV would have it, he introduces a fresh and striking term for God, 'my steadfast love' (see RSV mg.), which NEB renders as 'my help that never fails'.[1] In quoting 18:47 he again brings in a change (which RSV again resists, but this time not without some ancient support), saying now 'who subdues my people under me'. It is order and peace at home, not only in his empire, which now occupies his thoughts, as it will in the expansive verses at the end.

3, 4. Now *man*, so full of himself, is seen to scale, first in a free quotation of Psalm 8:4 (where see comment and a note of similar passages), then in phrases which recall Psalms 39:5 (*a breath*) and 102:11; 109:23 (*a . . . shadow*).

144:5–11. A pattern of rescue

Recollection is now the springboard for intercession. Where Psalm 18 had looked back in wonder ('He bowed the heavens, and came down; . . . he drew me out of many waters', 18:9, 16), this psalm looks steadfastly up to heaven for a comparable act of rescue. All these verbs are now imperatives. And while Psalm 18:44f. (45f., Heb.) told of foreigners cringing before their conqueror, verses 7c, 8 and 11 point to them again (RSV *aliens*, translating the same expression), this time as an insidious and mortal threat.[2] The *right hand* (8, 11) was commonly raised towards heaven (Dt. 32:40) in swearing an oath, or offered to one's fellow to shake hands on an agreement (*cf.*, *e.g.*, Pr. 6:1b, lit.).

9. This verse shares its most striking features, the *new song* and the *ten-stringed harp*, with 33:2f. A psalm which draws so

---

[1] This bold term for God is not unique: *cf.* Jon. 2:8 (9, Heb.), where it should again be taken as a designation of the Lord and His loyalty, rather than of man's loyalty to Him.

[2] The *lies* and *falsehoods* here are the arrogant counterpart to the element of falsehood implied in the Heb. verb translated 'come cringing' in 18:44 (45, Heb.). See p. 96, footnote 1.

much on other poems is likely, though not certain, to be the
borrower rather than the source of these expressions; but there
is no sure means of dating Psalm 33[1]. The *new song*, in the
context of this hope of victory, evidently means a song to be
composed for the occasion; other suggestions seem over-
elaborate for this psalm, *e.g.*, that it is one to accompany a
covenant-renewal, or a song for the age to come (a sense which
it has more naturally in the eschatological atmosphere of
96:1; 98:1; 149:1; *cf.* Rev. 5:9; 14:3).

10. *Victory*, or salvation, *to kings* is an echo of 18:50 (51,
Heb.), somewhat closer in Hebrew than in RSV. Once more
David is treating 'former mercies' as a measure of what God
can do.

144:12-15. A people at peace

This tranquil scene is all the more attractive for the turmoil
and treachery it replaces, just as the prayer which embodies it
is thereby all the more heartfelt.

12. The prayer[2] starts with the family and its rising generation—not with dreams of empire. Here, as 127:3-5 points out,
is God-given, living strength. The sons, as the young olive shoots
of 128:3, are now pictured as sturdy, well-established saplings,
and the daughters as the very picture of statuesque elegance
and strength, 'like sculptured pillars at the corners of a palace'
(NEB). There has been nothing slipshod in their upbringing.

13, 14. After touching on the human resources of the
kingdom, the psalm looks to its material wealth, which the
Old Testament values realistically as the gift of God—to be
delighted in, but not presumed on. Verse 14, as translated in
RSV, NEB, TEV, calls to mind the conditional blessings of, *e.g.*,
Deuteronomy 28:4; Exodus 23:26. But the second line of this

---

[1] It could even be Davidic (as LXX alleges) since it is found in the First
Book of the Psalter; the title could conceivably have been omitted by
accident in MT (*cf.* Anderson, *ad loc.*).
[2] Whether it is a prayer or a beatitude (anticipating verse 15) is debatable,
since there are no finite verbs in this stanza, only a series of word-pictures
expressed by participles. But the series is introduced by the particle *'ašer*,
which is flexible in meaning, corresponding in some measure to our word
'that', both as a relative pronoun (*cf.* LXX here, implausibly) and in the
sense 'in order that' (*cf.*, *e.g.*, Gn. 11:7; Dt. 4:40). Although it is not found
elsewhere in the latter sense when followed only by participles, this seems
the most likely continuation from the prayer of 11a. (NEB, with 'Happy
are we . . .', emends *'ašer* to *'aš⁽e⁾rê*.)

verse (14) is more likely to be speaking of security, as in AV, RV, JB, Gelineau. The last-named translates it 'no ruined wall, no exile'. The *cry of distress* may be suggested by the agony of defeat, but need not be limited to it. It is true kingship to say with Paul, 'Who is weak, and I am not weak? . . . offended, and I burn not?'

15. Having begun with human, not material values, in the soundness of the family (12), the prayer ends at the source of the harmony it has visualized. For while it treasures the gifts, it reserves its final beatitude for the relationship behind them: that of being the people who know the Lord as their own. This, as a later man of God would fervently declare (Hab. 3:17f.), can outweigh the loss of everything else.

Psalm 145

An Alphabet of Praise

This great outpouring of worship is the last psalm of David in the Psalter, and the last of the eight acrostics found there (see the first footnote to Ps. 119), of which no less than five bear his name. One letter of the alphabet (*nûn*) is lacking from the standard Hebrew text; but most of the ancient translations and now a text from Qumran (11Q Ps^a) supply the missing verse, which RSV and subsequent translations include at the end of verse 13 (*i.e.*, the couplet beginning with 'The Lord is faithful . . .'), either as 13b (RSV, JB, TEV) or as 14a (NEB).

Title
On *A Song* and *David*, see Introduction, pp. 37, 33.

145:1–3. An opening doxology
The praise of God which came most readily to David's lips in other psalms made use of expressions such as 'Rock', 'Fortress' and 'Deliverer', words which sprang from personal experience. Here he broadens his approach, to glory in God's greatness and universal care. Throughout the psalm his personal praise will mingle with that of all generations and all creatures.

145:4–7. A theme for all men

Even David could have had little inkling of the fulfilment in store for his words, not only in the fact that his *generation* still speaks to ours, and his small circle (the other nuance of this word for generation) to the world, but in that God's *mighty acts*, *wondrous works* and *terrible* (or 'awesome') *acts* would reach a new climax in the gospel events, and still be moving now towards their consummation.

With the exception of *thy majesty* (5) and perhaps *thy greatness* (6; but *cf.* its dynamic meaning in 2 Sa. 7:21), all the matters for praise in this stanza are God's saving interventions, of which the various terms here bring out different aspects. In verse 7, the two main nouns still have this redemptive thrust, speaking respectively of God's kindness or generosity in taking action (*thy . . . goodness*), and of His concern to set matters straight (*thy righteousness*: see on 24:5; 65:5).

145:8, 9. God the compassionate

Verse 8 repeats God's self-revelation at Sinai (Ex. 34:6) almost word for word. It was one of the most quoted sayings in the Old Testament:[1] a rich yield from the prayer of Moses, 'Show me thy glory', to which it was the answer. When Jonah quoted it back to God with disapproval, he received a reply which confirmed not only this but the truth of our verse 9, by revealing God's pity for the very cattle of Nineveh (Jon. 4:2, 11).

145:10–13a. King for ever

The expression, *All thy works*, picks up the thought of 9b, where 'all that he has made' uses the same Hebrew term. Perhaps 'declare thee' would be truer here than *give thanks to thee* (see on 136:1; 138:4), since only man can know true gratitude (10b), while the rest of God's works proclaim Him by what they are, and will do so perfectly in the end (Rom. 8:21).

This part of the psalm uses several of the terms of verses 4–7, but now the stress on the word *kingdom* (four times: 11, 12, 13, 13) brings out the theme of rule rather than redemption. The reappearance of verse 13 in Daniel 4:3 (MT 3:33) on the lips of Nebuchadnezzar confirms this emphasis and points us to a part of Scripture which expounds this sovereignty at

[1] *Cf.* Nu. 14:18; Ne. 9:17; Pss. 86:15; 103:8; 111:4; 112:4; Joel 2:13; Jon. 4:2.

length and on a world scale. It is as much a cause for joy as is the compassion proclaimed in verses 8 and 9.

145:13b–20. God the Provider

This passage enlarges on the theme of verses 8 and 9 with examples from life's emergencies and regularities alike. Verses 13b[1] and 17 sum up the divine qualities which are most apparent here, laying their chief stress on God's dependability, since *gracious* (13b) and *kind* (17) represent the single word *ḥāsîd*, which might be better rendered 'loyal' or (NEB) 'unchanging'. It is a frequent term for God's devoted servants (see on Ps. 18:25), but is used of God Himself only in these two verses and in Jeremiah 3:12, where NEB renders it by the phrase 'my love is unfailing'.

Four aspects of life testify to this concern and constancy:

14. Help for the inadequate. The phrase, *all who are falling*, is unusually expressive; and this timely help at an early stage is coupled with God's power to revive lost hope and failed abilities: *cf.* NEB, 'and straightens backs which are bent'.

15, 16. Food for all creatures. This complex and exuberant provision—so unlike the standardized dietary units of farming technocrats—reflects the Creator's generous joy in His world, a theme developed at length in Psalm 104, and used for our emulation and encouragement in the Sermon on the Mount (Mt. 5:45; 6:25ff.).

18, 19. Answers for those who pray. The symbolism of the word *near* is not confined to the thought of being within earshot, but may include that of the closeness of friends ('the haughty he knows from afar', 138:6; *cf.* 25:14) and the boon of help that is ready and waiting (Pr. 27:10b; Is. 50:8). But note the warning of Isaiah 55:6.

20. Protection for those who are His. This verse has the only direct mention of *the wicked* in the psalm. But it would hardly be a psalm about life (or a psalm of David!) without this shadow; nor would God's faithfulness be fully seen without reference to His uncompromising judgment. *Preserves* may be a little misleading, as though it promised the godly a charmed life. 'Watches over' (NEB) is better; see again Luke 21:16, 18.

---

[1] On this extra couplet of verse 13 see the comments introducing the psalm, above.

145:21. A closing doxology

So ends David's contribution to the Psalter, on a note of praise
which is wholly his own (21a), yet as wide as mankind and as
unfading as eternity.

Psalm 146

'I'll praise my Maker'

Five joyous psalms of praise, each of them beginning and
ending with Hallelujah, bring the Psalter to a close. So in this
respect as in many others, the Psalms are a miniature of our
story as a whole, which will end in unbroken blessing and
delight.

More than one German hymn, and in English the verses b,
Isaac Watts, 'I'll praise my Maker while I've breath', owe their
inspiration to this psalm.

146:1, 2. A lifetime of praise

The opening call, *Praise the Lord* (Hallelujah), is plural, a
summons to all, but within the chorus each one can make an
offering which is all his own (1b, 2). There is an emphatic ring
to the resolve of verse 2 (*cf.* 104:33), which JB catches with its
rendering, 'I mean to praise . . . all my life, I mean to sing . . .
as long as I live.' It puts the matter on a broader base than
the mood of the moment: *cf.* 34:1 and comment.

146:3, 4. Man, the false hope

The word *princes* may seem to remove this advice from the
plane of ordinary folk and their needs; but a modern equivalent would be 'the influential', whose backing may well seem
more solid and practical than God's. Isaiah 32:5 reminds us
that the big names are not always what they seem,[1] but the
present passage goes deeper with its sombre play on the words
man ('*āḏām*) and *earth* ('*aḏāmâ*) derived from Genesis 3:19.

146:5-9. God, great and good

Verse 5 is the last beatitude in the Psalter (see the list in the

[1] The word 'noble', there, is the singular of the word used here for
'princes'; and the 'fool' is the arrogant evil-doer portrayed in Psalm 14:1.

footnote to Ps. 1:1), and it unfolds its implications in the whole length of this stanza.

5. *Jacob* is probably meant collectively, as the people of God; but it may carry a reminder of the man whom God befriended and transformed. Certainly the beatitude is for the individual, who is understood to be in personal covenant with God. The next verses will show how immense this privilege is.

6. As Creator, God stands in sharp contrast to the ephemeral helpers of verses 3 and 4; but not only as Creator: equally as the One who *keeps faith*.[1] With men, the will is lacking as often as the power. *Cf.* Paul, on his trial: 'All deserted me. . . . But the Lord stood by me' (2 Tim. 4:16f.).

7ff. Like Father, like Son. For us, these lines may bring to mind the oracle of Isaiah 61 by which Jesus announced His mission, and the further clues to His identity which He sent back to John the Baptist (Lk. 4:18f.; 7:21f.). What is added here is judgment, two statements of it which flank the story of compassion and are indeed part of it (7a, 9c). The relation between judgment and salvation in the work of Christ is one of the themes of the gospel: *e.g.* John 3:17-19; 5:25-29. The eventual finality of both is a clearer prospect there than in the psalms.

146:10. An eternity of praise

The personal and lifelong praise vowed in the opening stanza now opens out into that of *Zion, i.e.*, the people of God (see on Ps. 87), and that of eternity. Whether the individual singer of verse 2 saw himself included in these endless generations or not, such was in fact his destiny, for God is 'not the God of the dead, but of the living'.

> 'My days of praise shall ne'er be past,
> While life, and thought, and being last,
> Or immortality endures.'[2]

---

[1] NEB gratuitously emends *ever* ('*ōlām*) to 'wrongdoers' ('*awwālîm*), paraphrasing the line as 'who serves wrongdoers as he has sworn'. This makes link with 7a, but is pure speculation.

[2] I. Watts, 'I'll praise my Maker'.

Psalm 147
'Lift up your eyes on high'

At times this psalm takes up the rhetorical questions of Isaiah 40, and at times the challenges of the Lord to Job, turning them into praise, and linking the wonders of creation with the glories of providence and grace.

The Septuagint treats this as two psalms, of which the second begins at verse 12. So its numbering of the Psalter, which has diverged from that of the Hebrew Bible (familiar to Protestants) from Psalm 10 onwards, comes into step again for the last three psalms, 148-150.

147:1-6. The God who redeems

1. Before turning to particular matters for praise, the psalm pauses to consider the delightfulness of praise itself. While it must always be a 'whole offering', never self-regarding, the very act of responding articulately to God's pure glory and goodness is enlivening and emancipating; see on 92:1-4. Verse 1 may be translated, 'How good it is[1] to sing psalms, how pleasant to make fitting praise.'[2]

2ff. Now follows the first motive for such an offering, namely gratitude. The promises of Isaiah 40ff. to a homeless generation are here reflected back to God as praise—either in naked faith or in response to their fulfilment. We are singing to the same tune as the prophet: compare verse 3 with Isaiah 61:1, but chiefly verses 4 and 5 with Isaiah 40:26, 28c, where the point is made (more explicitly than in the psalm) that One who marshals the host of stars, 'calling them all by name' (as here, 4b), is more than equal to the problems of His people, both in *power* and *understanding* (*cf.* 5). It turns upside down the familiar argument that in so great a universe our small affairs are too minute to notice.

---

[1] Lit. 'Surely it is good', understanding the particle *kî* here as a mark of emphasis rather than an explanatory conjunction.

[2] This follows Anderson (on the basis of J. Blau, *VT* 4 (1954), pp. 410f.) in taking *nā'wâ* as an infinitive.

147:7-11. The God who cares

The theme at first is that of Job 38ff. and of Psalm 104: the immense range of God's operations, equally wonderful for their vastness and their attention to detail. This is divine care on a scale to evoke wonder and worship; but verses 10 and 11 give a fresh turn to it, that so great a Giver looks for humble response, not the benefit of our prowess ('as though he needed anything', Acts 17:25), and for trust, not self-sufficiency. The thought is expressed at greater length in Psalm 33:16ff., and with more positive emphasis in Matthew 6:25-34.

147:12-20. The God who commands

The psalm continues to hold together the vision of God as Lord of the covenant and as Lord of creation. Verses 12-14 may be either a thanksgiving for what has been received, *e.g.* in the days of Nehemiah, or else a confident prediction; in either case we delight in the characteristic gifts of God, and confess that these basic requisites of any people, namely security, spiritual health, concord and prosperity, are His to give, not ours (as experience shows) to achieve.

15ff. The unifying theme of the final verses is the *word* of God (15, 18, 19) in its two great functions: to command and to communicate. Verses 15-18 show God's effortless control, in terms which recall Job 37 and 38; they also remind us of the single will and intelligence behind the diversity we see. The cold is *his cold*,[1] the wind which thaws it is also his.

But verses 19, 20 are the climax. Here is no merely activating word, but, amazingly, the meeting of minds. It has been well pointed out that, purely as the means of getting things done, *statutes and ordinances*, or even appeals and encouragements, are most uncertain tools. So by addressing us, not programming us, God shows that He seeks a relationship, not simply a sequence of actions carried out. 'God does not wish to have my obedience as something which is valuable in itself. He wants me.'[2]

So verse 20, which may at first sound self-satisfied, is an

---

[1] The emendation of NEB in 17b, 'the water stands frozen', represents a fairly small textual change (*mayim*, 'waters', for *mî*, 'who', followed by a plural verb). It makes an easy link with 18a (lit. ' . . and melts them'), but as 'them' can refer back to the snow, frost and ice, the alteration is not by any means a necessity.

[2] E. Brunner, *The Divine Imperative* (Lutterworth, 1937), p. 145.

exclamation of wonder. If pride were to creep into it, the very name *Jacob* (19) should silence it, and the call to be 'a light to the nations' (Is. 49:6) re-direct it.

Psalm 148

Choir of Creation

Starting with the angelic host, and descending through the skies to the varied forms and creatures of earth, then summoning the family of man and finally the chosen people, the call to praise unites the whole creation. If any notion of a colourless or cloistered regime were associated with the name of God, this glimpse of His tireless creativity would be enough to dispel it.

The *Benedicite* (from the Song of the Three Servants, in the Apocrypha) is an expansion of this psalm.

148:1-6. Praise from on high

Not only in Old Testament times but in the Christian era, men have been tempted to worship *angels* (Col. 2:18), who are our fellow servants (Rev. 22:8f.), and to treat the *stars* as arbiters of destiny. The psalm sweeps away such folly with two gestures: first with its call to this heavenly host, animate and inanimate, to praise the Lord—indeed to initiate the praise which we will echo back to Him, as shown in the twin expressions 'from the heavens' (1) and 'from the earth' (7)—and secondly with its reminder that they, like us, were *created* with a word (5) and allotted their stations at His will.

2. *Host*, which to us is merely synonymous with a multitude, is the normal word for an army (as is also its Greek equivalent, Lk. 2:13; *cf.* Mt. 26:53), a further token that, in Milton's words, God's 'state

> Is kingly; thousands at his bidding speed,
> And post o'er land and ocean without rest'.[1]

4. *Highest heavens* is literally 'heaven of heavens', a similar superlative to 'holy of holies', or perhaps an expression for 'heaven itself' (*cf.* Anderson, referring to J. Gray). The *waters*

---

[1] John Milton, Sonnet 'On His Blindness'.

above the heavens are a poetic or popular term for the rain clouds; *cf.* Genesis 1:6–8.

6. The word translated *bounds*, *i.e.*, a prescribed limit, also means decree or statute; hence rsv mg., 'he set a law which cannot pass away'. As the final verb is singular, the latter translation is more accurate; but the sense remains much the same.

148:7–14. Praise from the earth

Now comes the answering antiphon *from the earth* (7; *cf.* 'from the heavens', 1), the mirror-image of that of heaven, in that the praise which was passed down from conscious to unconscious participants in verses 1–6 is now passed up the scale to man, who is aware of God, and ultimately to the people who are in covenant with Him.

11, 12. In these few lines there emerges, quite incidentally and with unforced simplicity, the only potential bond between the extremes of mankind: a joyful preoccupation with God.

13, 14. It is instructive to compare these verses with their counterparts, verses 5 and 6. In verse 5 the celestial bodies are called to praise God simply by the fact of their existence ('For he commanded and they were created'). But in 13, man may praise Him consciously, since He has revealed Himself ('For his name . . . is exalted'). Similarly, God's glory in the natural world is the reign of law (6), the regularity which invites us to 'search out' His works (Ps. 111:2); but among His people His glory is redemptive love (14), in raising up *a horn* for them, *i.e.*, a strong deliverer (Lk. 1:69); above all, in bringing them *near to him*. That is the climax of the psalm, as it is of the gospel: 'Behold, the dwelling of God is with men. He will dwell with them, and they shall be his people' (Rev. 21:3).

Additional note on verse 14

Some commentators have queried whether the lines 14b, c ('praise for all his saints . . .', *etc.*) are an integral part of the psalm, suggesting that they were a rubric or an appended title, like Habakkuk 3:19b (see Introduction, p. 39). R. A. F. MacKenzie[1] brings another angle to this by arguing that these lines were in fact the title to the next psalm, isolated from it by a misplaced Hallelujah, which should have followed 14a

[1] *Biblica* 51[2] (1970), pp. 221–224.

instead of 14c. The most impressive part of his argument is his observation that of the seven Hebrew words of 14b, c, six occur in Psalm 149, but only one in the rest of Psalm 148.

If, however, we regard Psalm 149 as a composition *generated* by 148:14, written to enlarge on the subject which emerged only in that final verse—the special calling of Israel—these verbal links will be equally well accounted for. Moreover, Psalm 148 will retain a conclusion worthy of the theme of a growing intimacy of praise and response.

Psalm 149

Victory Celebration

While the previous psalm summoned the whole creation to worship, reserving Israel's share in it for the final verse, here it is her praises and her calling that fill the picture. The verse just mentioned, Psalm 148:14, with its joy of deliverance and its sense of vocation, may possibly have been the seed from which this psalm developed; see the Additional note on it, above.

149:1-5. The church jubilant

A new song suggests a new situation, and this has all the marks of victory, including the time-honoured way of celebrating it with *dancing* and the *timbrel* (*cf.* Ex. 15:20; Jdg. 11:34; I Sa. 18:6). The scale of it is orld-wide (7ff.), and we are evidently singing of no less an event than God's advent, as in Psalms 93, 96–99 (*cf.* the 'new song' of 96:1; 98:1; songs of the new age).[1]

5. The *couches* may refer quite simply to the fact of being able to lie down at night without fear and with a good conscience (*cf.* 4:8; Ho. 7:14). But the picture may be of reclining at a festal meal (*cf.* also the 'hymn' sung in Mk. 14:26), especially if the theme of such a festival was the final victory of God. (A further suggestion, that the reference is to prayer-mats—*cf.* JB, 'prostrate before him'; NEB, 'kneel before him'—

---

[1] The sense in which 'a new song' is to be understood probably varies with the contexts in which it occurs. See on 144:9.

is open to the objection that the root of this word means to lie down, not to bow down or prostrate oneself.)

149:6–9. The church militant

Now, in terms of a holy war, such as those of Israel against the Canaanites, we sing of the retribution which will overtake the enemies of God. As a nation, Israel had been charged with executing this in literal fact at her entry into the promised land; and at the last day the angels, the armies of heaven, will accompany our Lord to judgment (2 Thes. 1:7ff.; *cf.* Rev. 19:11ff.). By contrast, the church's enemies are 'not . . . flesh and blood, but . . . the spiritual hosts of wickedness'; and her weapons are not those of the world. Our *two-edged sword* (*cf.* 6) is the word of God, created to 'destroy arguments (or 'sophistries', NEB) and every proud obstacle to the knowledge of God'. Our equivalent of binding *kings with chains* (8) is to 'take every thought captive to obey Christ' (2 Cor. 10:5; *cf.* Eph. 6:12; Heb. 4:12). The Apocalypse, for all its fiery imagery of final judgment, describes the church's victory as congruous with that of Cavalry. 'They have conquered . . . by the blood of the Lamb and by the word of their testimony, for they loved not their lives even unto death' (Rev. 12:11).

This is *the judgment written* by the cross against 'the ruler of this world' (Jn. 16:11), who is the power behind the kings of verse 8. God has appointed *glory for all his faithful ones* at a higher level than was clearly visible in the Old Testament. Such are the battle-honours of the genuinely holy war.

Psalm 150

Hallelujah!

While the first four books of Psalms each ended in doxology, the fifth rounds off the whole Psalter with an entire psalm of praise. Its brevity is stimulating. There can be no fear of flagging; besides, all has been said, and we can give ourselves to a sustained *fortissimo* of response.

150:1. The 'where' of praise

Coverdale's Psalter (PBV) has 'Praise God in his holiness',

which is a feasible translation; but the matching line, '. . . in his mighty firmament', suggests that 'holiness' has its secondary meaning here, *his sanctuary*. So the call is to God's worshippers on earth, meeting at His chosen place, but also to His heavenly host (the *firmament* is the sky, the vault of heaven) to mingle their praises with ours. Earth and heaven can be utterly at one in this. His glory fills the universe; His praise must do no less.

150:2. The 'why' of praise

Throughout the psalm, except in 2b,[1] the same Hebrew preposition persists, taking different shades of meaning from its contexts. In 2a it clearly means *for*, but we can get the feel of its primary sense of 'in' by remembering our own expression 'to rejoice in'—*e.g.*, to rejoice in 'his mighty deeds', somewhat as in this verse. Here there are two comprehensive matters for praise, of which the second, *his . . . greatness*, dwells on what He is in Himself (*cf.* the phrase in the *Gloria in Excelsis*, 'we give thanks to thee for thy great glory'), while the first, *his mighty deeds*, means primarily His saving acts (*e.g.* Pss. 20:6c (7, Heb.); 145:4, 12), though secondarily, too, His might as Creator (65:6 [7, Heb.]) and Sovereign of the world (66:7).

150:3-5. The 'how' of praise

The answer to the question 'how?' is: 'with everything you have!' Various sides of life are touched on in this short list: great national and sacred occasions, by the *trumpet* blast (this was the curved horn used, *e.g.*, to announce the year of jubilee, Lv. 25:9; see on Ps. 81:3); joyous celebrations, *e.g.*, of a victory, by the *timbrel and dance* (see on 81:2; 149:3); simple music-making, to judge by the everyday associations of the *pipe*[2] or flute (Gn. 4:21; Jb. 21:12; 30:31). But these are not distinctions to be pressed, beyond the fact that every kind of instrument, solemn or gay, percussive or melodic, gentle or strident, is rallied here to the praise of God.[3]

---

[1] In 2b the preposition *ke* ('according to') replaces *be* (translated 'in', 'for' and 'with' in verses 1, 2a and 3–5 respectively). But these two consonants look very much alike in Heb., and possibly 2b should conform to the rest, as one ancient version (the Peshitta) suggests.

[2] AV, misleadingly, has 'organs', derived from the Vulgate.

[3] For further details of the instruments, see *NBD*, article 'Music and Musical Instruments'. The Heb. terms and RSV equivalents here are as follows: *šôpār* (trumpet); *nēbel* (lute); *kinnôr* (harp); *tōp̄* (timbrel), *minnîm* (strings); *'ûḡāḇ* (pipe); *ṣelṣelîm* (cymbals).

150:6. The 'who' of praise

While some would hold that *everything* should be translated
'every*one*' here,[1] this seems an unduly narrow view of the
phrase, which is literally 'Let all breath praise the Lord'.
Rather, let it sum up the glorious variety that was glimpsed in
Psalm 148:7–12, with 'sea monsters . . . , beasts and all cattle,
creeping things and flying birds', joined by the whole family
of man from kings to children—indeed, as Psalm 8 declares,
to babes and sucklings.

'And I heard every creature in heaven and on earth and
under the earth and in the sea, and all therein, saying, "To him
who sits upon the throne and to the Lamb be blessing and
honour and glory and might for ever and ever!" '

Amen!

---

[1] See T. C. Mitchell in *VT* 11 (1961), pp. 177–187, for the argument that
'breath' refers in the Old Testament to human life exclusively.